PLAYS BY
MARTIN JONES

BROADWAY PLAY PUBLISHING INC
224 E 62nd St, NY, NY 10065
www.broadwayplaypub.com
info@broadwayplaypub.com

PLAYS BY MARTIN JONES
© Copyright 2003 by Martin Jones

All rights reserved. This work is fully protected under the copyright laws of the United States of America.

No part of this publication may be photocopied, reproduced, stored in a retrieval system, or transmitted, in any form or by any means, electronic, mechanical, recording, or otherwise, without the prior permission of the publisher. Additional copies of this play are available from the publisher.

Written permission is required for live performance of any sort. This includes readings, cuttings, scenes, and excerpts. For amateur and stock performances, please contact Broadway Play Publishing Inc. For all other rights contact the author c/o B P P I.

Cover photo by Roman Duszek

First printing: September 2003
This printing: August 2016
I S B N: 978-0-88145-219-8

Book design: Marie Donovan
Word processing: Microsoft Word for Windows
Typographic controls: Xerox Ventura Publisher 2.0 P E
Typeface: Palatino
Printed on recycled acid-free paper and bound in the U S A

CONTENTS

About the Author v
WEST MEMPHIS MOJO 1
SQUATS 53
DARK RIVER 121
OLD SOLDIERS 181

the collection of plays is dedicated to the memory of
Scott Hudson

ABOUT THE AUTHOR

Martin Jones was born in Elizabeth, New Jersey, but has lived primarily in places such as Memphis, St Louis, Chicago, Michigan, Florida, Virginia, Maine, Vermont, and Italy.

In 1968 he received a B A in English and Theatre Arts from Hillsdale College in Michigan. He received an M A in Theatre from Eastern Michigan University, and a Ph.D. in Playwriting and Dramatic Literature from Southern Illinois University in Carbondale, Illinois. While at Carbondale he studied creative writing with the novelist John Gardner.

For ten years Mr Jones taught in academic theater. He was Playwright-in-Residence at Northern Illinois University, and a drama professor at the University of Virginia and at Bowdoin College.

In 1980 he left academic theater to work in Chicago as a playwright, actor, and director. He has worked as a performer at several regional theaters including the Victory Gardens Theater, the Wisdom Bridge Theater, the Theater at Monmouth, and the Portland Stage Company.

In 1980 his play, OLD SOLDIERS, premiered at the Performance Community in Chicago. OLD SOLDIERS was published in *Best Short Plays of 1983*.

His play, DAUGHTERS, premiered at the Guthrie Theater (Studio) in Minneapolis, and was later produced by Chicago's Victory Gardens Theater. In 1982 two of his plays were staged Off-Off Broadway—FLAMINGOS, at the Nameless Theatre, and SNOW LEOPARDS, at the 18th Street Playhouse. In October, 1983 his ZOOLOGY (a trilogy of plays) premiered in New York at the Stage Arts Theater Company. In 1985 Stage Arts also produced SNOW LEOPARDS, which was published later that year by Samuel French.

WEST MEMPHIS MOJO was selected in 1986 as a winner in the F D G/ C B S New Plays Program. In the spring of that year, Mr Jones co-authored a musical revue, FROM AWAY, which premiered at the Portland Stage Company.

Mr Jones received a Rockefeller Foundation Grant in Playwriting in 1986, and throughout the eighties served as Playwright-in-Residence at the Portland Stage Company and the Mad Horse Theater Company, where four of his plays premiered (VANISHING POINTS [also published by B P P I], SQUATS, DARK RIVER, and YOU CAN'T GET THERE FROM HERE.)

In 1991, Jones co-authored the screenplay for the H B O/Lorimar film *Prison Stories: Women on the Inside*, which had its premiere at the 1991 Sundance Film Festival, and was originally broadcast on H B O in January 1991. The film was nominated for a Cable Ace Award in the Best Dramatic Special category.

Two of his other film scripts, *Second Skin* and *Scarlet Moon* are under option in Hollywood.

Mr Jones currently lives in Springfield, Missouri, where he teaches creative writing at Southwest Missouri State University.

WEST MEMPHIS MOJO

WEST MEMPHIS MOJO was a winner in the 1986 F D G/C B S New Plays Program. It premiered at the Northlight Theater Company on 19 March 1986. The cast and creative contributors were:

TEDDY .... John Cothran, Jr
ELROI .... Don Franklin
FRANK .... Gregory Alan-Williams
MAXINE .... Lisa Dodson

Director .... Michael Maggio
Scenery design .... Gary Baugh
Costumes .... Kaye Nottbusch
Lighting .... Robert Shook
Production stage manager .... Anthony Berg

Song: *Can't Get Your Lovin' Off My Mind,* music by Rick Snyder, lyrics by Martin Jones

WEST MEMPHIS MOJO had its New York premiere at the Negro Ensemble Company as a co-production with Crossroads Theater Company on 22 May 1988. The cast and creative contributors were:

TEDDY ....Richard Gant
ELROI ....Tico Wells
FRANK .... Tucker Smallwood
MAXINE .... Kate Redway

Director ....Rick Khan
Set designer .... Charles McClennahan
Costume designer .... Judy Dearing
Lighting designer .... Shirley Prendergast
Sound design ....Rob Gorton
Stage manager .... Kenneth R Saltzman
Producing director of N E C ....Leon Denmark

CHARACTERS & SETTING

TEDDY, *(early forties) black, owner and barber of Teddy's Barber Shop & Records in West Memphis, Arkansas*
ELROI, *(late teens) black, shoeshine boy in* TEDDY's *shop. Fancies himself to be a songwriter*
FRANK JACKSON, *(early forties) black, a blues singer and recording artist. Admired by* ELROI
MAXINE PETTIBONE, *(late twenties) white, housewife from Senatobia, Mississippi. Likes black musicians*

Time: A cold November in 1955

Setting: Teddy's Barber Shop & Records in a poor black section of West Memphis, Arkansas

ACT ONE

(The set: consists of one main room: a barber shop with a record alcove.)

*(The shop is a storefront with a large bay window overlooking the street. The floor is worn linoleum, and the ceiling is made of painted tin, probably erected in the late 1920s. The walls are painted plaster and cheap wood paneling. There is a single barber chair of very old vintage, and a mirror, barber's sink, and shelves with clippers, razor, hair tonics on the wall behind the barber chair. A curtained doorway near the barber chair leads off to a back room. Against another wall is a shoeshine setup, with an elevated chair with brass footrests. At one corner of the shop there is an alcove with three small bins of phonograph records for sale. [In the South in the 50s, there were not many record stores, and as a result, most businesses in the black neighborhoods sold records as a sideline. People would purchase the latest R & B recordings in beauty parlors, drug stores, food markets, and barber shops.] Sitting next to the record bins is an old table-model record player, holding stacks of 78s, 45s, and a few albums. Nearby, there is also an amplifier for an electric guitar, and an old flat-top, acoustic guitar with an electric pick-up installed in the sound hole of the guitar. The walls of the shop are adorned with the usual assortment of sepia pin-up girls, and there are several posters advertising Rhythm and Blues shows that have played at the Palace Theatre on Beale St, across the river in Memphis. Some of the posters are of Ike Turner's Kings of Rhythm Revue, B B King, Louis Jordan, and Joe Turner. On one section of wall there is a special section devoted to local deceased singing star, Johnny Ace—including a black and white autographed picture of the singer, a show poster, and the record cover of his major album—*Johnny Ace—Memorial Album.*)*

(Music: prior to the beginning of the play, Guitar Slim should be heard playing on the on-stage record player. As the lights dim to begin, his song, The Things That I Used To Do, *can be heard.)*

(At rise: TEDDY, *a burly man in his early forties, is seated in his barber chair, reading the Memphis World—the local black newspaper.* TEDDY *is dressed in dark slacks and an open-necked white shirt with a vest. He twiddles with his mustache and taps his foot along with the music as he reads. He turns and looks at himself in the mirror on the wall.* TEDDY *rises and moves closer to study his face in the reflection, as he hums along with the song. He takes some small barber's scissors from the shelf and trims his mustache. Finished, he smiles at himself. He goes to the window, looks out at the street, hands in pockets, rolling back and forth on the balls of his feet. The song ends.* TEDDY *goes to the record player and starts the record over*

again. He sits in the barber chair and resumes reading the paper. There is a knock at the front door of the shop. TEDDY *tries to ignore it.)*

TEDDY: We're closed. It's Sunday. *(Knocking continues)* You hear me? We closed. Who's out there?

ELROI: *(Outside)* Teddy. Open the door. It's me, Elroi.

TEDDY: *(Slowly rising)* That you, Elroi?

ELROI: It's me. Open the goddamn door. Freezin' my ass off out here.

TEDDY: *(Opens door.)* Don't be cussin' out in the street. It's Sunday. Somebody's Mama be on her way to church...the whole neighborhood be on my butt.

(ELROI, *a young man in his late teens enters. He wears a light jacket and carries a brown paper sack with a change of clothes.* ELROI *has a "do" rag on his head to protect his processed hairstyle.)*

ELROI: Ain't nobody on the street. Too damn cold. Brr.

TEDDY: Where's your key?

ELROI: I gave it to Frank.

TEDDY: He'll probably lose it. Close the door. You're lettin' all the heat outside.

ELROI: Damn it's cold. *(He closes the door, rubs his hands together, flaps his arms to warm up.)*

TEDDY: You get my licorice?

ELROI: *(Tosses him a sack)* Yeah, I got it...had to go three places...find somethin' open.

TEDDY: *(Savoring a piece)* Thanks. Well, don't stand there flappin' your arms. Get over here, stand on the hot air vent.

(ELROI *stands over the heating vent.)*

ELROI: Coldest damn winter I ever seen. Radio says it gonna snow.

TEDDY: It ain't gonna snow. It's only November.

ELROI: Said it on W D I A...

TEDDY: Ain't never snowed in November...

ELROI: All I know...it's cold in Tennessee!!

(ELROI *elongates the word "Tennessee".)*

TEDDY: Why you always say that?

ELROI: What?

TEDDY: *(Mimics* ELROI*)* "Tennessee!" We's in Arkansas, fool! Cross the river, or has you got chillbrains too? *(He laughs at his own joke.)* "Cold in Tennessee". You got that from Frank...that's where you got that from. I heard him say it too.

ELROI: Yeah. He says it sometimes.

TEDDY: Where'd he get it?

ELROI: Dunno. Have to ask him yourself. Somethin' he heard...I guess.

TEDDY: You want some coffee? I got water on in the back room. You want... I get you a cup...

ELROI: That be great. With lotsa sugar.

(TEDDY *goes off through a curtained area that leads to a back room-his living quarters in the back of the shop.* ELROI *hangs up his jacket on a hook on the wall. He picks up* TEDDY's *copy of the paper, sits in the barber chair.)*

ELROI: Anything in the paper?

TEDDY: *(Off, teasing)* What do you care? You can't read.

ELROI: Hell, I can't.

TEDDY: *(Off)* Guitar Slim's playin' at the Pearl Lounge next week.

ELROI: *(Scanning the paper.)* I know, Frank told me. Hey, there be somethin' 'bout Big Boy Crudup...

(TEDDY *enters carrying* ELROI's *coffee, and a cup for himself.)*

TEDDY: Where? Lemme see that.

ELROI: No, man. I found it. I get to read it first.

(They struggle over the paper.)

TEDDY: Now, give me my paper. C'mom give it up...

ELROI: *(Holding it away from* TEDDY.*)* You had it all mornin'. I want a chance. I been out runnin' your errands. I should get to see the *World*.

TEDDY: You gonna be seein' stars in about one second. Gimme my paper.

(To keep it from TEDDY, ELROI *sits on the newspaper.)*

ELROI: You want it? You reach your hand under my butt for it. Come on. *(Laughs)* I been workin' up a big ol' fart for when you do.

TEDDY: All right, fool! Take the paper. But, first...you get outta my chair. You can read it to me...you need the practice. Begin with the story about Big Boy Crudup.

(ELROI *rises, moves to the shoeshine chair.* TEDDY *sits in the barber chair.)*

ELROI: It says here that Mr. Elvis Presley has made Arthur Big Boy Crudup a famous man, by recordin' one of his songs...*That's All Right, Mama*... *(Pause)* What about *Milk Cow Blues*?

TEDDY: Just read the article.

ELROI: *(Reading)* "Crudup was not even aware that his song had been recorded until he heard Presley's version of *That's All Right, Mama*, on a radio broadcast from W L A C in Nashville..."

TEDDY: John R's show, I bet. "Brought to you by Randy's Record Mart in Gallatin, Tennessee..."

ELROI: You wanna hear the article or not?

TEDDY: Go on.

ELROI: *(Reading)* "Arthur Crudup, or Big Boy, as his friends call him, is not currently active in the recording industry. He was known for many recordings on various "race record" labels made during the 1940s. Crudup now lives on a sharecropper farm near Greenwood, Mississippi. He says that he is rather bewildered by all the attention that Mr. Presley has brought to him. But, as he says, "I'll be glad if they send me some money."

TEDDY: Yeah, I bet. Big Boy Crudup got enough socked away to buy him a whole fleet of Cadillacs. Can't tell me he's choppin' cotton in Mississippi, not a big star like that. Naw, I bet he just says that so every freeloadin' nigger in the Delta don't come hittin' on him for a handout.

ELROI: You think so?

TEDDY: Sure. Crudup ain't nobody's fool. Before the war...I seen him once...at the Palace over on Beale...him and Louis Jordan. Hell of a show. Limousines all lined up at the curb...women in fur coats...nothin' like it. They was popular with white folks too. Had to do two different shows every night-one early for the whites, and one later for the coloreds. Standin' room only a whole week runnin'. Them singers get rich, boy, and that's a fact. *(Pause)* So, read me the rest of it.

ELROI: That's all it says.

TEDDY: That's all?

ELROI: Ain't nothin', but about two inches in here.

TEDDY: Hmmm. Ain't that somethin'?

(They are quiet. ELROI turns on the radio. Gospel music is heard coming from the radio. TEDDY looks at the radio.)

TEDDY: What the hell is that on my radio?

ELROI: Sounds like Rosie Wallace.

TEDDY: *(Rises)* I hate Gospel music. Screamin' 'bout Jesus...makes me jumpy. *(Turns off radio)* Got no sophistication. Ain't got no uptown rhythm. You know what I mean?

ELROI: Oh yeah. Not like what we can do.

TEDDY: *(Crossing to window)* Not hardly. *(Looks at street)* Terrible lookin' day...even for a Sunday. *(Pause)* What time did Frank say he was gonna get here?

ELROI: About noon, I guess. The session is at two. Why? You nervous?

TEDDY: Me, nervous? Naw. What do we do if he don't come by here first? Suppose he goes right over to Memphis?

ELROI: He ain't goin' nowheres without his amplifier and guitar...

(TEDDY *looks skeptically at the guitar.*)

TEDDY: So, where the hell is he?

ELROI: You is nervous.

TEDDY: No...I just need me a taste, that's all. *(Looks out window)* Goddamn Blue laws. I wish I had me some corn liquor.

(ELROI *chuckles gleefully, rises, and goes to his sack of clothing on the floor near the coat rack.* ELROI *pulls out a fifth of Heaven Hill bourbon, holds it proudly.*)

ELROI: Suppose I said I have a surprise for you? Somethin' better than a twenty-five cent slab of corn...look here.

TEDDY: Where the hell'd you get that on a Sunday? You bust in a liquor store?

ELROI: No, Teddy. This is somethin' I been savin'...for a special occasion...Heaven Hill. What do you think about that?

TEDDY: You done stole it off a truck somewhere.

ELROI: What do you care where I got it? Give me your cup. We give you a taste right now. Come on. *(He opens the bottle.)*

TEDDY: I know where you got that...one of them bootleggers on President's Island. Probably been watered...cut with tea.

ELROI: No, sir. Genuine...bottled in bond. Ain't no bootlegger's keep. Stuff is smooth...goes down like honey-dew rind water. You gonna like this. *(He pours them both a cup of bourbon.)* Try that on.

(TEDDY *drinks slowly, savoring the whiskey.*)

TEDDY: Mighty fine. I know you stole this shit. Pour me another.

ELROI: Take it slow. We gotta be sharp today.

TEDDY: I'm always sharp, boy. Wherever you got this bourbon...I hope you had the good sense to walk off with a couple of dozen cases...

ELROI: Naw, I only got two bottles. A waiter over at the Peabody Hotel sneaked 'em out after work. Pretty good, huh? I figured that since you and me is about to get ourselves famous like Big Boy Crudup...I thought we should celebrate with the good stuff.

TEDDY: Yeah, could be our lucky day...*(He pours himself another drink.)* You better watch Frank around that bottle. He'll drink it all...

ELROI: Be our secret.

TEDDY: So where do you think he is? Probably some gin mill!

ELROI: Maybe he got a woman shacked up in Memphis.

TEDDY: Better get his butt over here...after twelve now...

ELROI: Why don't you just sit and relax, Teddy. He'll be here.

TEDDY: What if he comes in drunk? And he can't sing?

ELROI: Then we sober him up.

TEDDY: What if he's in jail?

ELROI: Then we get ourselves another singer.

TEDDY: Like who?

ELROI: You and me.

(TEDDY *guffaws.*)

ELROI: Why not? We can sing 'em. We wrote 'em, so we can sing 'em too. *(Sings)*
She got a mean disposition
She's the meanest gal I ever seen
I asked her for some whiskey
And all I got was kerosene
Hey, darlin', why you gotta be so mean?

Take it, Teddy...Dee, dee, da, dum...

TEDDY: Dee, dee my ass...I ain't no singer. And I don't play that damn guitar.

ELROI: Me, neither. *(Pause)* All right, so we need Frank. Aw, don't get riled up. Frank ain't no fool. This is his big chance too. He knows Sun Records ain't gonna come lookin' for him...that's why I know, he's gonna show up. You gotta have some faith, Teddy. You turnin' white.

TEDDY: *(Pouring a drink)* I don't know why I let you talk me into this. All your big ideal...writin' rhythm and blues songs...nobody ever heard of us.

ELROI: But they done heard of Frank. And soon, they gonna hear of us. We all be rich men. *(Laughs)* Can I use the back room for a minute?

TEDDY: What for?

ELROI: I wanna change my clothes. Gotta look sharp when we get over to Memphis.

TEDDY: Go ahead.

(ELROI *picks up his sack of clothes, looks at* TEDDY.)

ELROI: You goin' like that?

TEDDY: What's wrong with this? It's clean shirt.

ELROI: You might wanna wear a tie. We just might be talkin' to white folks.

TEDDY: I got nothin' to say to them white folks.

ELROI: Then, you keep quiet. Me and Frank will do the talkin'.

TEDDY: You pretty sure of yourself, ain't you?

ELROI: *(Exits to back room.)* Why not? What we got to lose?

(*Offstage,* ELROI *sings* Can't Get Your Lovin' Off My Mind—*see lyrics on page 30.* TEDDY *looks at himself in the mirror. He opens a drawer and finds a bow tie. He puts on the tie, looks at himself, feels foolish, loses his nerve, and removes the tie.*)

TEDDY: Oh, what am I doin'? Who am I foolin'? I ain't no songwriter. I'm a barber...that's all.

ELROI: *(Off)* Seems I recall you sayin' somethin' different, last time you heard Frank rehearsin', *Can't Get Your Lovin' Off My Mind.*

TEDDY: Yeah...*(Pause)* Did sound pretty good, didn't it?

ELROI: *(Off)* Better song than, *That's All Right, Mama.*

TEDDY: That be true! But, then Big Boy Crudup had that Presley kid to help out.

ELROI: *(Off)* You'll see...gonna be the same for us. We get some white guy to sing the songs...we be right up there. We gonna make it, Teddy. You just gotta keep tellin' yourself that the three of us come up with somethin' that's good. Gonna change our lives!

(ELROI *enters wearing orange pants, a dark silk shirt, and a white tie. He struts in front of the mirror. He still has the handkerchief tied over his head.*)

TEDDY: You gonna wear the rag on your head too?

(ELROI *removes the handkerchief from his processed hair. He primps in the mirror.*)

ELROI: This here, keeps the rain offa my "do"...keeps it just perfect.

(ELROI *primps his head in the mirror. He dabs a place with one of the hand towels.*)

TEDDY: Hey, don't be gummin' up my clean barber towels with that process junk. I'll never get them towels clean.

ELROI: My hair is clean.

TEDDY: Can't believe you'd put that junk on your hair...

ELROI: Man, it's in style.

TEDDY: Gonna make all your hair fall out, you'll be bald-headed.

ELROI: Not my hair.

TEDDY: What do you think they put in that stuff, huh? It's lye...that stuff is poison, boy...you can kill varmints with it. I ain't lyin' to ya...I'm a barber... I know somethin' about hair. Stuff will kill your scalp. *(Long pause)* Okay so don't listen to me. You'll see what I'm talkin' about.

ELROI: You just tryin' to scare me. Probably ain't even true. You just sayin' that cause you ain't got a "do" like mine. You jealous...that's what.

TEDDY: That'll be the day.

ELROI: You gonna be a wooly head 'til the day you die.

TEDDY: Coloreds ain't meant to have straight hair. Ain't natural.

ELROI: *(Points to photo on wall)* What about Johnny Ace? Look at his picture! You can't tell me that's natural. That hair done been played with.

TEDDY: Johnny mighta put a hot comb through it once, or twice, but he wasn't no conk head...Look like some Eye-talian!

(ELROI *douses himself with some lilac aftershave.*)

TEDDY: Go easy on that lilac vegetal. Got to last me 'til the end of the month.

ELROI: Now I smell pretty.

TEDDY: Won't have to take no bath 'til Christmas, right? Fool! Usin' up all my inventory!

ELROI: *(In mirror)* I be lookin' bad, just like Chuck Berry. *(Sings)*
Maybellene why can't you be true?
You done started back doin'
The things you used to do.
Maybellene...

(ELROI *does the Chuck Berry Duck Walk.*)

ELROI: *(Strikes a pose)* So, what do you think? Has you ever seen anything look so good in your entire life?

(TEDDY *regards the image for a moment, breaks into a wide smile, and then laughs hysterically.*)

TEDDY: Lawd, have mercy!

ELROI: What's wrong: Why you laughin'? What's so funny?

TEDDY: *(Pointing at the pants.)* You be Orangebird! With them skinny legs, and all....

ELROI: Knock it off. You and Frank been callin' me that Orangebird.. .and I'm sick of it...

TEDDY: *(Laughing)* An Orangebird...that's what you is...

ELROI: Don't start that shit, again. My name is Elroi...I don't like that other name...

TEDDY: Well, look at yourself in the mirror, fool! You ridiculous! Am I right? Ol' Crazy-legs Orangebird!

ELROI: That ain't my name! Now, cut that shit, Teddy. I don't like it.

TEDDY: Everytime you wear them pants, I'm gonna call you Orangebird.

ELROI: How you like it if I call you fat nappyhead?

TEDDY: *(After a pause.)* You'd be lookin' to swallow some teeth.

ELROI: Then, you lay off, man! My name is Elroi. E-L-R-O-I. My Mama said my name means, The King...in French. You know that? You wanna call me somethin' else...you call me, The King! That's what!

TEDDY: You lucky your Mama ain't alive to see the mess she raised.

ELROI: Okay. You wanna talk about your Mama...we talk about your Mama...

TEDDY: Hey! Don't be startin' no dozens with me, boy! I don't allow that...not in here! I mean it! I don't tolerate the dozens...not outta your mouth! Where's your respect?

(Silence. ELROI moves away, sullen.)

TEDDY: You hear me?

ELROI: I hear ya. Then, you lay offa that Orangebird crap!

TEDDY: All right...I'll do that.

ELROI: I can't help it. I got skinny legs. I had rickets when I was a kid. Ain't my fault.

TEDDY: I know. All right, I'm sorry...shouldn't have started that...

ELROI: I spent ten dollars on these pants...and I like 'em. They sharp. I only got two pairs of pants...these, and them ol' black ones.

TEDDY: I said I was sorry, Elroi...let's just drop it, okay?

ELROI: Okay.

TEDDY: Let's have us a drink. "C'mon." *(He pours the drinks.)* To us...and to The King!

ELROI: That's right, The King!...El-Roi! And to Nappyhead Teddy...and to Guitar Frank Jackson, our partner!

(TEDDY *downs his drink.*)

TEDDY: I'm gonna call that guitar playin' low life...

(TEDDY *gets a coin from his change drawer, goes to the pay phone on a wall near the door. He finds a piece of paper in his vest pocket with the number.* TEDDY *dials the number, after dropping in the coin.*)

TEDDY: *(To* ELROI*)* If he's still sleepin', then it's time to be gettin' up. It's ringin'...*(To phone)* Who's this? Is this the King Cotton Hotel? Get me Frank Jackson's room, please. Jackson, like Stonewall! That's right...tell him it's an emergency. What? When? Son of a bitch! No...that's okay. Did he say where he was goin'? Well...is he comin' back? I see. Well...if he does, you tell him to call Teddy over in West Memphis. It's real important. 'Bye. *(He hangs up.)*

ELROI: He ain't there?

TEDDY: He done checked out of the King Cotton last night.

ELROI: Last night. What the hell for?

TEDDY: I dunno. The man at the desk don't know nothin'. Frank jes up and left in the night...took all his shit outta the room.

ELROI: Maybe he's plannin' to move it over here...

TEDDY: What for?

ELROI: I dunno...just an idea.

TEDDY: I don't like it. Maybe we oughta called the recordin' studio...in Memphis...that Sun Records. You got the number?

ELROI: There ain't no point in callin'. It's Sunday. They gonna be closed.

TEDDY: How can they be closed? We gotta recordin' session at two!

ELROI: Front office gonna be closed. Only the engineer be there to meet us this afternoon.

TEDDY: What are you sayin'?

ELROI: We're goin' in kinda on the sly. The only reason we gettin' in to record is 'cause Frank knows this engineer guy...and there ain't nobody usin' the studio on Sunday. See, Frank got it set up so we get in, cut our songs, and get gone 'fore anybody knows nothin'. Then, sometime next week, or two...the recordin' engineer...he take our record in to Sam Phillips...say, "Hey, I found this...Listen to these guys...This is some great shit." So, Sam Phillips, he listens to the songs, he digs it, and he flip out, sayin' he gotta give us a big contract right away...and there you are! We be set...we on our way!

TEDDY: Why we gotta sneak in the back door?

ELROI: 'Cause that's the way it works. Frank says we go in the front we get thrown out on our ass. These cats at Sun, they got Elvis Presley.... They big time now. You think they gonna give a damn about three coloreds from nowhere 'cross the river? No way.

TEDDY: They gonna change their tune when they hear them songs we wrote!

ELROI: Of course...but, we got to go 'bout it the right way. Frank says it's the best shot...go through the engineer.

TEDDY: I don't know...I'm gonna call the studio, jes' see if he's over there.

ELROI: Don't do it, Teddy. What if there's somebody in the office...like one of those white guys...and you get the wrong guy on the line...?

TEDDY: So. I ask to speak to the engineer. What's his name?

ELROI: I dunno. Frank didn't tell me.

TEDDY: So...how many colored engineers they gonna have?

ELROI: That's not cool. What you gonna say? "Hello, can I speak to the nigger in the booth?" You do that, it be fucked and we out for good. No record. Give him some time. Shit, it ain't but half past now...I know Frank...he ain't gonna cut an' run...I say we sit tight...wait a spell.

TEDDY: Okay, okay...maybe you right. *(Pause)* Son of a bitch, got forty dollars of mine!

ELROI: What?

TEDDY: Said he had to get his Gibson guitar out of hock.

ELROI: What Gibson guitar?

TEDDY: You tell me.

ELROI: What's the matter with this here guitar?

TEDDY: That's what I asked him. He said that ol' flat top model ain't got the right tone. He says he got an electric one on ice with one of them Jew stores on Beale street...said he need forty dollars to get it out. I tried to call him on it, he said to talk to you 'bout it...said you'd know what guitar he was talkin' about.

ELROI: Ain't never seen Frank play no Gibson 'lectric guitar.

TEDDY: Me neither. Didn't know he owned one. *(Looks at guitar)* This one sounded fine to me. He played on it all last month. Nothin' wrong with the tone...not in my ear...*(Pause, then a recognition)* He done stole my money to get hisself a new guitar! That's what that lyin' mutha done...

ELROI: Wait a minute...don't go flyin' off. We don't know what's what!

TEDDY: I been suckered! That's what! Cheat me out of my money...Well, I tell you that forty dollars is comin' out of his cut...ain't comin' out of mine!

ELROI: Okay. We work it out when he gets here. Calm down, Teddy. You gonna get your blood pressure up.

TEDDY: That no-count done piss me off! Never shoulda listened to his stories...and yours too!...let you drag my butt into this foolishness...

ELROI: You gotta relax, Teddy. Frank ain't gonna pull a fast one on you.

TEDDY: You ain't known him as long as I have. He's just a no-count drifter, that's what he is. You's a fool to believe anything he says. I know him boy, he ain't nobody's angel.

ELROI: *(Massaging* TEDDY*)* Hey! Hey! Cool out, Teddy. You're gonna have a stroke or somethin'. We gonna cut our songs today. So, you just save it. Look at you...you're sweatin', breathin' hard, your knees are twitchin'...

TEDDY: Then quit shakin' me, boy!

ELROI: Maybe you need one of your pills.

TEDDY: They on the dresser in the back room.

(ELROI *goes off.* TEDDY *wipes his face, fans himself with the newspaper, and breathes heavily.* ELROI *re-enters with a pill bottle of blood pressure medicine. He goes to the sink, finds a glass, fills it with water, and gives both to* TEDDY.)

ELROI: You gonna be okay?

TEDDY: Yeah. I be all right.

ELROI: You don't look so hot. You want me to get the chiropractor?

TEDDY: No, I be all right. Jes, let me sit a spell...get my wind.

ELROI: Can't have you dyin' on me, Teddy. Not today.

TEDDY: *(Fanning with paper.)* I made it through the war...I'll make it through this day. Don't worry 'bout me. Look out for yourself. Christ, it's hot in here. Crack that front door.

ELROI: You'll get a chill.

TEDDY: Open the door, Elroi!

(ELROI *opens the door slightly.*)

TEDDY: And while you're at it, pour me another Heaven Hill.

ELROI: That be a sure way to get to Heaven.

TEDDY: You gonna sass me? Do what I say. I know what I'm doin'.

(ELROI *pours another drink in* TEDDY's *glass.*)

TEDDY: Get yourself one, too.

ELROI: Seein' how it's my bourbon...you know, you worry me.

TEDDY: I been livin' with high blood all my life, boy. I'll be fine...soon as these pills kick in.

ELROI: How'd they ever let you in the service? Woulda thought they'd make you 4-F, or somethin'.

TEDDY: Hell...time I went in...1943...they woulda taken anybody...even a cripple. They was desperate. They didn't put me in the fightin' troops. Put me in the Quartermaster Corps. Did my time at a base in England. They made me a barber...heard my Daddy cut hair, guess they figured I cut hair, too. But, I ain't complainin'...Army was good to me. Didn't get my ass shot up by no Nazis. I did okay. After D-Day, in '44, most of the regular troops was over on the Continent...that's what they call Europe... the Continent! Anyway, there wasn't too many haircuts to be givin' for about eight months. So, I fixed it so I spent most of my time on leave. In London. Nice city, London. Met me some pretty girls.

ELROI: I bet they got some pretty gals over there.

TEDDY: Sure they do...white, Chinese, African, Jamaicans, Hindu...Siameses... they got 'em in all colors over there, boy! A veritable rainbow! They look so fine, look like God done thrown down some angels out of heaven.

ELROI: Sounds like the place for me.

TEDDY: Yeah, I liked it over there in London...seemed like paradise, you know? First place I ever been where folks didn't treat ya like you was some ol' dog. See, it's different over there...color don't seem to keep folks apart like it does back home. You see men like Duke Ellington, and Louis Armstrong-they're treated like kings over there. I seen a picture in the paper...Duke Ellington kissing the hand of the Queen of England! Imagine that! Kissin' her hand...and it's on the front page of the paper! Try that over in Memphis...they'd nail your carcass to the bridge, 'til the buzzards picked you clean. *(Pause)* Yeah...England...spent the finest eight months of my life there. *(Reminiscing)* I had me a nice little Irish girl for a while, name of Marie...coal black hair, blue eyes...skin like alabaster. I coulda married that girl if I'd wanted to...her family didn't mind...and she was Catholic. But I didn't care about that, you know? (TEDDY *broods into his drink.*) Sometimes I wonder what it would have been like if I'd just stayed on over there after the war...lot of our boys did, you know?

ELROI: Why'd you come back? I woulda stayed....

TEDDY: I had responsibilities back here in West Memphis...when my father took sick...wasn't nobody to run the shop *(Pause)* maybe I'll take you over there sometime...

ELROI: Yeah...just as soon as we get Elvis Presley to sing our songs. Yes, sir...I be out of here for good. London, here we come!

TEDDY: Last week we was goin' to Chicago. Week before that, it was where? Harlem?

ELROI: Hell, I go anyplace outta the South. Someplace where I don't have to keep my eyes down just cause there's somebody white in the room.

TEDDY: You dreamin'...'taint never gonna be that way in this country.

ELROI: Unless you a big star...like Johnny Ace! He didn't have to take crap from nobody...white, or colored.

TEDDY: Johnny was different...the exception. Not many like him.

ELROI: First time I heard him sing, I knew that's what I wanted. Just like that. Everybody know my name...walk down the sidewalk with a gal on each arm...stroll right on up to the front door of the Peabody Hotel, walk right past the doorman, on up to the register desk...get me a suite of rooms...with champagne to boot! Jes, like that!

TEDDY: Even Johnny Ace never got in the front door of the Peabody Hotel.

ELROI: Someday...it gonna happen.

TEDDY: Not in my lifetime.

ELROI: Maybe I be the one...

TEDDY: You drunk with glory, boy.

(TEDDY *goes over to the record player and plays the second side of the Johnny Ace single. The song* Never Let Me Go *begins.*)

ELROI: *(Recognizing the tune)* My man...Johnny.

TEDDY: Best of the uptown singers.

(TEDDY *leans back, closes his eyes, and listens to the plaintive tone of Johnny Ace's singing.*)

ELROI: *(Nostalgic)* Man, he could sing...

TEDDY: The best of the best...

ELROI: Why did the fool wanna kill hisself? He had it all...money, women, sharp cars...everything. *(Pause)* I remember the night I heard he was dead...last year... what was it?...New Year's Eve...

TEDDY: *(Correcting)* Christmas Eve.

ELROI: Right, Christmas Eve.

TEDDY: *(Reclining, with eyes closed.)* Backstage at the City Auditorium, Houston, Texas...intermission of the Christmas show...Johnny put a bullet in the chamber of his pistol, spun it around, put the gun to his head, and pulled the trigger. *(Pause)* Never finished the show.

ELROI: What a waste. Playin' Russian Roulette...You knew the guy... why he wanta do somethin' crazy like that?

TEDDY: I dunno...folks said he did it to impress some girl...

ELROI: White girl, I bet.

TEDDY: Pink Miller says it wasn't no accident...he was just bored... bored with livin'. I remember him from the ol' days in Memphis... he always liked to play cards...and he carried a pistol, even back then... always pullin' it out, twirlin' it around...cockin' that piece, like he was crazy or somethin'. You shoulda seen him the last time he played the Palace in Memphis...The whole crowd was real impatient during the opening act... Big Mama Thornton, had to get off early...Then Johnny come out and all hell broke loose. He had all the girls up close, crowdin' the edge of the stage, and on them ballads he'd lean over to 'em...real close and sexy, like he was singin' just to them. Girls would start screamin' like a snake bit 'em.

ELROI: Man, I wish I'd been there.

TEDDY: Couldn't half hear the music...bitches swoonin' in the aisles. *(Laughs)* Women was always chasin' after Johnny Alexander...that was his real name, back when he went to Washington High School.

ELROI: How'd you meet him?

TEDDY: I met him after he come back from the Navy. Every Friday night, Frank, and me, and Johnny, Pink Miller, and some other guys...we used to play cards over in the back room of Dinky's Tavern...offa Lamar Boulevard. Them was some nights, I tell you. And Johnny...he was always showin' off that pistol.... *(Long pause)* Them days is gone now. *(Pause)* I went to the funeral. Everybody in Memphis...seems like was there...never seen so many flowers. And the fans...shit, girls was weepin' and moanin'...tryin' to throw themselves on top the casket. Police had to come...pry 'em off...just to get the coffin in the ground.

(The record ends. ELROI *goes to the record player.)*

ELROI: You want hear the other side?

TEDDY: Yeah, that be fine. But, keep your greasy fingers offa the record surface. I can't sell those things to folks if they got your finger prints all over them.

ELROI: You ain't gonna sell this record, been played so many times, the grooves 'bout done wore out.

(ELROI *puts record on.* Pledging My Love, *Johnny Ace's most famous song.* ELROI *mimes a singing routine in the mirror.* ELROI *gets an idea for a song, he turns off the record, finds a pencil, and his well-worn songwriting notebook.*)

ELROI: Teddy, we gotta write us a ballad like that. Now, help me out...

(ELROI *sits near* TEDDY. ELROI *hums a tune similar to a Johnny Ace ballad tempo.* ELROI *struggles to find the first line of the song.*)

ELROI: *(Sings as he scribbles)*
Don't leave me my darlin'
Why won't you be true?

(TEDDY *watches, helpless to add any idea to the process.*)

ELROI: Come on, Teddy...help me out...

TEDDY: I'm thinkin' Elroi...I'm thinkin'...

ELROI: *(Sings and scribbles.)* I always think of you...

TEDDY: *(Following* ELROI's *lead)* ...always think of you...

ELROI: *(Starts over-singing)*
Don't leave me my darlin'
Why don't you be true?

(TEDDY *joins in, unsure*)

ELROI & TEDDY: I always think of you....
Don't make me feel....

(Pause)

TEDDY: *(Blurts out gleefully.)* BLUE! Blue...that's it..."Don't make me feel blue!"

ELROI: *(Sings and writes.)* "I always think of you...don't make me feel blue..." All right, that's the first verse....

(ELROI *repeats the phrase, and slowly realizes that it sounds exactly like Johnny Ace's,* Pledging My Love.)

ELROI: Wait a minute...that sounds like....

(TEDDY *and* ELROI *slowly look toward the record player, and sink in despair.*)

ELROI: Oh, shit! *(He scratches out the page of lyrics.)* Naw, I don't copy nobody's style. No way. We can do better than that. Come on, Teddy... follow this groove with me...we'll make up our own beat.... Boom, Boom, diddy boom...diddy....you followin' this with me? Come on, help me out, Teddy. Boom, diddy, boom, diddy, diddy...Teddy? You listenin' to me? Talk to me...

TEDDY: *(After a pause.)* We dreamin'...that's all we doin'.

ELROI: *(Throws pencil down.)* You gettin' in a funk on me again?

TEDDY: We ain't got no experience as songwriters. Who we kiddin'? I can't come up with songs like that, Elroi. Not a chance.

ELROI: Hey, where's your confidence?

TEDDY: Done been kicked outta me. I ain't as young as you, Elroi. I been around. I seen what's possible...and what ain't...

ELROI: Man, what is wrong with you? We got talent.

TEDDY: Just foolin' ourselves...

ELROI: You got a bad attitude, Teddy. You gettin' sad-eyed drunk on me, and you not makin' sense...just feelin' sorry for yourself. We gonna make it with a charm...see, we got a special kind of luck on our side. I wanna show you somethin'....

(ELROI *goes to his jacket hanging on a hook. From the pocket, he pulls out a "mojo hand"—a talisman, wrapped in red flannel with a dark string attached.* ELROI *shows the mojo to* TEDDY.)

ELROI: Look here...we got magic with us.

TEDDY: What is that thing?

ELROI: It's a mojo.

TEDDY: Aw, for Chrissake!

ELROI: I was gonna give it to Frank...but, I reckon you need it worse than him...it be a charm, see...

TEDDY: Get that thing away from me.

ELROI: C'mon, I went to the conjure woman, and she made it up special for us.

TEDDY: Ol' conjure woman is nothin' but a fake.

ELROI: She is not.

TEDDY: How can you believe in that voodoo?

ELROI: Ain't voodoo. It's powerful medicine. I know, 'cause my Mama went to the conjure woman when I was bad sick...conjure woman made up one of her spells...put a mojo on my body...and them rickets, just cleared up. It's the truth...done went away. I could walk normal again...Doctors said I might never get outta the bed...and the conjure woman, she cured me.

TEDDY: You's a fool to believe that.

ELROI: It's good magic. She done fixed it up, and it's guaranteed. She say it bring back a lost love, give a person good luck...can even chase out the devil.

TEDDY: Them things is curses too.

ELROI: Not this one. I told her...we be needin' good fortune. Now, you put this on...you see if it don't change your whole outlook...maybe even lower your blood pressure, too.

TEDDY: I ain't gonna wear nothin' made by that ol' witch.

ELDOI: C'mon, it ain't gonna bite you. Try it on.

TEDDY: *(Moves away)* Conjure woman is the ugliest lookin' woman on God's Earth. Face like a monkey...scrawny legs...look like a twisted 'possum...

ELROI: You scared of the mojo, ain't you? You scared it might have the power...ain't that right?

TEDDY: I ain't scared of that little sack.

ELROI: Then why won't you touch it?

TEDDY: Damn foolishness.

ELROI: Touch the mojo.

TEDDY: It's a sin against the Lord.

ELROI: Since when you go to church?

TEDDY: It ain't right.

ELROI: Look at you. You is scared.

TEDDY: No I ain't.

ELROI: Okay, then...put out your hand. Take the mojo...jes hold it in your hand. It ain't gonna hurt you.

(Reluctantly, TEDDY *takes the sack.)*

TEDDY: What she put in here?

ELROI: Potions.

TEDDY: *(Sniffs the mojo.)* Smells like somethin' rotten.

ELROI: Means it's doin' its work.

TEDDY: What's in this thing...make it smell so bad?

ELROI: I don't know what all...some herbs...Samson's snakeroot, Devil's shoestring, some flour, a lump of coal...drippings...I don't know everything...but it works. She said some words over it, and it give off smoke. I swear...I seen the smoke.

TEDDY: *(Tries to hand it to* ELROI*)* Here...take it back.

ELROI: Say your full name.

TEDDY: What?

ELROI: Just say your full name. Come on...say it...

TEDDY: What for?

ELROI: Just do it. Full name...not just Teddy.

TEDDY: Theodore Booker Nalls. Satisfied? Now, take this stupid thing back.

ELROI: I can't.

TEDDY: Why not?

ELROI: It's yours now. The spell be workin'. See, you done said your name over it...it belongs to you...won't work for nobody but the name it hears last.

TEDDY: Well, I don't want it.

ELROI: Too late now. You got it.

TEDDY: I ain't wearin' this thing!

ELROI: You got to. Put it 'round your neck.

TEDDY: What if I say your name over it?

ELROI: Won't work right. I'd have to be holdin' it, and I'd have to say it... besides, a mojo ain't supposed to change hands, once they been adopted... be like throwin' out a child...maybe bring on a curse.

TEDDY: Are you shittin' me?

ELROI: No, that's what the conjure woman say, and she don't lie. The mojo is yours...better put it 'round your neck.

TEDDY: What happens if I don't?

ELROI: I dunno. I ain't sure I wanna find out.

(TEDDY *looks at the mojo, and finally slips the string over his head.*)

TEDDY: Are you happy now? Do I have to wear it all the time? Even when I'm sleeping?

ELROI: Don't know...I'll have to ask the woman...you best keep it on 'til we find out what to do next.

(TEDDY *tries to hide the mojo, placing it inside his shirt.*)

TEDDY: People see this thing...they think I'm nuts. (*Pulls out the mojo from inside his shirt*) Damn thing itches. You talk to her first thing tomorrow, 'cause ain't no way I'm gonna wear this thing all the time.

ELROI: I'll ask her. So...how you feelin'?

TEDDY: I feel like an idiot.

ELROI: You know...different? Relaxed?...what do you feel?

TEDDY: Nothin! Was you expectin' smoke?

ELROI: Maybe we done it wrong...left somethin' out...

TEDDY: If I get poisoned, or I die from this thing...you gonna be in some big trouble.

(Pay phone rings. They stare at it for a moment. It rings again.)

ELROI: Frank! It's Frank...see, the charm is workin'.

TEDDY: I'll get it. *(Answers phone.)* Hello...who? This is him...speakin'.

ELROI: Is it him?

(TEDDY nods.)

Where is he? Is he comin'?

(TEDDY shoos him away.)

TEDDY: Operator, where is this call coming from:

ELROI: Long distance?

TEDDY: *(On phone)* Helena? You mean Helena, Arkansas?

ELROI: What the fuck he doin' in Helena?

TEDDY: *(To phone.)* Yes, ma'm...I'm sorry...I didn't mean to cuss in your ear...

ELROI: Don't he know we gotta make a record in an hour?

TEDDY: *(To phone.)* 'scuse me a minute, ma'am.

ELROI: He supposed to be here...

TEDDY: *(Covers receiver, to ELROI)* Stop your jabberin'...and just maybe I can find out what's goin' on! Move away from here...I'm talkin' long distance...

(ELROI moves away, TEDDY turns back to phone.)

TEDDY: Yes ma'm. Put him on. Hello, Frank? What is goin' on? Unh-huh...unh-huh. We been waiting to go to the studio and...

ELROI: What's goin' on?

TEDDY: *(On phone)* Your sister? What about her?...so? Ain't you got sense, nigger? We supposed to be in Memphis at two o'clock. Elroi says the engineer is waitin' on us...He what?...When? If it was last night...Why didn't you call me, fool? We was supposed to be there, too...

ELROI: What about the session? What he say? They change it on us?

TEDDY: *(On phone.)* I don't care 'bout that...I wanna know about our songs. SON OF A BITCH!

(TEDDY slumps, letting the phone drop from his hand. The receiver bounces against the wall. TEDDY walks away from the phone, unable to talk. He stares vacantly out the window. ELROI is confused.)

ELROI: What he say about our songs?

(TEDDY *doesn't answer.* ELROI *grabs the dangling receiver.*)

ELROI: Frank...Frank...you there? This is Elroi...Frank.

(*The line is dead.* ELROI *replaces the receiver, looks expectantly at* TEDDY.)

ELROI: What he say?

(TEDDY *remains turned away from* ELROI.)

TEDDY: Ain't gonna be no recordin' session.

ELROI: How can that be? We had it all set up...

TEDDY: The engineer changed the time...it was last night...that's why he done left the hotel.

(*Turns to* ELROI)

ELROI: Last night? How can the session be last night? He woulda called us...what about our songs...we was supposed to be there, too...

TEDDY: Frank done his own songs...we been scratched offa the list.

ELROI: I don't believe it...Frank ain't like that...

TEDDY: (*Exploding*) WAKE UP, BOY! WE BEEN CUT!

(ELROI *stands frozen, shaking his head, unable to fathom the idea.*)

TEDDY: Our partner...Guitar Frank Jackson...the big man, you always talkin' up...done SOLD US OUT! (*Pause*) AND STOLE MY FORTY DOLLARS! To boot!

ELROI: No...can't be...no...

TEDDY: Yes, Elroi, yes....

(TEDDY *tears at his own shirt, sweating profusely. He grabs the mojo, and rips the cord from around his neck.*)

TEDDY: Mojo hand...ignorant voodoo! (*He hurls the mojo down.*)

TEDDY: Good luck, my ass! Give me the bad luck! Bring it on, Goddamn it, bring it on!

(TEDDY *and* ELROI *look at each other. Slowly,* ELROI *bends to pick up the mojo, holds it in his hand...*ELROI *looks at* TEDDY, *as the lights fade out.*)

END OF ACT ONE

ACT TWO

Scene One

(Time: A week later. Late evening)

(Scene: The same)

(At rise: Most of the lights in the barber shop have been turned off. ELROI is lying on the reclined barber chair, arm covering his face. He is listening to Johnny Ace playing quietly on the record player. The front door opens quietly. FRANK JACKSON steps into the shop, carrying a guitar case. FRANK is a tall black man in his early forties. He wears a new winter coat, a new cowboy hat, and a pair of new cowboy boots. He sets down the guitar case and closes the door quietly. ELROI does not hear him come in. FRANK takes off his gloves, blows on his hands, rubbing them together. He crosses to the heating grate and stands over the blowing heat.)

FRANK: *(To himself)* Brr! Cold in Tennessee!

(ELROI sits up suddenly.)

ELROI: Frank?

FRANK: Who's there? That you, Teddy?

(ELROI rises, turns on a light. He is still wearing the orange pants, but now with a different shirt. FRANK sees him and smiles broadly.)

Well, I'll be...Orangebird, hisself. You glad to see me again, boy?

ELROI: *(Surprised)* Frank.

FRANK: Here I be...done blown across the river to see you special. And I brung somethin' for you. Bet you know what I'm talkin' about don't you?

ELROI: Where the hell you been?

FRANK: Is that any kind of greetin' for your partner? Lighten up, Orangebird...I come back from down the Delta.

ELROI: You been gone over a week.

FRANK: I know that. Was you expectin' me for dinner or somethin'?

ELROI: Where you been?

FRANK: I been with my sister down in Helena...then I been in Memphis, and I played a few joints...both sides of the river, work my way north...and now I'm standin' here. What's with you? Where's Teddy? He in the back room?

ELROI: He ain't here right now.

(FRANK *hangs up his coat on the hooks, strolls into the back room, comes back out.*)

ELROI: What's the matter? Don't you believe me?

FRANK: Sure, boy...sure. So, where's Teddy?

(ELROI *shrugs.*)

FRANK: Out drinkin', huh? What you been up to?

ELROI: I should be askin' you that.

FRANK: *(Walks around the room.)* Makin' money, my man...earnin' my daily bread.

(FRANK *goes to the barber sink behind the chair, takes off his shirt, and fills the basin with hot water. He removes his cowboy hat and places it on* ELROI's *head.*)

FRANK: How you like that? Genuine Stetson. Got that hat in a a Jew shop over on Beale Street. You like it? Looks real good on you. *(Indicates the mirror.)* Check yourself out. See? Pecos Pete...*(Laughs)* Orangebird on the range!

(ELROI *removes the hat, sets it aside,* FRANK *lathers his face with shaving cream. He finds one of Teddy's razors, begins stroking the razor on a strap on the chair.*)

FRANK: Five whole days now, I been dreamin' about a nice hot bath...and a good shave. Teddy ain't here...guess I have to shave myself. Where you say he is, Orangebird?

ELROI: I dunno...he went out after supper...maybe he gone for a walk.

FRANK: He say anything about me?

ELROI: Not much.

(FRANK *starts shaving. After a few strokes, he looks at* ELROI *in the mirror who is staring at him.*)

FRANK: You be awful quiet, Elroi...You be thinkin' mighty hard on somethin', what might that be?

ELROI: I don't want you to call me Orangebird no more.

FRANK: *(After a pause.)* All right, if that's what you want. I was only funnin' ya...What you want me to call you?

ELROI: Nothin'.

FRANK: Nothin' it is, then. You wanna hand me that towel, over there?

(ELROI *gives him the towel.*)

FRANK: What's the matter with you? Ain't you never seen a man shave before? Somethin' buggin' you?

ELROI: You lucky you didn't come back here last Sunday night. Teddy was hot...he mighta killed you.

FRANK: Yeah, I know he wasn't too pleased...way things turned out. Not my fault...just happened, you know? My sister took sick...they done put her in the hospital...

ELROI: If I was you, I'd get out of here, 'fore he comes back.

FRANK: Oh? Teddy gonna start in a cuttin'...huh? *(Laughs)* I don't think so. He change his tune, when I show him what I got in that guitar case over there.

ELROI: I know what you got in there.

FRANK: What might that be?

ELROI: You know! Why'd you steal his money for a new guitar...then have to lie about it?

FRANK: New guitar? That what he told you? Shit! Ain't no new guitar...

(FRANK *opens the case, removes a red electric guitar, he plugs it into the amplifier...and tunes it.*)

FRANK: This here, ain't new...this is my "Emma-Jean", my ol' guitar. She done been locked up in the pawnshop for almost seven months... had to get her out. Never made a record without my Emma-Jean... kinda superstitious about things like that...she's my charm. You like her?

ELROI: If you got Teddy's forty dollars...

FRANK: I got it.

ELROI: Then leave it on the shelf...and you better get your butt back cross the river...he mad about that money....

FRANK: Forty dollars! That all he worried about? That ain't squat! How about I leave two hundred and forty there on the shelf. Maybe that make up for some of his troubles.

ELROI: You ain't got that kind of money.

(FRANK *reaches into his trouser pocket and removes a roll of bills. Places money on the shelf.*)

FRANK: Count it, boy.

(ELROI *counts the money,* FRANK *crosses to shoeshine chair, sits, and rolls a cigarette.*)

ELROI: *(Finished counting.)* You rob a bank?

FRANK: Bet you ain't ever seen that much money in one place. That ain't even includin' your share, boy.

ELROI: My share?

FRANK: Yeah. Your wages...from them songs I recorded...*Can't Get Your Lovin' Off My Mind...Mean Disposition...Short-Haired Gal.*

ELROI: You jivin'...

FRANK: No, I ain't.

(ELROI *whoops.*)

FRANK: See these boots? Brand new. (*Laughs*) Got kinda scuffed up in that Delta mud...maybe, you give me a quick shine job...I leave you a big tip. (*He laughs, picks up the guitar, strums a few chords.*)

ELROI: Tell me the truth, man....Where did you get all this money?

FRANK: I done told you...makin' records, my man. That's what I do! (*He plays a fast blues run and begins singing,* Can't Get Your Lovin' Off My Mind.)
I woke up with the blues on a Sunday
Had the same ol' thing on Monday
Now, Lordy, it's Tuesday already
I still ain't feelin' too fine
I think I smell me some trouble
It's got me seein' double
I just can't get your lovin' off my mind.

(FRANK *stops;* ELROI *jumps with excitement.*)

ELROI: You done it! You recorded my song!

FRANK: What I been saying to you?

ELROI: You gone and done it...DAMN!

FRANK: I strolled right in there...pulled out ol' Emma-Jean, plugged her in, fired her up...and the man started ravin' about my sound. Just can't get enough of it. The man sends out for a bottle of Wild Turkey and some hush puppies, and I set there over three hours, and I set down...oh, I don't know...must've been seventeen or eighteen numbers....Man says he loves my sound. (*Laughs*) We rich now, Orangebird...I mean Elroi...we rich men. Pretty slick, huh? (*He plays a fancy guitar figure.*)

ELROI: Goddamn! I can't believe it! (*Pause*) But, you was supposed to take us along...that was part of the deal.

FRANK: Had to change it, boy. Man says he only got one microphone...and besides ain't much room in that recordin' booth...but, hell I brung ya the record...the first one they gonna release this week.

ELROI: They gave you the record? (*Looks in* FRANK's *guitar case.*) Where is it? Lemme see...

(FRANK *closes the guitar case with his foot, holds it closed.*)

FRANK: Hold on...be plenty of time for that later. First, how about that shine I be needin'?

ELROI: I wanna hear our song.

FRANK: You get to it in a spell. How about you cleanin' the Mississippi offa these boots now? Maybe I give you an extra ten dollars, if you do a good job.

ELROI: You got a deal!

(ELROI *grins, grabs his shoeshine brushes, and goes to work furiously.* FRANK *lays a blues run while* ELROI *works.*)

FRANK: C'mon, boy...this is your song, sing it with me...

(*They sing together as* ELROI *works.*)

FRANK & ELROI: I woke up with the blues on a Sunday
Had the same ol' thing on Monday
Now, Lordy, it's Tuesday already
I still ain't feelin' too fine
I think I smell me some trouble
It's got me seein double
I just can't get your lovin' off my mind.

Went to see my doctor just the other day,
Now I gotta tell ya what the man had to say,
He said, "You'll be feelin' funny
'Til you find that lovin' honey.
Got no pills to cure the achin',
My hands and feet are shakin',
Got these tears flowin' from my eyes,
My knees are feelin' weak.
Ever since you left me, baby,
I got a bad luck streak.

Can't nobody help me with this pain of mine?
Just can't seem to get her lovin' off my mind.
(*They laugh at end of song.*)

ELROI: So, tell me what happened. What the man say? What he say about the songs? He say he gonna show 'em to Elvis?

FRANK: Elvis? Hey, hold on....All I done was cut some blues numbers. That's all. Weren't no Elvis Presley where I was...

ELROI: What did the engineer say? He like them songs?

FRANK: He loved 'em. The man said we might even get a hit record outta one of them songs.

ELROI: *(Whoops)* All right! Damn! You mean we gonna hear my song on the radio? Right here in Memphis?

FRANK: Sure. You just wait, Elroi...it be on the radio before you know it.... Hell, folks all 'round the South gonna hear it....They be singin' *Can't Get Your Lovin' Off My Mind* on their way to work every mornin'. It'll be on so many juke boxes...you'll get tired of hearin' it...be drifting outta every joint on Beale Street....You'll see.

ELROI: Damn! We done it! I can't believe it. *(Pause)* You ain't just fuckin' with me are ya?

FRANK: No...I told ya...I recorded them songs.

ELROI: Man, what was it like?...I mean in the recordin' studio?...Did they make ya sign a contract?

FRANK: Contract! Shit, boy! I made 'em pay me cash. Never did trust them white boys' contracts. They pay me after each song....I sing one, I gets the money...then I do another one. They wants a third, they pay me right then...cash up front. Long as they keep the money comin' and the whiskey flowin' I play all night long. No white record company gonna cheat me again. I learned my lesson the last time I cut some sides, back in the forties. Always take the cash. I take a piss on their promises. See, you gotta let 'em know what's what.

ELROI: Right!

(FRANK *notices the cord under the collar of* ELROI's *shirt.*)

FRANK: What's that?

ELROI: What?

FRANK: That rope 'round your neck. What's that? *(He pulls it out.)*

FRANK: Well lookee here...got yourself a mojo. Where you get that?

ELROI: I found it.

FRANK: Conjure woman make that up for you?

ELROI: Yeah...she said it bring us luck. I was savin' it for you.

FRANK: Them things don't work. Few years back in Alabama, an ol' conjure woman give me a mojo....said, "Son, you wear this thing, and you can "pass!" *(He laughs.)* Conjure woman was full of shit!
(He plays and sings a quick ditty.)
If you black, well get back,
If you brown, stick around,
If you white, well that's all right....

(ELROI *finishes shining the boots.*)

ELROI: There...it's done.

FRANK: Mighty nice. Thank you, dad.

ELROI: Now, c'mon, I wanna hear that record. You promised...

(FRANK *steps down from the shoe shine chair. He takes a roll of money from his pocket, peels off a few bills, hands them to* ELROI.)

FRANK: I keep my promises, boy. Here's two hundred and ten dollars.

(ELROI *stares at the money, astounded.*)

FRANK: Well, ain't you gonna say somethin'? Or you gonna stand there with your mouth open? That there is more money than you ever made shinin' shoes. Go on, put it in your pocket.

ELROI: You mean, I get all this money?

FRANK: I told you. You earned it. For helpin' me out...you and Teddy... lettin' me store my gear in your place...feedin' me some meals...and...

ELROI: And them songs...

FRANK: And for that too. That's your cut.

(TEDDY *comes in the front door, stops, looks warily at* FRANK.)

ELROI: Teddy, Frank...

FRANK: *(To* ELROI.*)* I got it, I got it...jes' be cool.

(ELROI *puts the cash in his pocket.* TEDDY *seems a bit tipsy.*)

TEDDY: Saw all these lights on...shoulda known you'd be back.

FRANK: Yeah. I come in tonight. Me and Elroi was just talkin' about you. He says you missed me. That true?

(TEDDY *ignores him. He hangs up his coat on the hook next to* FRANK's. TEDDY *touches* FRANK's *hat.*)

FRANK: That there's a new Stetson. You like it...I let you have it. Try it on.

TEDDY: Already got me a hat.

(TEDDY *removes a slab bottle of corn liquor from his hip pocket. He gets a glass from the shelf, and pours a drink.* TEDDY *notices the money lying on the shelf by the sink. He picks up the money, looks at* FRANK.*)*

FRANK: That's the forty dollars I borrowed...and some interest.

TEDDY: So, you done struck it rich, huh?

ELROI: Frank recorded them songs we wrote, Teddy. He says they gonna be on the radio this week. Teddy, we gonna be famous.

FRANK: Yeah. I come by to pick up my stuff...think I'll be movin' on soon....maybe go to Houston for a bit.

TEDDY: Good. When you leavin'? Tomorrow?

(FRANK *looks at* TEDDY *for a long moment.*)

FRANK: Okay...tomorrow. Hey, why I get the treatment from you? I come back and I brung you money...lots of it. I cut those songs we been workin' on...I thought you'd be happy about that.

TEDDY: I been listenin' to KWEM this week. I ain't heard it yet.

FRANK: Record just come out...in a coupla days maybe they play it...

ELROI: Frank brung the record, Teddy. I want to hear it.

(FRANK *opens his guitar case, takes out a 78 R P M record.*)

FRANK: Teddy, here 'tis. You want me to put it on?

TEDDY: Well it ain't gonna play itself, is it?

FRANK: *(To* ELROI*)* Nigger's jaws is tight.

(FRANK *goes to the record player, puts on the record.*)

FRANK: You gonna like this. Got a nice deep sound...bluesy like.

(*The song begins. A loping guitar figure.*)

ELROI: What the hell's that?

FRANK: That's the intro...just wait...

(FRANK*'s voice is heard singing. The song is a medium-tempo blues shuffle, much in the style of Lightnin' Hopkins or John Lee Hooker.*)

That's me...motherfucker! What you think? Sound good, huh?

TEDDY: Shut up...I'm listenin....

ELROI: Man, it's too slow...too fuckin' slow. You got it on the right speed?

FRANK: Yeah, it's on seventy-eight.

ELROI: Can't be...it's too slow...that ain't the right tempo...lemme see.

FRANK: *(Irritated)* Motherfucker, this is the way I recorded the song. I know if it's right.

TEDDY: Shut up.

ELROI: Man, it's all wrong! Teddy, it's wrong! That ain't the way it goes. It's supposed to be faster, like a jump tune.

FRANK: Jump tune...shit! It's the blues.

ELROI: Not even fast...farm-boy shuffle music...

FRANK: It ain't no rock-and-roll song! So just shut your face, 'fore I close it for you.

ELROI: You done it all wrong! Jive Ass! He done it all wrong!

TEDDY: *(Bellowing)* I'M TRYING TO HEAR THE FUCKING SONG!!!

ELROI: *(Kicks the wall.)* It ain't like we rehearsed it!

FRANK: We rehearsed it? What did you do, boy?...Jes slap your hand on your knee while I played the guitar...that's all you did.

ELROI: You fucked it up!

FRANK: Who you be? You the expert on music? Jive ass, Orangebird!

(ELROI *is furious. He kicks* FRANK's *guitar case.*)

ELROI: LYIN' MOTHERFUCKER! YOU RUINED MY SONG!

TEDDY: Elroi!

FRANK: Hey, don't you ever kick my guitar case! Boy...I'll cut your ass!

(FRANK *picks up* TEDDY's *straight razor from the shelf.* TEDDY *tears the record from the turntable with a loud scratch sound.*)

TEDDY: That's enough! Put it down!!

FRANK: This dumb nigger done kicked my case.

TEDDY: MOTHERFUCKER! Put it down!

(FRANK *stands holding the open razor.* TEDDY *steps in to him, a stern warning.*)

TEDDY: Don't make me get my pistol...

(TEDDY *stares* FRANK *down.* FRANK *lowers the razor, closes it and puts it back on the shelf.*)

TEDDY: Frank...don't you ever touch no razor in my shop!

FRANK: Then you tell this kid to keep away from my stuff.

(FRANK *goes over to examine his guitar case.*)

FRANK: *(To* ELROI*)* You just damn lucky that guitar wasn't in there. You hurt my Emma-Jean...you be dead meat.

ELROI: He was gonna cut me! You believe that?

TEDDY: Okay, okay. BE QUIET! Both of you!

(ELROI *takes the money from his pocket and throws it on the floor at* FRANK.)

ELROI: Don't want your money, nigger! You cheatin' liar...

(TEDDY *grabs* ELROI *and slams him against the wall, hand around his throat.*)

TEDDY: I SAID BE QUIET!

ELROI: Didn't you hear what he done to the song?

TEDDY: *(Choking* ELROI*)* I SAID BE COOL! BE NO FIGHTIN' IN MY SHOP! YOU HEAR?

FRANK: Let the boy go, Teddy. You done choked off his wind.

(TEDDY *releases* ELROI, *who coughs and spits into the sink.* TEDDY *gives* ELROI *a swig of corn liquor.*)

TEDDY: Here...drink this. You gonna be all right. C'mon, Elroi...You sit down in my chair. I don't want to have to hurt you, but you out of control....

(ELROI *sits in the barber chair, face in his hands.* FRANK *slowly picks up the money from the floor.*)

TEDDY: Now, the three of us gonna start actin' civilized. I ain't havin' the po-lice come bustin' in here. *(Pause)* What's all that money on the floor?

FRANK: It's his. I give it to him for them songs. That's your split over there on the shelf.

TEDDY: Give it here.

(FRANK *gives him* ELROI's *money.* TEDDY *hands it to* ELROI.)

TEDDY: Go on, put it in your pocket.

(ELROI *hesitates.*)

TEDDY: Only a fool throw that much money on the floor.

ELROI: *(Pocketing the money.)* Still don't make it right.

FRANK: You's the strangest Orangebird I ever did see. Don't make no sense at all...

ELROI: That ain't my name. I'm Elroi...The King!

FRANK: King shit! That's what...

TEDDY: *(Warning)* Frank...lay off.

FRANK: Okay. I get my stuff, and I move on. That's what you want. You two done confuse me enough. Get me that record offa the victrola...You wreck it?

(TEDDY *goes to the record player, looks at the record.*)

TEDDY: Got a big scratch across it...

(FRANK *begins packing up his things which are stored near the amplifier.*)

FRANK: Then you keep it...a souvenir of our association. I can get me another one somewheres else.

TEDDY: *(Reading the record label.) Can't Get Your Lovin' Off My Mind.*

FRANK: *Mean Disposition* is on the other side.

TEDDY: Elroi, you wanna hear your song, *Mean Disposition*? I'll put it on if you wants.

ELROI: No, I don't wanna hear it...be the same crap as the other one...

(TEDDY *looks closer at the record label and frowns.*)

TEDDY: This ain't no Sun Records.... What the hell is Jewel Tone Records?

(ELROI *looks up.*)

ELROI: Jewel Tone...where's that?

FRANK: They a blues record company outside Helena.

TEDDY: *(Reads label.)* I thought you gone to Sun...in Memphis...by Smilin' Frank...who's that?

FRANK: That's me...my new stage name...Smilin' Frank.

ELROI: Yeah, I just bet you was smilin' when you ruined my song.

TEDDY: Elroi, be quiet...Frank...how 'bout you explainin' this...Jewel Tone.

FRANK: I went down to Helena to see my sister. I cut them sides down there.

ELROI: You said you was goin' to Sun...said you had this engineer friend who was gonna fix it so we get to record in there.

FRANK: No...I said maybe that be the case...as it turns out, that engineer was just talkin' in his hat.

TEDDY: Then why you lie to us?

FRANK: I said maybe we gets in and maybe we don't...that's all I said! Now if you want to turn it all around...

TEDDY: That's not what we understood.

FRANK: Well you been understandin' only the parts you want to hear. That be a big problem with you, Teddy. You don't hear what folks says to you...you gotta read somethin' else into it.

ELROI: You said the engineer could get to Elvis.

FRANK: No, you said that! I only said, that he had seen Elvis in the studio. See what I mean? You two...like peas in a pod...know about as much as that ol' conjure woman, and she don't know shit!

ELROI: But you said the engineer could get 'em to Sam Phillips...they get us writin' songs for all them white cats. They record 'em and then they hit records...

FRANK: Whoa! Hold on...I recorded them songs. Anybody gonna have a hit record, motherfucker, it gonna be me! Not some ofay hillbilly with sideburns. It's my record, see! Where you get this pea-brained idea? *(Looks at* TEDDY.*)* Need I ask! You been poisonin' this boy's mind, and that's a fact.

TEDDY: I wanna know why you had to sneak off to Helena...don't tell us one word 'bout what you doin'...

FRANK: You think back...you recall I told you last Sunday on the phone. But, do you listen? Hell, no! I done told you my sister took sick and they put her in the hospital...so, I grabbed a bus down there so there be someone to look after the kids while she's out. Now ain't that exactly what I said to you, Teddy?

TEDDY: I dunno...I don't remember.

FRANK: *(Mimicking* TEDDY*)* I dunno...I don't remember. *(Pause)* Damn good thing I ain't ever got any important messages for y'all.

TEDDY: I remember you said the time of the session was changed.

FRANK: It was. I went in Saturday night...instead of Sunday...

TEDDY: You talkin' about Jewel Tone! I'm talkin' about Sun...in Memphis! That's what we talkin' about! Don't weasel me...what about Sun Records? Let's get this straight. I know you said Sun...on the phone to me...

FRANK: *(Fed up)* Christ Almighty! All right...you wanna hear it? I give it to you...but you ain't gonna like it. *(Calmly rolls a cigarette)* I went over to Sun...to talk to the engineer...just to make sure it was all set for Sunday.

ELROI: When was that?

FRANK: I dunno...musta been last Thursday.

TEDDY: What happened?

FRANK: Engineer said no go! Somebody in the office got wind of it and the word come back...Sun Records ain't interested in recordin' colored singers no more...

ELROI: That ain't true...they got Howlin' Wolf...and Junior Parker.

FRANK: That was before...before this Presley kid got so big on them blues numbers he done stole from Big Boy Crudup. Engineer guy says they only recordin' these hillbilly cats now...this Carl Perkins, and a Johnny Cash... said they don't need us no more. Said Sam Phillips been sayin' for years if he could just find him a white man who could sing like a colored...he could make a million dollars. Well, I guess he done found one.

ELROI: But those is colored songs they recordin'.

FRANK: So? When you see a white man pass up somethin' he wants for hisself?

TEDDY: *(Slow recognition)* You mean they ain't give no money to Big Boy Crudup for his song?

FRANK: Oh...you just figurin' that out? You learnin'!

ELROI: *(Looks at the record label)* Nobody done heard of Jewel Tone... Who's gonna play it?

FRANK: What do I care as long as they pays me.

ELROI: And why you let them call you somethin' stupid like Smilin' Frank?

FRANK: 'Cause it don't matter, boy. The last time I recorded they call me "Lonesome Frank"...time before that..."Blind Boy Jackson." White man can call me whatever suits his fancy...as long as he come up with the bread. Who the fuck you think runs this world, Orangebird?

ELROI: They done turned you into a joke!

FRANK: *(After a pause)* Yeah...so I be a joke to the white man. Don't mean I like it...but I do it...just like they wants. I stamp my foot to the music, I whoop and holler, flash a big ol' smile...I do what they says, 'cause they still runnin' this plantation, boy...and they pays my livin' expenses...you understand?

ELROI: You let 'em tell you how to sing 'em, too?

FRANK: *(Proud)* I plays the straight natural blues! I ain't no rock and roller! Not for nobody.

ELROI: Well, they ain't gonna turn me into no clown. Not me and Teddy...Not our songs...they're gonna sing 'em the way we want, I'm gonna use my name...they gonna pay us royalties.

FRANK: Royalties? *(Laughs)* Royalty is for kings, Motherfucker! And contrary to what your Mammy done told you...you only the king of the shoeshine! And that's all you gonna be!

TEDDY: Frank...ease off!

FRANK: Who you think you are? The two of you...puttin' on airs...You some special type of niggers? *(Pause)* You done sold your shit...just like me...you no different.

TEDDY: What you mean?

FRANK: Them, songs, man...

ELROI: They our songs...we wrote 'em...we done the arrangements....

FRANK: Whoa! Hold on! What's this we stuff? We done this...we done that....I'm the man with the guitar...I'm the one on the record...not you! I made the deal with Jewel Tone...What did you do?

TEDDY: We done helped you write those songs.

FRANK: You helped on two songs. And I appreciate that, and you done been paid for your help. Thank you very much!

TEDDY: Three songs!

FRANK: How you get three?

TEDDY: *Short-Haired Gal*. Did you record that one?

FRANK: Yeah...so?

TEDDY: I done give you the title. You was gonna call it, *Big-Legged Woman*, but you done used my title instead.

FRANK: Oh, well, excuse me, Mr Nalls, sir! You so right. I must owe you somethin'.

TEDDY: Damn right.

(FRANK *peels off a fifty-dollar bill from his roll of money.*)

FRANK: How about fifty dollars? That take care of you for today? I thought so. Everything fine now.

TEDDY: Don't get smart with me.

FRANK: *(Holding out money)* There's your fifty. Take it. I only gets a hundred for each song, so I figure fifty be worth more than the title. Don't you?

ELROI: How you figure a hundred for each song?

FRANK: 'Cause that's what the man pays me. I go in there with maybe twenty songs...I record seventeen of 'em...and the man give me seventeen hundred dollars. I done give each of you two hundred...more than two hundred...seems more than fair to me.

ELROI: You mean you sold my songs to the man? He owns them?

FRANK: That's right...he owns them.

TEDDY: Frank, you can't do that.

FRANK: Well, it's done. He do whatever he wants with them. They his now.

(ELROI *lunges at* FRANK, *knocking him off his feet.* TEDDY *struggles to pull* ELROI *off* FRANK.)

ELROI: You can't sell my songs...they mine...I'm gonna kill you.

TEDDY: Hey...c'mon...Elroi...stop it...

FRANK: Get that crazy fool offa me!

(TEDDY *holds* ELROI's *arms, but he struggles violently.* FRANK *gets up, grabs* ELROI, *and speaks directly in his face.*)

FRANK: Hey! Hey...you listen to me, Boy. I done you a favor. Did I ask you to write songs for me? Did I ask you? No. I had my own songs...but here you come...stickin' 'em in my face... "Here, sing this...how about this?"... So, I did. Just like you wanted, Elroi. I done right by you. And now you been paid for your work! What more you want, nigger?

(TEDDY *glares at* FRANK. *He releases* ELROI. ELROI *collapses to the floor, howling and moaning.*)

TEDDY: Frank...you done gone too far!

FRANK: Time this boy growed up...see things for what they is. And that goes for you, too!

(ELROI *rolls around on the floor, crying. He curls himself into a ball.* FRANK *walks away in disgust, crosses to the shelf and takes a long swig from* TEDDY's *pint of corn liquor.* TEDDY *kneels next to* ELROI, *trying to comfort him.*)

TEDDY: Elroi...listen to me. It's gonna be all right. We write some new songs...you and me...we write 'em together...what you think? Come on... get up off the floor.

(TEDDY *helps* ELROI *to his feet...*ELROI *stands for a moment staring with hatred at* FRANK. FRANK *does not respond.* ELROI *spits at the floor by* FRANK's *feet.*)

ELROI: LIAR!

(ELROI *turns and runs out the front door of the shop.* TEDDY *goes to the door calling after him.*)

TEDDY: ELROI...don't run off... Come on back here...Elroi...ELROI!

FRANK: You be wakin' up the whole neighborhood.

TEDDY: He run out in the cold without his jacket.

(TEDDY *goes to the hooks and puts on his own coat and scarf.*)

FRANK: Jes...let him be.

TEDDY: I gotta go find him.

FRANK: He's long gone by now. You'd be lookin' all night. He'll come back when he gets cold.

(TEDDY *stands by the door for a long moment, then turns back to* FRANK, *who is by the sink, drinking from the corn liquor slab.*)

TEDDY: You shouldn't have done that.

FRANK: Teddy...the man would have stolen them songs anyway...put his name on 'em....they always do. At least I got somethin' for 'em.

TEDDY: Two wrongs don't make it right.

FRANK: He get over it. Just his pride, that's all that hurts.

TEDDY: He just a kid.

FRANK: *(Pause)* You been soft on him ever since his Mama died.

TEDDY: I said I'd look after him. *(Pause)* No reason for it....What you done to that boy tonight...there ain't no excusin'.

FRANK: Time some folks learned they ain't hangin' the moon for us out there.

TEDDY: We know that, but there's nothing wrong with him hoping and you done spit in his face.

FRANK: No...I done showed him how it is.

(TEDDY *looks at* FRANK *for a long moment, then turns, and goes out the front door to find* ELROI. FRANK *shakes his head, and drinks from the pint of corn liquor. The lights fade out.*)

Scene Two

(*Time: that same night, almost four in the morning.*)

(*Setting: the same*)

(*At rise: a single light over the sink, is the only illumination in the shop.* FRANK *is seated in the barber chair, alone with his red electric guitar, which is plugged into the amp nearby.* FRANK *is wearing trousers, his boots, and undershirt, and his new cowboy hat. The empty pint bottle is on the floor by the chair.* FRANK *is quietly strumming and improvising bluesy runs on the guitar.* FRANK *reaches down for the bottle. After draining the last drops from the pint, he tosses the bottle across the room toward the record alcove.* FRANK *broods. He plays another blues run, and breaks into a boogie-woogie rhythm. He taps his foot to the beat, and starts singing in a deep, menacing voice.*)

FRANK: (*Singing*)
I'm goin' to Louisiana
Gonna get me a Mojo Hand
I'm goin' to Louisiana
Gonna get me a Mojo Hand
I'm gonna fix my woman
So she can't love no other man.
(*Instrumental break*)
I'm layin' down thinkin'
'Bout that Mojo Hand
I'm layin' down thinkin'
'Bout that Mojo Hand
I'm gonna fix my woman
So she can't love no other man.

(FRANK *plays a bridge to the song as the phone rings.* FRANK *stops playing, looks at the phone. He sets the guitar side, turns off the amp. He ambles to the phone, and answers.*)

FRANK: Teddy's Barber Shop...Hey, Teddy...where are you! It's almost four in the morning. You see Orangebird, yet? No, he ain't called here. Why don't you come on back...be sunrise in an hour or so...he'll come home when he's good and ready. You just wastin' you time...the streets is empty, everybody sleepin'...

(FRANK *notices something outside the window. Headlights and the sound of a pick-up truck outside.*)

FRANK: Hold on a minute...

(FRANK *looks out the window, goes back to the phone.*)

FRANK: You know anybody with a red pick-up truck...Mississippi plates? Naw, me neither...well, one just pulled up outside. Can't tell who...I dunno. Where you keep that pistol of yours? Well, you better get your butt back here. They gettin' outta the truck now...two people...comin' this way... I gotta go now.

(FRANK *hangs up the phone, and stands to one side where he will not be seen. He looks at the figures outside the window. As they approach the front door,* FRANK *slips quietly into the back room. The front door opens and two people stumble into the dimly lit shop. It is* ELROI *and a white woman,* MAXINE PETTIBONE. *She is holding him up.* ELROI *is very drunk and he sings incoherently. They stumble toward the barber chair. She struggles to get him to the barber chair.* ELROI's *face has many cuts and bruises. His shirt and trousers are soiled and torn.* MAXINE *is a somewhat pale and plain girl in her late twenties. She wears a dress and cloth coat, carries a purse.* MAXINE *speaks with the unmistakable accent of poor people from the Delta area.*)

MAXINE: This is it. We made it. (*Calls out*) Anybody here? Come on, into this chair...just a few more feet. Up you go. That's it. (*She maneuvers him into the barber chair, tries to find the lever to tilt it back.*) There...now where the hell is the control lever on this thing? Here it is....

(*The chair reclines half way.* FRANK *watches from the curtain area.*)

MAXINE: (*Calling out, again.*) Anybody here? (*To* ELROI) You sure this is the right place? There's nobody here. Maybe this ain't the right barber shop.

(ELROI *mumbles.*)

MAXINE: What you sayin'?

ELROI: Get Teddy....

MAXINE: Who is Teddy? I don't know no Teddy. You want a teddy bear? Is that what you want?

(FRANK *steps into the room. He turns on the light switch.* MAXINE *turns quickly, scared.*)

MAXINE: Oh, Jesus, save me! You scared me half to death....

(FRANK *moves toward her and* ELROI.)

MAXINE: Who are you? You Teddy?

FRANK: No, I'm Frank.

MAXINE: I...I brung him home...he got in some trouble.

FRANK: What happened to his face?

MAXINE: He got in a fight with some white boys.

FRANK: Friends of yours?

MAXINE: No...God, no...we were mindin' our own business...I swear... and these boys come and start sayin' stuff...I brung him in my truck. He asked me to take him home. I didn't know what else to do.

FRANK: This boy smells like a still.

MAXINE: He drank himself a whole pint of corn liquor.

ELROI: *(Singing)* She got a mean disposition...meanst gal' I ever seen...

MAXINE: Shh. You gotta settle down now, Elroi.

(FRANK *gets a bottle of peroxide from the shelf.*)

FRANK: I'll take care of him.

(MAXINE *steps aside as* FRANK *tends to* ELROI.)

FRANK: Now shut up, boy. Quit your singin'...Now this is gonna sting a bit...but it'll be okay....

ELROI: Ow!...

FRANK: Now hold still, Elroi. I'm tryin' to fix you up.

MAXINE: Elroi told me he was a singer. Said he used to sing in a group with Johnny Ace. You know Johnny Ace?

FRANK: Yes, ma'am. He dead now. Shot hisself.

MAXINE: I know. I cried when I heard that on the radio. I was listenin' to WDIA that night....They was playin' *Pledgin' My Love*, and Jimmy Mattis, he come on the air after the song, and all he could say was, "...Johnny's gone...Johnny's gone..." Kept sayin' it over and over...he started cryin', right there on the radio.

FRANK: *(To* ELROI*)* You're gonna have a hell of a head in the mornin'.

MAXINE: *(To* ELROI*)* You're gonna be all right. You just had too much to drink, that's all. *(Lullabyes* ELROI*)*
Forever my darlin'
Our love will be true....
(Again to ELROI*)* Shhh....
(She notices the posters of Johnny Ace on the wall.)

Wow! You got his picture, and his record album on the wall. God, he was really somethin'...I seen that show! That one right there! God, was it great! I drove all the way up here...wanted to stay for both shows, but, I couldn't...besides...second show was only for the coloreds, you know? *(She discovers the record bin.)* Damn! Look at all these records. Golly, look at this stuff-Joe Turner, Ray Charles. You can't buy these records for love nor money down where I live. Folks down there...they hate this kind of music. "Coon jump", that's what they call it. What do they know? Ain't ever heard nothin' but Roy Acuff and the Grand Old Opry—bunch of stupid yodellin' peckerwoods—if you ask me. Hey, how much you want for that B B King picture?

FRANK: Not for sale.

MAXINE: Oh. *(Pause)* Tell me somethin'...was Elroi just talkin', you know, when he said he sung with Johnny Ace? He just make that up?

FRANK: Elroi ain't no singer. He's a songwriter.

MAXINE: I see. You're the singer, ain't ya?

FRANK: That's right.

MAXINE: I figured. You look like a singer. *(She starts to pick up* FRANK's *guitar.)* I bet this is your guitar. Real purty...

(FRANK *takes the guitar from* MAXINE *and puts it away in the case.)*

MAXINE: Would I know any of your songs?

FRANK: No, Ma'am.

MAXINE: So tell me...where the hell am I?

FRANK: I think you on the wrong side of town. This is West Memphis.

MAXINE: Arkansas?

FRANK: Yes, ma'm. West Memphis, Arkansas. You ain't from around here.

MAXINE: No. I come from Mississippi...Senatobia. You know where that is?

FRANK: Yes, ma'm, I do...north end of the Delta.

MAXINE: That's right.

FRANK: You work down there?

MAXINE: Me? Work? *(Laughs)* No...my husband does...he's a salesman... farm machinery. We got ourselves a little place down there. Sometimes on the weekends...I...uh...

FRANK: You drive up to Memphis...have a little fun...

MAXINE: Yeah, somethin' like that. *(Pause)* Tonight I come up to hear Guitar Slim. He's got that hit record out now, *The Things That I Used To Do*. You know that song?

(MAXINE *sings the opening lines.* FRANK *tries to cover his amusement at her singing.*)

MAXINE: *(Singing)* "The things that I used to do...Lawd, I don't do no more...." God, I love that song. He's playing at the Pearl Lounge this week. Did you know that?

(FRANK *shakes his head, "no".*)

MAXINE: Heard all about it on Rufus Thomas' radio show. You know— *Hoot and Holler*...I listen to it every night. Well, nights when, Earl...that's my husband...nights he ain't in the house. He can't stand all that colored music, ya know?

FRANK: Where be this husband of yours? He out in the truck?

MAXINE: In the truck? No...he's down in Jackson, 'til tomorrow...on business. So...I come up to Memphis. I like to hear them singers in the juke joints. *(Pause)* Nothin' wrong with that...

FRANK: No, ma'am.

MAXINE: I just love them rhythm and blues songs. Makes you wanna get up and dance. Sometime a person's just gotta let loose...have a good time...right?

FRANK: Yes, ma'am.

MAXINE: Don't say that: "ma'am." I hate that. Nigras back home say that all the time. Why don't you call me...Maxine. That's my name...Maxine Pettibone. Some of my friends call me, "Maxie"...I don't mind...

(FRANK *regards her for a long moment.*)

MAXINE: Why you lookin' at me so funny-like?

FRANK: I don't think I'll be callin' you nothin'.

MAXINE: What do you mean by that?

FRANK: I knowed a white woman like you before...was nothin' but trouble.

MAXINE: What are you insinuatin'?

(Front door opens, TEDDY *enters. He stops when he sees* MAXINE.*)*

TEDDY: What the hell is goin' on here? *(Pause)* Who's she?

FRANK: This is Mrs. Maxine Pettibone, from Senatobia, Mississippi.

MAXINE: Hi!

TEDDY: What's she doin' in my shop?

MAXINE: I brought Elroi home. Are you his father? Are you a singer too?

(TEDDY *moves to the barber chair, and examines* ELROI.)

TEDDY: Elroi. What happened to him? Who did this?

FRANK: Got drunk and got his ass beat.

TEDDY: *(To* MAXINE*)* You responsible for this?

MAXINE: *(Follows* TEDDY*)* No...I was tryin' to help him.

TEDDY: Elroi...you hear me? How you feel?

FRANK: I put some peroxide on them cuts...he'll be all right.

TEDDY: Elroi...talk to me, boy...

MAXINE: I think he done passed out.

FRANK: He was dead drunk when she brought him in here.

TEDDY: You get him drunk?

MAXINE: No, I did not.

TEDDY: Suppose you tell me exactly when you done.

MAXINE: I was drivin' in Memphis...when I seen him hitchhiking on the road...lookin' all cold and pitiful...so, I gave him a ride...just like any decent Christian woman would do...

FRANK: Then they went to some gin mill.

MAXINE: That ain't what happened! Were you there? No, you weren't. He bought the corn liquor himself.

TEDDY: But you done drunk it with him.

MAXINE: I don't like what you're suggestin'...not one bit!

TEDDY: Just tell me what happened after you picked him up...on the road.

MAXINE: Well...he got into the truck...and then I asked him where he was goin'...and he asked me if I could take him to some recordin' studio...over near the Memphis 'Lectric Company....

FRANK: Sun Records.

MAXINE: That's the one...

TEDDY: In the middle of the night? Why'd you go over there?

MAXINE: I dunno...I tried to tell him...I thought they'd be closed, but he kept insistin' that he knew somebody in there...and they was gonna let him in...so he could sing his song...or somethin'...

FRANK: Fool idea...

MAXINE: So, we pull up...and all the windows are dark, but he gets out and starts bangin' on the door. He was makin' a terrible racket...I just knew the po-lice was gonna come by any minute...so, I went out on the sidewalk... and I was tryin' to get him back in the truck 'fore somebody come to see what all the hollerin' is about...and then these boys came down the street.

TEDDY: White or colored?

MAXINE: White...'bout five of 'em...and they been drinkin' too...and they seen me tryin' to pull him into the pick-up truck and they started sayin' things...you know. And then, Elroi...he sees 'em and he gets it in his head that one of these fool boys is Elvis Presley....Now I knew it wasn't Elvis, 'cause I seen pictures of him. You know? Well, Elroi started talkin' back, smart like...and they got to pushin' and shovin'...suddenly, they were all on top of him...I started yellin', and they took off...I put him in the truck and I brung him over here....

TEDDY: Why didn't you take him over to the hospital...and get them cuts tended to?

MAXINE: I don't know where the colored hospital is. I ain't from Memphis.

(TEDDY *starts for the pay phone.*)

MAXINE: Hey, what are you doin'?

TEDDY: I'm gonna call the po-lice.

MAXINE: No...You can't do that. I mean...they see me here...what are they gonna think?

TEDDY: What do I care what they think?

MAXINE: Now, look, my husband would kill me iffin' he knew I was here. You can't get me involved.

TEDDY: You already involved...you done got him drunk...got his ass kicked.

MAXINE: I already told you...that ain't my fault! Now, I brung him here...that's all I'm gonna do.

TEDDY: Oh, no. You gonna tell the po-lice what you know about them boys. They ain't gettin' away with this.

FRANK: Teddy...careful...

MAXINE: Now, I'm warnin' you...you call the po-lice, and I'll tell 'em that three niggers kidnapped me....brung me across the river to rape me. You'll get yourself in a lot of trouble. You understand?

TEDDY: Woman, I'm done foolin' with you!

(TEDDY *drops the phone, starts toward* MAXINE.)

MAXINE: You stay away from me. Don't you dare touch me. Don't you ever try to touch me, boy!

(TEDDY *lunges for* MAXINE. FRANK *jumps between them, grabs* TEDDY *and pushes him away from her.*)

FRANK: NO! Teddy...NO! You can't do this! Now, stop! The lady's right, Teddy. There be trouble for us all. Besides...you call 'em, what they gonna do when they hear some colored boy done got his ass beat by some hillbillies? They laugh...that's what they do.

(FRANK *settles* TEDDY *into a chair.* TEDDY *is breathing heavily.* FRANK *turns to* MAXINE.)

FRANK: Lady, you better get the hell home 'fore your husband finds out what you been up to.

MAXINE: *(Moves toward the door.)* I done nothing wrong with this boy!

TEDDY: Go on...get outta my shop! There be plenty of farm bucks down there in the Delta to occupy your time...don't have to drive all the way up to Memphis...

MAXINE: *(Moving toward door.)* I'm sorry as hell about what happened to this boy, but it ain't my fault. I just come up here to hear some music...that's all.

(MAXINE *exits.* TEDDY *slams the door.*)

TEDDY: Music, my ass!

(FRANK *looks at* TEDDY *for a long moment. Sound of truck engine starting up outside.*)

FRANK: Is you crazy, nigger? Where's your sense? All that woman has to do is tell the po-lice...

TEDDY: I don't care what she says.

FRANK: Yeah, well, you'd sing a different tune with a rope around your neck. Now, you better cool off, Teddy....You playin' with the Devil.... What the fuck is wrong with you?

(TEDDY *doesn't answer. He puts a cold, wet compress on* ELROI's *face.* TEDDY *puts on his coat and scarf.*)

FRANK: Where you think you're goin'?

TEDDY: I'm goin' after them white boys.

FRANK: Oh, and how you gonna find 'em? They be long gone, now.

TEDDY: I'll find 'em....

FRANK: You plannin' to walk to Memphis in the middle of the night?

TEDDY: If I have to. Done walked farther in boot camp.

(TEDDY *finds his pistol in a box on one of the shelves. He puts the pistol in his coat pocket. He turns.* FRANK *stands in front of the door, blocking his way.*)

TEDDY: Now, get outta my way, Frank. I know what I'm doin'.

FRANK: I ain't lettin' you walk outta here. You crazy, Teddy. Now, calm down, man.

TEDDY: Stand aside, Frank.

FRANK: No, Teddy. I ain't gonna let you get yourself shot by no cracker over in Memphis. You wanna kill somebody? Then kill me. Kill me, goddammit! I ain't movin'.

TEDDY: I'm mad, Frank! I'm mad.

FRANK: I know it...but you can't do this....You know it, Teddy. You can't. This ain't London...Ain't never gonna be like it was back then.

(*Tears well up in* TEDDY's *eyes. He throws a 78 RPM record against the wall in frustration.* TEDDY *howls in anguish. He thrashes wildly about the shop. He rakes the items off a shelf.*)

TEDDY: Goddamn them! Goddamn it...

(TEDDY *smashes one of the records on the floor.*)

TEDDY: Lyin' cheatin' motherfuckers!

(TEDDY *hurls a record at the wall with the picture of Johnny Ace.*)

TEDDY: Fuckin' Johnny Ace!

(TEDDY *is winded by his outburst.* TEDDY *gasps for air, holding his chest.* TEDDY *sits heavily on the shoe shine stand, trying to control his breathing.* FRANK *goes to the sink, fills a glass with water.* FRANK *brings the water and* TEDDY's *blood pressure medicine to* TEDDY.)

FRANK: Easy, Teddy...easy now, man...take your medicine.

(TEDDY *takes the pills, washes them down with water.* TEDDY *takes off his coat, fans himself with a newspaper.*)

FRANK: You want me to get you a doctor?

TEDDY: No, I'll be okay in a minute. Just let me sit a spell.

(*They are silent for a long moment.*)

FRANK: I know how you feel, Teddy.

TEDDY: Do you?

FRANK: Yeah.

TEDDY: (*Gestures to* ELROI) I can't let nobody shame this boy...nobody.

FRANK: Well, this boy mighta got some of them starry ideas knocked outta him tonight, but Elroi gotta take his lumps just like the rest of us.

TEDDY: Oh, yeah...you's a fine one to talk. You ain't the one that's been here with him every day. I'm the one that buys him a new pair of shoes. I'm the one that makes sure he gets somethin' to eat...I'm the one who's gotta put him back together tomorrow.

FRANK: I see. You be thinkin' maybe somebody owes you somethin'... I see how it is.

TEDDY: Nobody owes me nothin'.

FRANK: That a fact?

TEDDY: I only want what's best for him.

FRANK: No, I think maybe you wants a little bit for yourself, too...

TEDDY: What the hell you mean by that?

FRANK: Elroi ain't the one, Teddy. It's you, I'm talkin' about....You been kickin' my butt 'bout lettin' the boy down...steppin' on his hopes...but, you been wantin' that hit record more than him.

TEDDY: You's full of shit!

FRANK: That may be! But there was a time when you wanted more than this barber shop. Back in the old days when we was runnin' around Beale Street...we'd see Louis Jordan at the Palace, or you'd catch my act at Dinky's...I watched you listenin' to the music, all the time knowin' that wished it was you up there on the bandstand.

(*Long pause*)

TEDDY: And, if I could've played the guitar as good as I cut hair, I'd've put you outta business.

FRANK: I believe that. But what would it've gotten ya'?...a beat up old suitcase full of dirty clothes...an old guitar...that needs a new set of strings.

TEDDY: And your pockets full of money!

FRANK: Shit, the money's nothin', Teddy. It be gone in a month or two...then I be three steps ahead of the revenue man...money just slips through my fingers like rainwater. I don't even know where it goes...some juke joints along the river...a woman over in Hot Springs...some whore down in Mobile...I ain't in one place long enough for the dust to settle.

TEDDY: Why you live like that?

FRANK: So I can make music...that's what I do. The cards have been dealt, Teddy...you cut hair...I play music.

(TEDDY *looks at* ELROI.)

TEDDY: What about this boy? He ain't gonna grow up shinin' shoes forever...and I sure as hell don't want him takin' over this shop after I'm gone. What's he gonna do?

FRANK: First thing he gonna do...is get over the hangover he's gonna have.

TEDDY: *(Chuckles)* Yeah, his ass gonna be sore in the mornin'.

(They laugh.)

TEDDY: Tell me straight, Frank...his songs...are they good enough to get on the radio? Are they?

FRANK: I went into Jewel Tone...I recorded seventeen songs...and outta them seventeen...the only two they pressed into records was *Mean Disposition* and *Can't Get Your Lovin' Off My Mind*. You figure it out.

TEDDY: The boy's got talent.

FRANK: Yes, indeed.

(TEDDY *rises, goes to barber chair.* TEDDY *looks at* ELROI *for a moment.*)

TEDDY: I'll tell you one thing, Frank...I'm gonna make sure he gets his chance. He's gonna do it. I'll see to it, he does...

FRANK: Yeah, I bet you will.

TEDDY: We oughta get him outta this chair. Come on, help me lift him up. We'll put him on the bed in the back room....Let him sleep it off.

FRANK: You get the top, I'll get these ol' orange legs.

(FRANK *and* TEDDY *lift* ELROI *from the barber's chair.*)

(FRANK *sings,* Can't Get Your Lovin' Off My Mind—*at the slow bluesy tempo.*)

FRANK: Well, I woke up with the blues on Sunday
I had the same ol' thing on Monday...
Now, Lawd it's Tuesday...

TEDDY: Frank. If you're gonna sing the boy's song, then you sing it the way he wrote it.

FRANK: You got it.

(FRANK *sings the uptempo version, and* TEDDY *joins in as they carry* ELROI *toward the back room.*)

BOTH: Woke up with the blues on Sunday
I had the same ol' thing on Monday
Now, Lawd, it's Tuesday. I still ain't feelin' so fine
I think I smell me some trouble

It's got me seein' double
I just can't get your lovin' off my mind.

(Lights fade as FRANK *and* TEDDY *continue to sing the song.)*

END OF PLAY

SQUATS

SQUATS premiered at the Mad Horse Theatre Company of Portland, Maine, on 28 September 1989. The cast and creative contributors were:

CHARLIE . . . . Donald Jellerson
HOLLY . . . . Randy Aromando
CECE . . . . Terry Drew
JACKIE BLUE . . . . Tony Owen
TUCKER . . . . Walter Dunlap
MOIRA . . . . Pam Montanaro
ELLEN . . . . Cynthia Barnett
SALLY/LINDA . . . . Lew-Ann Leen

Director . . . . Michael Rafkin
Costumes . . . . Sue Picinich
Sound . . . . Cliff Rugg
Set/light design . . . . Michael Rafkin
Stage manager . . . . Joan Sand

CHARACTERS

CECE, *sixteen, a homeless teenager*
CHARLIE, *seventeen, CECE's boyfriend, also homeless*
HOLLY, *eighteen, a transvestite. Homeless*
TUCKER, *thirties, a homeless mental patient. An ex-con*
JACKIE BLUE, *forties, a black street musician. Homeless*
ELLEN, *forties, a bag lady. Homeless*
MOIRA, *thirty-nine, CECE's mother*
SALLY, *thirties*, night manager of a twenty-four-hour donut shop*
LINDA, *thirties*, a social worker.*

* *The same actress should play* SALLY *and* LINDA.

Time: late fall, winter. The present

Setting: various locations in a large port city in New England.

Note on the setting: A unit set would work best, with the overall feel and look of an urban junkyard. Let found items serve as the furniture pieces—an abandoned car seat becomes a sofa, a spool table, abandoned crates and boxes become tables and chairs in various scenes. Be inventive, let the play flow from scene to scene without cumbersome set changes. Scaffolding and chain link fence can also be used to add levels and texture to the design.

Home is the place where, when you have to go there,
They have to take you in...

Robert Frost from *The Death of the Hired Man.*

for Giulia

ACT ONE

Scene One

(Pre-show music: Joanna Dean's Gimme Shelter *[Mercury Records, 1988])*

(Scene: Congress Street—The Strip. The Friday night meat rack. HOLLY *and* CHARLIE, *two homeless teenage hustlers, share a quart of Miller High-Life in a paper bag.* CHARLIE, *seventeen, wears jeans and a denim jacket.* HOLLY *eighteen is a transvestite. He wears a mini-skirt, fish-net hose, and a black leather jacket.* HOLLY *will always wear a woman's wig and make-up.)*

*(*HOLLY *and* CHARLIE *watch the passing cars.)*

CHARLIE: Oh, whoo-wee...did you see that fuckin' monster? Four on the floor, cro-mags...put the pedal to the metal...I love cars like that.

HOLLY: Not bad...'cept for the paint job...too pussy.

CHARLIE: You would know.

(They playfully shove each other.)

HOLLY: So would you, "Hum Job." Oooooh, keep talkin', Mr. Charlie... it feels so goooood...please tie me up and hum in my ear.

CHARLIE: *(Shoving* HOLLY *away)* Dick-Head! The guy never said that. He didn't want me to hum. He wanted me to sing somethin'.

HOLLY: Oh, what?

CHARLIE: Some old song. I didn't know it.

HOLLY: Shoulda given him the Beatles... *(Sings)* I wanna hold your gland...

(Playfully HOLLY *grabs* CHARLIE's *crotch.* CHARLIE *shoves him away.)*

CHARLIE: Hey, will you cool it. I was tellin' ya my story.

HOLLY: You have so many stories, Charlie, I need a scorecard.

CHARLIE: 'Bout my old man...

HOLLY: The motel in Hartford?

CHARLIE: Yeah.

*(*HOLLY *spots a car on the street.)*

HOLLY: Uh-Oh, check this out...a low-rider special. Butch up your act... this looks like a denim dream date if I ever saw one.

CHARLIE: Naw, they're high school townies...cruisin' for burgers.

HOLLY: *(To passing car)* Hi, handsome...like my buns? Okay, fuck off!

CHARLIE: You wanna hear my story or not?

HOLLY: Sure. So, he just left you there?

CHARLIE: Yeah. Me and my little sister.

HOLLY: Nice parents.

CHARLIE: No, just my old man. I never knew my mom. She O D'd, or somethin' a long time ago.

HOLLY: Jees...

CHARLIE: I don't think he did it on purpose. He just sorta forgot.

HOLLY: *(Sarcastic)* Oh, right.

CHARLIE: He was in a hurry to get to the next Dead concert, which was in Buffalo, I think. So, I guess he got up, smoked a joint, maybe had breakfast in the diner, then he got on his Harley, unhitched the side-car, and drove off. Me and my sister were still sleepin' in the room....

HOLLY: A Harley? What is he, a biker?

CHARLIE: Yeah. Lots of bikers have kids...

HOLLY: *And* a fuckin' Dead-head... *(Screams)* Arrggh!

CHARLIE: He just forgot about us.

HOLLY: Yeah, but he did remember to unhook the side-car...as what? A sorta farewell gesture?

(CHARLIE *takes a drink and ponders this.*)

CHARLIE: Now that I think about it, I guess he was kind of a fuck-up.

HOLLY: Hey, here we go. This could be it. Smile pretty.

CHARLIE: *(To passing car)* Hey, man. Wanna party?

(*Car horn honks. It speeds away. Voices yell insults. A beer can lands near* HOLLY.)

HOLLY: Naval air-station jerkoffs! Drive up and down like they're shoppin' at Wal-Mart. *(Spots another car)* What's this? Another carload?

CHARLIE: Must be a fuckin' regiment in town.

(HOLLY *calls and waves to the car.*)

HOLLY: "I just love a man in uniform!" Hey, Dude, why don't you spend some money? Ahoy, sailor. I just love seafood.

(Car speeds away. HOLLY flips the bird.)

CHARLIE: Forget 'em, they're assholes!

HOLLY: This is the fuckin' dead zone. It's Friday night. Where is everyone?

CHARLIE: Not here.

HOLLY: Wanna try Cumberland?

CHARLIE: It's all the same big loop, Holly. It just ain't happenin' tonight.

HOLLY: I'm not goin' to the shelter again. Last time I found a turd in my cot. Had to sleep on the floor. Things were crawlin' on me in the night, and some old troll was coughin' up his lungs.... Jees, it's gettin' cold....

(They pace up and down, watching the street.)

HOLLY: So, did you ever see your old man again?

CHARLIE: Yeah, coupla summers ago, the Dead were playin' up at Oxford Speedway. We got high, hung out for two days. It was pretty cool. He looked real different...gotta long grey beard now, and he put on weight. Looks like Santa on a "hog". He gave me a nice bong for my last birthday.

HOLLY: I woulda asked for cash.

CHARLIE: Yeah. *(Pause)* Wanna hear the best part? My sister moved out to California...last I heard, she married a biker.

HOLLY: What goes around, comes around. *(Pause)* Wild fuckin' story. How come you never told me that before?

CHARLIE: You never asked. Besides, you ain't my social worker.

HOLLY: Ain't that the truth. *(They spot a car cruising them.)* Oh, boy... what's this one? It's slowin' down. Oh, fuckin' tourists.

(CHARLIE and HOLLY couple obscenely for the passing car.)

HOLLY: Come on, come on...take a picture, why don't ya? *(She coughs.)* Shit, I think I'm gettin' a cold. We gotta find a squat.

(CECE enters carrying CHARLIE's skateboard like a serving tray. She has coffee and a bag of donuts on the skateboard. CECE [16] is a pretty girl who is beginning to show the signs of wear and tear from street life.)

CECE: Midnight snack?

HOLLY: Took you long enough.

(CHARLIE embraces CECE, gives her a long kiss.)

CECE: How's it goin?

CHARLIE: Slow motion.

HOLLY: Pitiful. I see more action in the Christian Science Reading Room.

(CHARLIE *kisses her again.*)

CHARLIE: You taste good.

CECE: Hall's mentholyptus cough drop.

(*They kiss again.*)

HOLLY: Jesus, will you two chill on the tongue wrestling, and give me my fuckin' donut. I'm starvin' here.

(CECE *sets down the skateboard, and hands out coffees and donuts.*)

HOLLY: What'd ya get?

CECE: Boston Cream. They were out of crullers. (*Hands coffees to them*) One cream, four sugars. Black, no sugar.

CHARLIE: Thanks, Ceec.

HOLLY: (*Sips coffee*) Oh, damn, the inside of my mouth hurts. Look in my mouth. What do you see? What's it look like?

CECE: Raw meat.

HOLLY: Sore...Christ.

CHARLIE: Any change?

CECE: No, I was twenty cents short. Sally let me have it on credit.

CHARLIE: We gotta score some cash.

(HOLLY *spots a car.*)

HOLLY: Here we are. Pucker up! Hello, there, handsome. Come on, make up your mind. O K, get lost.

CHARLIE: Wanna try the tunnel?

HOLLY: No way. We'd get mugged down there.

CHARLIE: (*Spots a car*) Oooh! There is my car! Black Porsche with a Targa top.

HOLLY: Awesome!

CHARLIE: Great machine, but mine's gotta have a spoiler, and mag-reverse wheel covers. And a sun roof.

CECE: Sun roofs are stupid. Just get a convertible.

HOLLY: Porsches are for yuppies. Give me a black Trans-Am.

CHARLIE: (*Spots a car*) Wait! What's this? I think we got one. He's slowin' down.

HOLLY: Me? I think he wants you, Charlie.

CHARLIE: See ya later, girls.

(CHARLIE *saunters off toward the car.*)

CECE: *(Glum)* Shit!

HOLLY: You can have the next one.

CECE: I don't want the next one, or any of 'em.

HOLLY: What's eatin' you?

CECE: Not feelin' so great. My crotch itches somethin' wicked, and, I think I got a fever.

HOLLY: Yeah. Somethin's goin' around. I got sores in my mouth that won't heal. *(Watches* CHARLIE*)* What's he doin'? Tellin' his life story? Come on, either get in the car, or take a walk. What's it gonna be?

(CHARLIE *returns.*)

HOLLY: What's the deal?

CHARLIE: Changed his mind. *(To* CECE*)* He wants you.

CECE: I'm not interested.

CHARLIE: Ceec, it's fifty...straight.

CECE: No.

CHARLIE: The guy looks okay. Really.

CECE: I can't tonight. I got a yeast infection.

CHARLIE: He don't care.

CECE: Well, I do. *(Yells at car)* HEY, BUDDY! I GOT THE CLAP!

CHARLIE: Jees, Ceec! We need the fuckin' money!

CECE: Then you earn it.

(HOLLY *spots a police car, starts walking away non-chalantly.*)

HOLLY: Disperse. We got John' Law at three o'clock. Time to stroll, kiddies.

(They split off in different directions.)

CHARLIE: Meet by the library.

(HOLLY *saunters and talks like John Wayne.*)

HOLLY: You betcha! See ya' later, Pilgrim.

(Fade to black)

Scene Two

(Scene: a drainage culvert near an overpass. Sound of cars passing overhead. It is late at night. JACKIE BLUE, *forties, a black street musician, stands by a rusty metal oil drum. A fire is burning in the barrel.* JACKIE *is dressed for winter—a worn topcoat, scarf and a hat.* JACKIE *finishes the last drops of a pint of Wild Irish Rose. He tosses the empty bottle into the oil drum.* JACKIE *opens his coat. Inside he has an old saxophone on a lanyard around his neck.* JACKIE *sings the* Boll Weevil Song *at the moon.)*

JACKIE: *(Singing)*
Well, the boll weevil is a little black bug
Comes from Mexico they say
Came all the way to Texas
Just lookin' for a place to stay
He was lookin' for a home
Just lookin' for a home.

Well the first time I seen the boll weevil
He was sittin' on the square
The next time I seen the boll weevil
He had his whole family there.
Just a lookin' for a home, just lookin' for a home...

*(*TUCKER *appears from the shadows under the culvert.* TUCKER, *thirties speaks with a slight southwestern drawl. He wears a soiled olive drab field jacket. He carries something in a greasy brown paper bag, tucked under his arm.)*

TUCKER: *(Applauds slowly)* Mighty nice, my man. "Just lookin' for a home."

JACKIE: Amen, brother.

TUCKER: What was that song?

JACKIE: The *Boll Weevil*...about a little black bug from Texas.

TUCKER: Texas song, huh? My ex-wife was from Texas. *(Pause)* I hate fuckn' Texas.

JACKIE: I learned it in the army...in Oklahoma...Fort Sill.

*(*JACKIE *lights a smoke with a stick from the barrel.* TUCKER *moves closer.)*

TUCKER: You mind if I get warm?

JACKIE: "Take a load off, Annie..."

*(*JACKIE *chuckles to himself, puts another piece of wood on the fire.* TUCKER *watches* JACKIE *smoke.)*

TUCKER: You got another one of them cancer sticks?

(JACKIE *takes a half-smoked butt from the brim of his hat and hands it to* TUCKER.)

JACKIE: Got your name on it, brother.

TUCKER: Thanks, man.

(TUCKER *bums a light from* JACKIE's *cigarette, inhales deeply, savoring the taste.*)

JACKIE: Feels good, don't it?

TUCKER: Yeah...Man, I think I know you.

JACKIE: Maybe. Maybe not.

TUCKER: Oh, yeah. I seen you...state hospital. You were on the third floor. I was on the fourth.

JACKIE: Fourth ward was for schizos.

TUCKER: Yeah, well, I was mis-diagnosed. I was manic-depressive all the way. They just put me in the wrong place. I shoulda been downstairs with you guys. That's where I belonged.

JACKIE: Sorry, don't think I know you.

TUCKER: Yeah, you do. You're Jackie Blue. I recognize the sax. *(He whistles the first three notes of* Parker's Mood.*)* Parker's Mood. Remember? You taught me that? You said that's how junkies used to identify each other. You whistle the first three notes, and if a guy whistles back, that's how you know he's holdin'. You told me that.

JACKIE: I said that? Don't remember it.

(TUCKER *whistles the notes, waits for a reply*)

JACKIE: I ain't holdin'. Don't even chip the shit no more.

TUCKER: Yeah. Who can afford it? I'm straight too. *(He takes out a bottle of pills, and swallows one. He offers a pill to* JACKIE.*)* Thorazine. Want one?

JACKIE: Got my own pills.

TUCKER: What'd they give you?

JACKIE: Lithium.

TUCKER: Popular pill. You wanna sell any?

JACKIE: Naw, man. I need 'em.

TUCKER: Wanna buy some of mine?

JACKIE: No bread.

TUCKER: Me neither.

JACKIE: Life's a bitch! *(He places a piece of wood in the fire barrel, hums and sings the chorus of an old song*—Until The Real Thing Comes Along.*)*

JACKIE: *(Singing to himself)*
I'd sigh for you, I'd cry for you
I'd lay my body down and die for you
If that isn't love, it's gonna have to do...

(TUCKER *joins in on the last line.*)

BOTH: Until the real thing comes along.

(JACKIE *laughs. They slap "Five".*)

JACKIE: That's right. *(Pause)* You just get out?

TUCKER: 'Bout a month. You?

JACKIE: 'Bout a year.

TUCKER: Got a place to squat?

JACKIE: You're lookin' at it.

TUCKER: Here?

JACKIE: That ol' car back there under the bridge. I live in the back seat. Times get rough, I rent out the front.

TUCKER: How much?

JACKIE: Three dollars a night.

TUCKER: Whew, kinda high.

JACKIE: The heater still works.

TUCKER: That ol' car still run?

JACKIE: Yeah. I got two gears-Park and Neutral. Beats the shelter. Got my stuff ripped off in there. Guys like to fight and shit.

TUCKER: Yeah. *(Shivers)* Damn, it's freezin'.

JACKIE: Gonna get a lot colder. *(Pause)* I know where you can get a set of long-johns.

TUCKER: Where?

JACKIE: Health-tex.

TUCKER: They went outta business.

JACKIE: Yeah, but I know where they stored all the old inventory. Yessir, a little warehouse by the docks. You oughtta see the stuff they got piled up in there-sleep wear, kiddie clothes, piles of long-johns, just sittin' in bales, gatherin' dust. A smart guy might know how to get inside, do a little midnight shoppin'.

TUCKER: Show me.

JACKIE: Man...things cost.

TUCKER: How much you want?

JACKIE: Ten bucks.

TUCKER: If I had ten, I'd go to Sears.

JACKIE: O K, a pint of Chivas.

TUCKER: I'm fresh out. *(Pause)* Just show me the warehouse. Take me over tonight.

JACKIE: Too early. Nightwatchman ain't done his rounds yet. Besides, I gotta stay here. I'm workin'.

TUCKER: *(Confused)* You're workin'...where?

JACKIE: Right here. *(He puts another piece of wood in the barrel.)*

TUCKER: I don't see nothin'.

JACKIE: *(Touches his head)* In my head, I'm workin'. Practicing scales. Improvising. Gotta practice. Coltrane's comin' to town next week. This time I'm gonna be ready for him. Shut that mutha down.

TUCKER: John Coltrane?

JACKIE: The only and only. Comin' here. We're gonna jam. *(He hums a few bars of* Giant Steps.*)*

TUCKER: Coltrane's dead, Jackie.

(JACKIE *looks at him for a long moment.)*

JACKIE: You lyin' sack of shit! You just sayin' that so I'll go with you to that warehouse. My mama didn't raise no fool.

TUCKER: OK, maybe I'm wrong. You'll whip his ass, 'cause you're the best damn sax player in the universe.

JACKIE: You better believe it.

(JACKIE *fingers a few runs on the sax keys, an hums the chord changes.* TUCKER *watches him, wondering why no notes come out of the sax.)*

TUCKER: Why you hummin'? Play me somethin', Jackie.

JACKIE: Naw, it hurts to play...makes my gums bleed. Need to see a dentist, get me some new choppers. I get me some new teeth, I'll be ready for Trane...just need some bread, that's all....

TUCKER: New teeth cost a bundle, Jackie.

JACKIE: Then I'll play in pain if I have to...gonna beat him this time.

(JACKIE *hums another tune, fingers the sax keys.* TUCKER *watches him sadly.)*

TUCKER: Jackie, why don't you tell me where that warehouse is. I'll go in alone.

JACKIE: I'm a businessman. You want a free lunch, go to the soup kitchen.

TUCKER: Look, I got money socked away, but I can't get to it right now. It's all tied up in a Swiss Bank account, and I can't remember the number. I gotta call my brother in Kansas City. He's got the number.

JACKIE: Yeah, I got the same problem, man. All my bread is tied up in real estate in the Bahamas. My uncle got me into a bad deal, and I'm still payin' for it.

TUCKER: Yeah. Life's a bitch!

(They watch the fire for a few seconds.)

TUCKER: You got an extra sweater?

JACKIE: No, I got mine at the Public Library...by the newspapers. People are always leavin' somethin' in there. Once I got a nice pair of gloves. Butterscotch leather, and real rabbit fur inside. They were warm, but I lost 'em. *(Pause)* What you got in the bag?

TUCKER: Car stereo. *(He takes it out of the bag.)*

JACKIE: Nice.

TUCKER: SONY. Digital, quartz-lock. The best.

JACKIE: Very nice. Just what I'll be wantin' soon as my new Camaro gets delivered.

TUCKER: You can hook it up to the car battery. Worth at least a hundred. O K, for you—fifty.

JACKIE: Maybe worth twenty. It's hot.

TUCKER: No. Somebody left it on a park bench. Left it in this bag. I'll let you have it. Go on, take it.

JACKIE: I still want the Chivas.

TUCKER: I'll owe you.

JACKIE: O K. The warehouse is on Pearl Street. Right behind the customs wharf. You go in the second floor window from the fire escape. It's unlocked. And when you leave, don't lock it.

TUCKER: You're a prince.

JACKIE: And, don't play me for no sucker.

TUCKER: You'll get your scotch. *(Looks up)* Jesus, look at the stars tonight.

JACKIE: *(Looking up)* Beautiful.

TUCKER: See that blue-green one. That one? That's my star.

(They watch the star for a long moment.)

JACKIE: It's moving.

TUCKER: No shit...it is...

(They watch it move across the sky and descend.)

JACKIE: It's falling.

TUCKER: It's a U F O.

JACKIE: Whatever it is, it's landing. *(Pause)* I think it was an airplane.

TUCKER: Oh, man...it's finally happened. They've landed. We're toast, man!

(TUCKER scurries off into the darkness. JACKIE looks around.)

JACKIE: Toast? *(Pause)* Crazy motherfucker!

(JACKIE places another piece of wood on the fire as the light fades.)

Scene Three

(Scene: a derelict fish shed at the end of a dilapidated wharf along the waterfront. Rotting pilings and piles of lobster traps and buoys. It is late at night. Sound of sirens in the distance. CECE and HOLLY enter running. They are carrying stolen items-a man's topcoat and a piece of designer luggage. They hide by the shed, out of breath.)

CECE: Whew...I think we lost him.

HOLLY: Did you hear that guy? "Come back here you punks, or I'll kill you."

CECE: Oh, stop. Don't make me laugh anymore. My sides are killin' me.

HOLLY: What a dork. *(Breathing heavily).* I can't get my wind. I'm gonna have to stop smoking. I can't run like I used to.

CECE: That jerk woulda chased us all the way to the west end.

HOLLY: 'Cept he fell on his fat butt.

(They laugh. Sirens pass by. CECE looks back to the street.)

HOLLY: No big deal. It's a fire engine.

CECE: That's the third one headin' that direction. Must be a big fire out that way.

HOLLY: You would know. You probably set it.

CECE: Get serious. I don't do that shit anymore. God, look at it. You can see an orange glow in the sky way over there. Maybe a whole lumber yard got torched!

HOLLY: You're just itchin' to go watch it burn, aren't you?

CECE: No. It's too far away...out past the airport. A real three alarm. That's wild.

HOLLY: What happened to Charlie?

CECE: I dunno. I thought he was right behind you.

HOLLY: I cut through the parking garage. He must have crossed Cumberland, goin' the other way. I thought he was with you.

CECE: Oh, no. Do you think he got caught?

HOLLY: Charlie? No way. He's too fast. He'll show up. That was so funny when the guy slipped and fell. I loved it.

CECE: Lemme see the coat.

HOLLY: I snatched it. I get the coat.

CECE: Hey, not fair. You've got a leather jacket. I'm freezin' in this denim. Come on, I bet it won't even fit you.

(HOLLY *tries on the coat. It is too small.*)

CECE: See, what did I tell you?

HOLLY: But, it's a *man's* coat.

CECE: Well, I guess that leaves you out.

HOLLY: *(Removing coat)* Too bad. Nice coat.

(CECE *tries on the coat.*)

CECE: What do you think?

HOLLY: Ugh! Definitely not. You can do better. Go to "Starvation Army", they're giving out surplus pea coats.

(CECE *removes the coat.*)

CECE: I guess we could sell it. Maybe it would look good on Charlie. Where the hell is he?

(HOLLY *starts going through the pockets. He finds a hotel key and a wallet.*)

HOLLY: Room 603, Sonesta Hotel. Rich out-of-towner. I told you.

CECE: Of course he was out of town, dip...he had Rhode Island plates. Gimme the wallet.

HOLLY: *(Opening the wallet)* The moment of truth...

CECE: Lemme see.

HOLLY: I get the honor.

CECE: *(Trying to grab wallet)* Yeah? Who elected you Queen?

HOLLY: *(Playing "keep away")* Gucci, Gucci, Gucci...

CECE: Come on, I spotted the car....

HOLLY: And who took the chance, huh?

CECE: Oh, big chance. The window was wide open. Did you chip a nail reachin' inside?

HOLLY: I took it. But out.

(CECE *and* HOLLY *wrestle for the wallet.*)

CECE: Give it up.

HOLLY: You give it up.

(*They each have a hand on the coat and the wallet as they struggle.*)

CECE: Dammit, leggo!

(HOLLY *pins* CECE *on the ground, twists her arm.*)

CECE: Hey, fuck...that hurts, Holly! Stop!

HOLLY: Then stop fighting.

CECE: Get off me.

HOLLY: Eat me.

CECE: Yeah, you wish.

HOLLY: Let go of the coat.

CECE: Gimme the wallet.

HOLLY: If you don't let go, you're gonna tear the lining.

CECE: I don't care.

HOLLY: You rip it, and you won't get shit for it.

CECE: Big deal, it's a man's coat. Who needs it?

HOLLY: Okay, then let go.

(CECE *releases her grip.* HOLLY *rises,* CECE *grabs the coat, giggling.* HOLLY *tosses the wallet to* CECE.)

HOLLY: Big baby...always got to have your way.

CECE: *(Searching wallet)*

HOLLY: There's no cash. Only credit cards... Yuppie scumbags.

CECE: American Express, Visa, Master Card...all right, a business card—"Arthur Klein, Architect".

HOLLY: I bet he designs all those ugly bank buildings.

CECE: *(Still searching wallet)* Triple A Card, aw, look...pictures of the wife and kids. Aren't they cute? Mrs Klein with the twins—Bobsie and Poopsie.

HOLLY: *(Looking)* Muffy and Buffy. *(Takes the photo)* The kids are cross-eyed.

CECE: *(Looks at photo)* No shit...they are.

HOLLY: And...I think Mrs Klein has a hare-lip.

CECE: You can't see that.

HOLLY: Sure. Look right there...the upper lip.

CECE: I know where it is! Naw, there's a smudge on the picture.

HOLLY: *(Talking with a "hare-lip")* No way, Jose. That's a fuckin' hare-lip. I know.

CECE: Lemme see. Maybe it's an over bite. Whatever it is, she's ug-lee!

(HOLLY *grabs the photo and pogo dances on it as he sings a chorus from a punk song by The Dead Milkmen.*)

HOLLY: I'm so bored, I got nothin' to do
Feel like takin' retards to the zoo.
(Pause) I love that song.

(Sound of a boogie box playing loud speed metal music)

HOLLY: That's Charlie!

(CHARLIE *enters on his skateboard, carrying his boogie box.* CHARLIE *dos a fancy "wheelie" on the skateboard, and jumps off.* CECE *runs to him, and kisses him.*)

CECE: Charlie! Where the hell have you been? I was worried.

CHARLIE: Did we score?

HOLLY: So far...zip. We haven't checked the luggage yet.

CECE: Where were you?

CHARLIE: I got stopped.

HOLLY: Oh, you took time out for a date?

CHARLIE: Fuck you, Holly. We were seen.

CECE: Nobody saw us...just the fat guy...

HOLLY: Arthur Klein, the asshole architect. We've been reading his life story.

CHARLIE: I'm serious. I ran into your mother.

HOLLY: My mother's dead.

CHARLIE: No, Cece's mom. I almost ran her down comin' out of 7-11.

CECE: My mom? No way...she's still in detox.

CHARLIE: Not anymore. I'm not kiddin'. She was right there...arms fulla paper bags...man, I almost creamed her when I came around the corner. She saw you guys runnin' across Congress Street. She was lookin' right at you. Didn't you see her?

CECE: No. Did she recognize you?

CHARLIE: Yeah. She gave me the third degree. She saw you guys with that coat. She asked me what you were doin'. I told her I hadn't seen you in a while. She knew I was lyin'.

CECE: How'd she look?

CHARLIE: I dunno, the same I guess...Ceec, we didn't exactly have lunch ya know...I was so weirded out, I didn't hang around.

CECE: I gotta go see her.

CHARLIE: Ceec, don't go back there.

CECE: I have to.

CHARLIE: No you don't. Stay with me.

HOLLY: Go back, see your old lady...maybe you can hit her up for some bucks. *(She turns on the tape player on* CHARLIE'*s boogie box. Loud rock music)* All right. Rock and roll!

CHARLIE: You don't need to see her, Ceec.

CECE: *(Yelling over the music)* Holly, do you mind? I'm tryin' to have a conversation here.

HOLLY: What? I can't hear you. I got a hare-lip, and I'm a retard.

(CECE *turns off the tape.*)

CECE: You're gonna be a retard in about one sec.

HOLLY: *(Sulks)* Spoil all my fun.

(CHARLIE *looks at* CECE *with disappointment.*)

CHARLIE: You gonna do it, aren't ya? Don't give a shit what I want...

CECE: *(To herself)* I just hope the "asshole rug" isn't there.

HOLLY: What's the "rug"?

CECE: Her boyfriend.

HOLLY: Why do you call him that?

CECE: 'Cause he's hairy as King Kong, and twice as stupid. Whenever he's around, all they do is get wasted, fight, and then fuck. If she hadn't thrown me out, I probably woulda left anyway. *(To* CHARLIE*)* Where you gonna be later?

CHARLIE: *(Stand off-ish)* I dunno. Depends on what happens.

HOLLY: Depends on who he can hustle tonight, eh, Charlie?

CECE: Charlie, don't go with anyone tonight. I wanna see ya later, O K?

CHARLIE: *(Reluctant)* O K.

HOLLY: True love is so touching.

CECE: Grow a dick, Holly! *(To* CHARLIE*)* Promise me you won't go with anyone tonight. Please... Maybe we can stay at Jackie's. He found a car.

CHARLIE: We'll see.

CECE: I'll be at the all-night donuts. Will you be there?

CHARLIE: I'll be there.

CECE: Ok, I gotta go.

HOLLY: Wait a minute, Cece. Don't you want see what we got in here? *(She tries unsuccessfully to open the piece of luggage.)* It's locked. You got a hairpin? If I had a hairpin, I could open it.

CHARLIE: Just rip out the side.

HOLLY: No way. This is a Louis Vuitton.

CHARLIE: A what?

HOLLY: Designer luggage.

CHARLIE: That? It looks like shit.

HOLLY: We can't ruin the bag. We can sell it to some yuppie in the Old Port.

(CHARLIE *picks up the set of keys on the ground, finds the suitcase key.)*

CHARLIE: Did you try the key? Amateurs!

(HOLLY *opens the lock with the key.)*

HOLLY: All right, cross your fingers...money...a kilo of "china white..."

(HOLLY *dumps the contents on the dock. It is a pile of clothes.)*

CHARLIE: Clothes.

HOLLY: This Klein guy is really weird. He leaves his car wide open, but he locks up his underwear.

CHARLIE: Shoulda boosted the tape deck.

CECE: We didn't have tools.

CHARLIE: Fuck tools...just slap the dashboard real hard, it'll pop out in your hand.

CECE: Nothin' but junk.

HOLLY: Not so fast. There's some good labels here.

CECE: I don't see nothin' I want.

CHARLIE: Me neither.

HOLLY: Ceec, take this blouse. It's you.

CECE: Holly...it's ugly.

HOLLY: All right, I'll keep it. You want a Brooks Brothers shirt, Charlie?

CHARLIE: I hate button-downs.

HOLLY: Oh, well, another lousy Christmas. What do we do now? You want hit the strip again?

CECE: I'm goin'. I'll see ya later.

(Loud crashing noise coming from inside the fish shed, followed by much cursing. TUCKER pounds against the door trying to get out)

TUCKER: Motherfuckin' cocksucker...son of a bitch!

CHARLIE: What the hell?

HOLLY: Jesus, run...

(TUCKER kicks out a section of boards. HOLLY, CHARLIE, CECE bolt, leaving their loot behind. TUCKER stumbles on to the stage, barefoot, and covered in fish guts and slime.)

TUCKER: GODDAMN YOU, JACKIE BLUE! It's a fuckin' fish shed. I stepped right into a tub of scrod, and fell on my fuckin' butt! I smell like shit! I'm gonna kill you, lyin' motherfucker! What happened to my shoes? Where are my shoes? Shit! *(He spots the clothing and bag lying on the dock. He looks at it in confusion. Slowly he picks up the top coat, and tries it on. He finds the wallet, opens it and reads the card.)* "Arthur Klein, Architect". *(He looks at the clothes again. He lifts a man's shirt and a woman's blouse, thinking that two people shed their clothes on this spot. He looks up at the sky with a sense of wonder.)* Wow! They zapped them. Slid their bodies right outta their clothes. Probably gonna do medical experiments on 'em. They'll find their carcasses down by the water, completely gutted...all the organs scraped out, clean...with a laser scalpel. Whew! Amazing! *(He gathers all the clothing into a bundle. He looks at the sky again and shakes his head, as the lights fade to black)*

Scene Four

(Scene: MOIRA's house. A worn sofa, a coffee table with a fifth of liquor still wrapped in a brown paper bag. Two cartons of cigarettes, a Bic lighter and a large ashtray. Late at night, CECE stands in the room, looking at the items on the coffee table. She removes two packs of cigarettes from the cartons, and slips them into her pocket. MOIRA enters from the hallway. MOIRA [39], is CECE's mother. She stands in the hallway in a bathrobe, drying her hair with a towel. MOIRA watches CECE take the cigarettes.)

MOIRA: So...help yourself.

CECE: I...I needed some smokes. You mind?

MOIRA: *(Shrugs)* No. *(Pause)* How'd you get in? You still got a key?

CECE: The door was unlocked. *(Pause)* You takin' a bath?

MOIRA: I was washin' my hair.

CECE: It looks different.

MOIRA: I got it cut. You like it?

CECE: It's okay.

MOIRA: Why'd you come back?

CECE: I heard you were out again.

MOIRA: Yeah.

CECE: Did they let you out? Or did you just walk?

(CECE begins to play nervously with the Bic lighter.)

MOIRA: I got a new job-cashier at Newberry's. Never ran a Datachecker before...real complicated...almost like a computer. It's real easy to screw up if you're not careful. *(She takes the lighter out of CECE's hand.)* Stop playin' with my lighter.

CECE: I wasn't hurtin' nothin'.

MOIRA: You ain't gonna burn down my house.

CECE: I was just flickin' it. Jeez...I don't do that stuff no more.

MOIRA: Yeah? What do you do now?

CECE: Nothin'. Just hang out. What do you care?

MOIRA: You still hang out with Charlie and that other one...the hermaphrodite...what's its name?

CECE: Holly! He's not a hermaphrodite. He's a cross-dresser.

MOIRA: Listen to you-little Miss Expert. What do you do-sneak in my house when I'm gone and watch Jerry Springer?

CECE: They're my friends.

MOIRA: And they're nothin' but trouble. Just like you, Cece. I seen you out on Congress Street. I know what's goin' on. I'm not gonna have the cops comin' here anymore about you. I've had it. I can't deal with your crap. I'm tryin' to get my own life back together now, and that's all I got time for. Understand?

(MOIRA lights a cigarette. There is already one burning in the ashtray.)

CECE: You already got one cig lit.

(MOIRA *stubs out the old cigarette.*)

MOIRA: I get so nervous. My hands shake when I ain't got a drink in 'em. It's real hard to stay sober, but I'm gonna do it this time.

(CECE *motions to the bottle on the table.*)

CECE: So, you bought this tonight...good move.

MOIRA: I'm expecting company. It's for him, not me.

CECE: Right.

MOIRA: *(After a pause)* He's comin' over...so if you don't wanna see him....

CECE: Yeah, I know...hit the road. *(She rises, stands for a moment looking down the hallway.)* What's all his shit doin' in my room?

MOIRA: He's storin' some stuff here for a while. He's leavin' his wife.

CECE: Oh, yeah? She throw him out? Did he beat the crap out of her too?

MOIRA: Watch your mouth! *(Long pause)* What do you want, Cece? Why'd you come back?

CECE: I don't know.

(MOIRA *watches her for a moment, then goes to her purse. She gets a ten dollar bill, and hands it to* CECE.)

CECE: What's that for?

MOIRA: They gave me an advance to tide me over till my first check. Go on, take it. Get yourself cleaned up or somethin'. You look like hell. It's all I can spare.

(CECE *holds the money, and looks at it.* CECE *lights the bill with the lighter. She puts it in the ash tray and watches it burn.* MOIRA *puts out the fire.*)

MOIRA: You never change, do you?

CECE: Neither do you.

(CECE *walks out.*)

MOIRA: WHAT THE HELL DO YOU WANT FROM ME?

(Blackout)

Scene Five

(Scene: the All-night Donut shop. Later that night. JACKIE *is asleep at one of the tables. A pile of donut holes on the table in front of him.* JACKIE *has his feet up, his head back, with mouth open, snoring loudly. His saxophone is draped around his neck.* CECE *sits at a table by the window with a cup of coffee. She is watching the street. At another table is* ELLEN *[forties], a regular.* ELLEN *is dressed in many layers, and has shopping bags at her feet.* ELLEN *sings* Jesus Loves Me, *lost in her thoughts. She stops. Suddenly, she laughs and begins talking loudly to the room, oblivious to anyone.)*

ELLEN: So, I told Anne Marie, if you're gonna have your baby around New Year's, then you gotta make sure that your baby is the first one born after midnight on December 31st. Can't be the second or the third...gotta be the first baby born in the new year. Number one. Because if you have the first one, oh, you wouldn't believe all the great gifts you get free. That woman last year who had those twins premature. They paid for all of her hospital bills, they put her on the eleven o'clock news, and she got all sorts of prizes. A pasta machine, an Amana freezer, bassinets, scholarships, and musta been a million coupons. Shop 'N Save gave her two years' worth of Gerber's Baby formula and Pampers. That's expensive when you add it up. Boy, did she make out. I heard they even got her a new apartment...just because she had the New Year's Twins. So, I told Anne Marie, you gotta deliver on the dot. She was takin' paregoric and laxatives for almost three days before New Year's Eve, and the baby wouldn't come no matter what she did.
By the time she went in the hospital, she was in labor for seventy-two hours. Thought she was gonna die. Had a C-section and everything. And wouldn't ya know...her kid was born on January second. After all that trouble she missed it by two full days. What rotten luck. She and that kid are gonna be miserable the rest of their lives. *(She sighs, and drinks her tea)* Well, maybe she can win the lottery. 'Cause she's gonna need it. She can't take care of that baby. She can hardly wash herself. Jackie, you gonna eat those donut holes?

*(*JACKIE *snores.* ELLEN *gets up, moves to his table, and looks down his throat.)*
Jackie? Jackie? I think he's dead. *(Suddenly upset.)*

CECE: He's just sleepin', Ellen.

ELLEN: Oh...can't sleep in here, Jackie. They'll throw you out. Do you think Jackie would mind if I was to borrow one or two of these donut holes?

CECE: I don't know.

ELLEN: I'll just take two. *(She takes four and shuffles back to her table. She dunks the donut holes in her cup.)* Ah, that's nice. Where's your boyfriend tonight, Cece?

CECE: I dunno. Said he'd be here later. You seen him?

ELLEN: No. I don't have time to look for anyone. I have to find my daughter. Have you seen her?

CECE: No, I haven't.

ELLEN: She's real pretty. You'd recognize her if you ever saw her. She's on TV. Did I ever show you her picture?

CECE: Yes, you have. Several times.

(ELLEN *rummages in her bags to find the photo. She finds it and crosses to* CECE.)

ELLEN: Her name is Connie. She's pretty enough to be a model, or an actress, which is what she is...in California. As soon as I get my money together, I'll be going out to Los Angeles to visit at Christmas. She lives in a house by the ocean...with flowers and hundreds, hundreds, and hundreds of cats, all running wild. She makes a million dollars a year.

CECE: That's nice, Ellen.

ELLEN: But now, Connie's missing. I think she was kidnapped by that horrible woman with all that blonde hair piled on top of her head. And that woman is now telling everyone that she is Connie's mother. But anyone knows I'm Connie's mother. I could tell you that. See the resemblance? So, I have to find her before that woman steals all of our money.

CECE: I haven't seen Connie this week.

ELLEN: Be sure now. Look at the picture.

CECE: Ellen, I've seen the picture. She's very pretty.

ELLEN: You haven't seen her? You're positive?

CECE: I'm sure of it.

ELLEN: Who does she look like?

CECE: Brooke Shields.

(ELLEN *pours an enormous amount of sugar in her tea as she rattles on to* CECE.)

ELLEN: That's right. But, Connie is her real name. They made her change it when she got to Hollywood. Everyone has to change their name out there. Did you know that? All of 'em...Tony Curtis, John Wayne, Janet Gaynor, Regis Philbin. You can't keep your own name for some mysterious reason. Maybe for tax purposes. I don't know. It's very complicated.

CECE: *(Trying to get rid of her)* Well, if I see Connie, I'll let you know, Ellen.

ELLEN: Would you? Thank you. *(She moves toward her own table.)* I have to find her. She has all my money and all my things. Once when I visited her she introduced me to Claude Rains and Caesar Romero. They are both in love with my daughter.

CECE: *(Looks at street)* Lucky her.

ELLEN: Lucky her, yes. And I'm the luckiest mother alive. And when I find her, we'll have a big reunion, and I'll invite everyone I know...even Anne Marie and her late baby. We'll be on the eleven o'clock news.

(HOLLY *enters singing a Lou Reed song.*)

HOLLY: Holly came out from the island
In the back room she was everybody's darlin'.

CECE: Holly! You seen Charlie?

HOLLY: Unh-uh! *(Singing, and strutting)*
She never lost her head
Even when she was givin' head.
I said, Hey, Babe,...take a walk on the wild side.
Hey, Sugar...take a walk on the wild side.
And the colored girls go-doo-tadoo, doo-ta-doo...

CECE: Who wound you up?

HOLLY: Ceec, I have made out like a bandit tonight. My ship is comin' in. I can feel it. How ya' doin, Ellen?

ELLEN: Fine, Holly. Have you seen my daughter?

HOLLY: Brooke? Not today.

ELLEN: Connie!

HOLLY: Right, Connie. No, sorry...last I heard she was doin' the U S O tour with Bob Hope.

ELLEN: That's right. I'm going to be on that show with her. If only I can find that awful woman who is impersonating me.

HOLLY: Go for it, Ellen! Kill the bitch!

ELLEN: I would if I could find her.

CECE: Don't encourage her.

HOLLY: Aw, lighten up. I'm havin' fun. Okay...okay. (HOLLY *crosses to* ELLEN, *hands her a dollar.*) Ellen...go buy yourself half a dozen at the counter. Live it up!

ELLEN: For me? Oh, thank you. *(She takes the money and goes off.)*

CECE: Where'd you get so flush? Do a date?

HOLLY: Not just any date...THE date! Check out the necklace. Solid gold. That is not cheap shit.

CECE: Who gave it to you?

HOLLY: An admirer, who just loves my ass!

CECE: I bet.

HOLLY: And get this...he's got a little condo down by the shore. Up here for the weekend on business. Guess who's been invited to the beach house for a little R & R? Can you picture it?...waves breaking on the shore, champagne by the fireplace, soft music on the stereo...

CECE: And you on your knees...lovely picture.

HOLLY: Do I detect some jealousy?

CECE: Holly, I hear this bullshit about ten times a week. You do a quicky hand job in the back row of the State Theatre and suddenly you're in love. *(Mimic)* "Oh, I've found *the* man."

HOLLY: Honey, he took me to three...count em!...*three*, expensive clubs tonight.

CECE: I'll believe this when I see the ring.

HOLLY: Well, you can hold your breath, he's coming tonight to pick me up.

CECE: Here?

HOLLY: Get some class! Not here. Lobby of the Holiday Inn.

HOLLY: We are talking major bucks.

CECE: Or major fucks. I've heard this before, Holly.

HOLLY: Want me to ask if he has a friend?

CECE: Forget it. I'm not doin' dates anymore.

HOLLY: Oh, did we inherit a trust fund?

CECE: I don't wanna hustle anymore. I'm not feelin' so great. I got an infection.

HOLLY: Ceec, this whole city is an infection. You wanna donut?

CECE: I can't keep anything down.

HOLLY: *(After a pause)* Uh-oh! Dead bunny time!

CECE: Oh, shut up! *(Pause)* Christ, I hope not.

HOLLY: Maybe you should go to the free clinic.

(CECE *stares out at the street.*)

CECE: I am late.

HOLLY: It's not late, the bars haven't even closed.

CECE: My period's late. *(Pause)* Oh, shit...what if I am?

HOLLY: *(Glossing it over)* Nah, I doubt it...you've been careful. You just ain't been eatin' right or somethin'. You oughta have a donut. Sugar's good for ya. (HOLLY *sips some of* CECE's *coffee.*) Damn, my mouth hurts. Hot or cold...drives me nuts. Lousy cold sores. What's with Jackie?

CECE: He passed out.

HOLLY: Hey, Jackie! Jackie Blue! Hey, you can't sleep in here, man!

CECE: Sssh! Leave him alone.

ELLEN: I think he's dead.

(HOLLY *crosses to* JACKIE, *looks at him.*)

HOLLY: No, he's still breathin'. (HOLLY *picks up some donut holes from* JACKIE's *table.*) You mind, Jackie? Thanks. Delicious grease. I love the chocolate ones.

CECE: You see Charlie tonight?

HOLLY: He'll show up after the bars close.

CECE: You've seen him.

HOLLY: Yeah, I saw him. He was workin' on some three-piece suit at the Castaways. Ah, don't worry. He never gets lucky in there. So, how was home?

CECE: The same.

HOLLY: Wouldn't let you stay?

CECE: Who wants to? The "rug" was comin' by later.

HOLLY: *(Bums a cigarette)* Home sweet home.

CECE: You ever go back to your family?

HOLLY: Once, about two years ago. My brother and my old man met me at the door. They had Louisville Sluggers in their hands. They said if I ever showed my 'queer face' again, they'd rip my nose off. They would too. The whole time I was grown' up there I thought my name was "Shut the fuck up!" *(Pause)* My mother was decent thought. But, she got cancer and died when I was twelve. So, I left, but I took most of her clothes. *(Laughs)* The rest of 'em are assholes. They could die and I wouldn't care. I know they feel the same about me. So fuck 'em. *(Pause)* Enough about me. Let's talk about you!

CECE: Let's not.

(HOLLY *holds the sugar container like a microphone at an interview.*)

HOLLY: So, tell us Miss, is it true that you once torched your entire neighborhood, because it was Monday, and you didn't like Mondays?

CECE: Stop it, Holly.

HOLLY: And what method do you prefer? The Ohio Blue tip kitchen match, or the trusty Bic lighter? Go on, speak into the mike.

CECE: You're not funny.

HOLLY: Ah, ha, the sore spot! Okay, I'm not funny. Sorry.

CECE: How come nobody lets me forget that stuff? It happened a long time ago. And I never burned down my whole neighborhood anyway. Whoever told you that, was a liar.

HOLLY: Charlie told me.

CECE: He would. Jerk! I suppose he told you the rest?

HOLLY: *(Revival preacher)* And, she found Jesus, Praise God!

CECE: Lay off, Holly. I didn't find Jesus...I just...forget it. Okay?

HOLLY: Okay.

(Silence. They look out at the street.)

CECE: It's startin' to rain. Shit.

HOLLY: *(As John Wayne)* Nice night for a hangin'...or maybe a gang bang.

(TUCKER *enters the restaurant, barefoot. He is wearing the camel topcoat.* TUCKER *immediately spots* JACKIE *and pulls up a chair next to him.* TUCKER *stares at the sleeping figure of* JACKIE.)

HOLLY: *(To* CECE*)* Ceec, check this out.

CECE: A guy with no shoes. Big deal.

HOLLY: Check out the coat. Look familiar?

(HOLLY *and* CECE *begin laughing.* TUCKER *glowers at them.)*

TUCKER: What are you laughin' at?

HOLLY: Nothin'. Nice coat, man.

TUCKER: Shut up, Homo!

(HOLLY *and* CECE *turn away to avoid trouble.* TUCKER *looks at* JACKIE. TUCKER *eats one of the donut holes on the table. He picks up the rest, and begins stuffing them into* JACKIE's *mouth.* JACKIE *awakes, gagging.* TUCKER *slips behind* JACKIE *and gets him in a choke hold.)*

JACKIE: What the fuck is goin' on?

TUCKER: You struggle, and I'll crush your fuckin' larynx. Funny man, Jackie. You sent me to a fish house! I lost my shoes. You owe me a pair of shoes, Jackie!

JACKIE: Leggo! I can't breathe!

CECE: Hey, leave him alone.

TUCKER: Who asked you? Where's my tape deck, Jackie? Huh? You sell it?

JACKIE: Get offa me! You stink like fish guts!

ELLEN: Go away! He's not hurting you!

TUCKER: He owes me. Where's my Sony?

JACKIE: Chill out, man. Before they call the cops.

(SALLY *[35], the night counter lady, comes out from the back of the shop.*)

SALLY: Hey! Hey! No fighting in here. I'll call the cops. You two break it up. Get out in the street. We don't have that in here. You wanna fight, you go outside.

TUCKER: He made me lose my shoes.

SALLY: I don't care. You have to leave. Read the sign. "No shoes, no service." Get out or I'll call the police. They'll pick you up.

(TUCKER *releases his grip.* JACKIE *jumps up, whirls around, and pins* TUCKER *to the floor.* JACKIE *whips out a straight-razor, and cuts* TUCKER *on the side of his neck.*)

JACKIE: Don't you ever touch me, man!

TUCKER: You cut me! You fuck!

(JACKIE *runs out of the donut shop.*)

SALLY: You get out now!

TUCKER: He cut me! I don't believe it! I'm bleedin'. He sliced my fuckin' neck!

SALLY: I don't care. You get out of here.

TUCKER: Jesus, I'm bleedin'. Give me a napkin.

SALLY: I'm calling the police.

TUCKER: *(Holds a napkin to his neck)* Good. Go call 'em. And get me an ambulance! I'm bleedin' to death. Go on, call the cops. I'm a crime victim. I got rights.

SALLY: *(Going off)* I'm calling them.

TUCKER: You do that! I ain't movin'. Shit! *(He looks at the bloodied napkin. He flies into a rage, and tosses a chair against the wall.)* GODDAMMIT!

HOLLY: I don't know about you, Ceec...but I think I hear my mom calling.

(CECE *nods. Quietly, they exit.* TUCKER *stands in the middle of the room breathing hard. He picks up the razor from the floor, pockets it. He picks up the cup from* CECE*'s table and drinks it. He sits in her chair, holding his wounded neck. He looks at* ELLEN, *who is sipping her tea.*)

TUCKER: What are you looking at? My feet? I lost my shoes.

ELLEN: I lost my daughter.

TUCKER: It's a bitch! *(He looks out at the street.)* You know that girl? The one who just left...you know her?

ELLEN: Maybe.

TUCKER: She reminds me of someone. What's her name?

ELLEN: Cece...Cecilia, I think.

TUCKER: Cece. *(Pause)* Cece what?

ELLEN: I dunno. Just Cece.

TUCKER: She live around here?

ELLEN: Nobody lives around here.

(TUCKER *watches the street. Sound of sirens approaching as light fades.*)

Scene Six

(Scene: the pier and fish shed. Late morning. CECE *is doing a headstand against a wall.* HOLLY *enters looking disheveled.* HOLLY *is coughing, and shivering.* HOLLY *watches* CECE *for a moment, then pushes her over.)*

CECE: Ow! Fuck. What ya do that for?

HOLLY: Felt like it.

CECE: Twat!

HOLLY: I wish. My life would be a lot easier. *(She is racked by a violent coughing fit.)* Oh, Jesus...my lungs.

CECE: Sounds great. Have another cig.

HOLLY: I got soaked in that rain. I think I got bronchitis or somethin'.

CECE: You look like shit.

HOLLY: Thanks. So do you. Where'd you crash?

CECE: Found an unlocked car. It was almost warm.

(HOLLY *removes his shoes and massages his aching feet.*)

HOLLY: I never went to bed. Spent five hours hanging on a parking meter. Then, I walked...up and down...more like fell down...my legs keep givin' out...maybe I need support hose.

CECE: Thought you had a magic weekend planned with Mr Wonderful.

HOLLY: The prick never showed up. You can say, "I told you so." Why am I so stupid? Why do I always think it's gonna be more than a blow job in a parked car?

CECE: He gave you a necklace.

HOLLY: Piece of shit. Turned my neck green. Musta been a two dollar special from Newberry's. *(He removes the necklace, throws it away.)*

CECE: Maybe the guy got the date wrong.

HOLLY: Sure. *(Pause)* They tossed me out of the lobby at four. Couldn't even get in the shelter last night. Some guy at the door says, "This is for men only!" *(Grabs his crotch)* I said—"So is this!" I can't find a decent squat anywhere in this town. Maybe I should hitch to Florida. At least it's warm there. Christ, I'm hungry. You got anything to eat?

(CECE does her headstand again.)

CECE: I told you, I can't stomach food.

HOLLY: Nothin'? Not even an old half-eaten candy bar?

CECE: Nope.

HOLLY: So, I guess a cup of coffee is definitely out of the question.

CECE: Try the donut shop. Maybe you can hit on Sally for a freebie.

HOLLY: Already been there. Sally wouldn't give me anything on credit.

CECE: Thought you had some cash.

HOLLY: Blew it on video games at the arcade. Dumb, huh? *(Pause)* I sat there in the donut shop, just smelling the grease. I think I fell asleep. I had this horrible dream. The world had ended in some nuclear war, or somethin'... the donut shop was gone...rubble in the streets. There was nothin' left in town except for one lousy restaurant. It was the last restaurant on earth that was still standing. And it was Howard Johnson's. And the service still sucked! God what a nightmare. *(Pause)* Pardon me for asking, but why the fuck are you upside down?

CECE: It's the only position I can get comfortable.

HOLLY: Jees...

CECE: It helps with the nausea.

HOLLY: Bonehead, why don't you go to the clinic?

CECE: I did, this morning. I was right. I had a yeast infection. They gave me some stuff for it.

HOLLY: What about the other problem?

CECE: I chickened out. I didn't say anything. *(Pause)* So, I swiped an E P T kit at the drug store. It changed color. I'm screwed.

HOLLY: What are you gonna do? I mean...have you thought about it?

CECE: What do you think?

HOLLY: You stay like that long enough, the little guy will suffocate.

CECE: Good.

HOLLY: Or, you'd get a freak. Last week, I was standin' in line at 7-11, and I was readin' one of those tabloids...it was all about this woman who slept on her stomach the whole time she was pregnant, 'cause she thought if she did that, she would give birth to a girl. I guess she already had five or six boys already, anyway, she slept on her stomach for like seven months, and you know what?

CECE: *(Coming out of the headstand)* She gave birth to a pancake.

HOLLY: No, but almost... She had twins, Siamese twins, and when they came out, they were all squashed together...like totally flat. They doctors couldn't separate 'em enough to find out what sex they were....

CECE: You're making this up.

HOLLY: No, I swear. I read it. It was true. They had photos and everything. It was wicked gross...these two poor little babies all smooshed together. They looked like Wylie Coyote in the Road Runner cartoons after he gets creamed by a steam roller. I'm not kiddin', they were totally flattened out.

CECE: That's the dumbest story I ever heard.

HOLLY: And they said the mother was gonna maybe give the kids to *Ripley's Believe It Or Not*...'cause she didn't think they'd ever be able to ride bikes, or have any normal sort of life...then, they locked up the mother for being a wacko.

CECE: What is the point of this? What has it got to do with anything?

HOLLY: *(After a pause)* I dunno. I thought it was interesting.

CECE: *(Upset)* Well, it's not.

(CHARLIE *enters upstage, unseen by* CECE.)

HOLLY: Hey, don't get shook. I was just foolin' around, Ceec. *(Pause)* Are you gonna tell Charlie?

CECE: *(Mimic)* "You gonna tell Charlie?" What are you, Ann Landers? I'm not gonna tell Charlie nothin', 'cause Charlie don't care. And I don't know for sure if I'm knocked up anyway. And if...I am...so what? What's Charlie gonna do? Marry me? Huh? *(Starts to cry)* I can't even be sure it's his. I've done favors I can't even remember. I've done things just to get a place to sleep for a night. I've done things I don't wanna think about....

(CECE *sobs.* CHARLIE *watches her, and* HOLLY *holds* CECE *in his arms.*)

HOLLY: Don't worry, Ceec. Charlie will come back. It'll be okay. We'll take care of you. You got friends. We care. We do. We won't let nothin' bad happen.

(Fade to black)

Scene Seven

(Scene: LINDA's *office in the Department of Family Services. A desk, file cabinet and chairs.* LINDA *[30s] a social worker sits behind her desk.* CECE *stands, looking out the window. A moment of silence before* LINDA *speaks.)*

LINDA: So what's been going on, Cece?

CECE: Nothin' much.

LINDA: Then why are you here?

CECE: I dunno. Maybe I missed your ugly face.

LINDA: What's going on?

CECE: I told you. Nothin'.

LINDA: Nothing. Okay, I guess we have nothing to talk about then. Close the door on your way out. I have work to do.

*(*LINDA *ignores her, reads a file,* CECE *finally speaks up.)*

CECE: I think I may be in some trouble.

LINDA: By the company you've been keeping that wouldn't surprise me.

CECE: You're angry with me.

LINDA: No, I'm just tired. Tired of all the lies and bullshit from the kids I'm trying to help.

CECE: You're pissed off 'cause I missed some appointments.

LINDA: Some appointments! Cece, the conditions of your release state that you are to check in with me at least once a week.

CECE: I know, I know, I know....

LINDA: You haven't been here in a month and a half.

CECE: And I haven't set any fires either! *(Pause)* Oh, you don't believe me? I'm a liar too? So, pick up the phone, call the goon squad, take me away. I'll do my time. Anything's better than sittin' around here with you given' me the evil eye just 'cause I forgot some appointments.

LINDA: Are you finished with your tantrum?

CECE: I'M NOT HAVING A TANTRUM! I'LL LET YOU KNOW WHEN I HAVE A TANTRUM! *(Pause. Softer)* I haven't been here...'cause I've had other things on my mind, ya know? All sorts of shit's been comin' down lately. You know how they say, "Shit happens?" Well, what do you do when shit happens on top of shit?

LINDA: You call me and we talk.

CECE: Sometimes talkin' in here doesn't solve anything.

LINDA: What does? Being out on the street?

CECE: No. *(Pause)* I don't know.

(LINDA *looks at her for a long moment.*)

LINDA: Are you pregnant?

(CECE *is momentarily stunned by Linda's blunt question,* CECE *sighs, and looks at the floor.*)

CECE: Yes...big surprise, huh?

LINDA: And how long do you think you can last out there, Cece?

CECE: I try not to think about it.

LINDA: Well, it might be time to give it some thought. Nobody's gonna take care of you on the street. Not even Charlie. *(Pause)* You know what happens to kids out there.

CECE: "They get old quick...and they die young." I know the drill.

LINDA: ...or they end up incarcerated. You don't want that, and I know you don't want to go back to jail. You're too smart for that, Cece. You have other options.

CECE: Yeah, real simple...I have the kid, or I don't.

LINDA: And have you made that choice?

CECE: Not yet.

LINDA: I think you'd better realize, you can't use public funds for an abortion. Medicaid won't pay for it.

CECE: I can always find money. That's no big deal.

LINDA: Oh, you like turning tricks?

CECE: What do you think?

LINDA: I think you should give some serious consideration to your health.

CECE: Yeah, yeah...I know all about condoms....

LINDA: Then why didn't you use them?

CECE: Some guys don't want you to. They pay you more if you don't. They say it ruins it for 'em...bunch of sick freaks.

LINDA: *(After a pause)* Cece, I'm worried about you.

CECE: Hey, I ain't gonna die...not yet anyway. I'll be okay.

(CECE's *bravado crumbles, as* LINDA *stares at her.*)

CECE: What can I do?

LINDA: First...you have to want to get off the street...and quite frankly, I'm not sure you're ready yet. Up till now, it's been a lot of fun, right? You've been having a blast. No school, no one to answer to, fast friends, easy money...you got a boyfriend who's a petty thief, and you've got a baby on the way. Sounds like the perfect life to me. What more could you want? It's total freedom. Isn't that what everyone wants, Cece?

(CECE *looks out the window as light fades.*)

Scene Eight

(*Scene: Donny's house. A living room with a couch, and a large T V monitor on a stand. Early evening. Thanksgiving.* CHARLIE *sits on the floor, leaning back against the couch. He is rolling joints from a stash in a plastic bag. The T V is playing.* CECE *sits on the couch holding the remote control for the T V.*)

CHARLIE: The people on these shows are so stupid. Why don't you buy a vowel, you dick-head! This great, huh, Ceec? T V, showers, clean sheets, a fireplace. Pretty cool, huh? (*He lights a joint, tokes, and offers it to* CECE.)

CECE: I don't want any.

CHARLIE: Why not?

CECE: It's not your stash. It's Donny's.

CHARLIE: He'll never miss it. I'll put oregano in the bag.

CECE: I don't think we should be here.

CHARLIE: Relax, it's safe. They'll be gone the whole weekend. The place is ours.

(*Sound of* HOLLY *coughing violently offstage in another room—the kitchen.*)

CHARLIE: Holly? Are you all right?

HOLLY: (*Off*) Fine. I just drank a bottle of Clorox, that's all.

CHARLIE: (*Calling to* HOLLY) Wise ass. What are you doing in there?

HOLLY: (*Off*) I'm cooking somethin' in the microwave. I'll be there in a minute.

CECE: What if they come back early?

CHARLIE: They won't. They'll be in Vermont till Sunday.

CECE: You don't know....

CHARLIE: Every year they visit Donny's mother for Thanksgiving. Always! Christ, I know what I'm talking about. They were my foster parents for three years. I know their routine. *(Pause)* What's buggin' you, Ceec? Are you pissed off because I didn't meet you when I said I would. Is that it? I told you, somethin' came up. I was busy.

CECE: Can I depend on you?

CHARLIE: What do you mean?

CECE: Once, you promised to take care of me.

CHARLIE: I am taking care of you. Good care. Look around, what's all this?

CECE: It's not yours.

CHARLIE: So...maybe the baby isn't mine either.

CECE: So, it's all my problem now, right?

CHARLIE: What do you expect me to do? You wanna get married, buy a house in the suburbs? I'll just walk in and get a job as a stockbroker, right?

CECE: What am I gonna do?

CHARLIE: Get rid of it. Have an abortion.

CECE: How are we gonna pay for it?

CHARLIE: I DON'T KNOW! Jesus! Steal this fuckin' television. It's worth something.

CECE: That's your answer for everything...steal somethin'.

CHARLIE: It used to be good enough for you. You got a better idea?

(HOLLY *enters from the kitchen with a huge bowl of popcorn.* HOLLY *is wearing a flower-print kimono and fuzzy slippers.*)

HOLLY: The wonders of microwave cooking. We have to swipe one of those some day. You should see all the stuff in the pantry. We can eat like pigs.

CECE: *(Indicates the kimono)* Where'd you get that?

HOLLY: Upstairs bedroom. You like it? Can I keep it, Charlie?

CECE: This is crazy. We don't belong here.

CHARLIE: Maybe you don't belong here.

(HOLLY *sits next to* CHARLIE *and picks up the remote control.*)

HOLLY: Don't be such a downer, Ceec. It's gonna be the best Thanksgiving I ever had. What are you watching? This is shit. *(She changes the channel:) Movie Loft*, all right. Maybe it's a Bruce Lee. What is this? A foreign film. Puke, I hate subtitles.

(CHARLIE *takes the remote, goes through the channels.*)

HOLLY: No...change it. Oh, wait, go back one. It's Gilligan. *(Hums the theme song)* Let's watch that. You want some popcorn, Ceec?

(CECE *rises, and paces around.*)

CECE: No.

HOLLY: What's got into you? This is great. (*To* CHARLIE) Do they have a dog or somethin'?

CHARLIE: I dunno. Why?

HOLLY: I saw a pet dish on the floor in there.

CHARLIE: Maybe they had a cat. I don't remember.

HOLLY: Neato. I like cats. If we get bored, we can put it in the microwave. (*Laughs*) Kitty? Here, kitty? Kitty? Probably hiding in the basement. (*She glances around the room, smiles.*) This is a great house, Charlie. You shoulda stayed with these foster parents.

CHARLIE: They changed their mind. Sent me back.

HOLLY: Why? Did you screw the old lady?

(CECE *wanders off toward the kitchen.*)

CHARLIE: I sold their sterling silver. Donny said, "He felt he couldn't trust me anymore." They never even used that silver set. It was a gift from a grandmother or somebody. Useless shit. I think Donny was more pissed that I ripped off his coin jar.

HOLLY: What coin jar?

CHARLIE: Donny had this big ol' jar fulla pennies and nickels sittin' on top of the fridge...musta been fifty dollars in coins. I spent it on video games. Donny flipped. I guess he had some rare coins in the jar.

HOLLY: (*Watching T V*) Oh, I've seen this one, Gilligan gets hit on the head with a coconut and falls in love with the professor. So bizarre. Where'd Ceec go?

CHARLIE: I dunno. (*Calls out*) Ceec? You in the kitchen? I better go find her.

(CHARLIE *rises, saunters off to the kitchen.* HOLLY *channel surfs with the remote control.*)

HOLLY: Oh, P B S...blow it out your ass!

(HOLLY *changes the channel.* CHARLIE *returns, sits next to* HOLLY.)

CHARLIE: She's gone.

HOLLY: Gone?

CHARLIE: She took off.

HOLLY: She's gonna miss the turkey dinner. What's with her?

CHARLIE: She's pissed off.

HOLLY: It's the baby thing. Hormones.

CHARLIE: Pain in the ass.

HOLLY: If she has the kid, maybe we can sell it. *Black Market Baby.* Did you ever see that one?

CHARLIE: You are a sick fuck.

HOLLY: But, a good fuck, Charlie.

CHARLIE: What are we gonna do about Cece?

HOLLY: I don't wanna think about it. *(She snuggles up in* CHARLIE'*s armpit.)* She's so weirded out. I'm not gonna let Ceec ruin my turkey weekend.

(CHARLIE *changes the channel.*)

HOLLY: Hey, I was watchin' that.

CHARLIE: You've already seen it. This is better.

HOLLY: *(After a pause)* I don't care what anyone says, the colorized movies are less boring. (HOLLY *is racked by a coughing fit.*)

CHARLIE: Jesus, are you sick?

HOLLY: I'll be okay. Don't look at my legs, they're ugly.

CHARLIE: Did you hear somethin'?

HOLLY: It's the T V.

CHARLIE: No, somethin' else. Turn it down. You hear that?

(HOLLY *mutes the sound on the T V.* CHARLIE *sits listening.*)

HOLLY: Maybe it's the cat?

CHARLIE: Sounded like a car door.

HOLLY: Oh, no.

(CHARLIE *gets up, goes into the kitchen*)

CHARLIE: *(Off)* Oh, fuck. It's Donny.

HOLLY: Damn it. What's he doing home?

CHARLIE: *(Enters quickly)* Grab your shit. Let's get out of here.

(*Blackout*)

(*Music: At the end of the* ACT, *Joan Jett's* I Hate Myself For Loving You.)

END OF ACT ONE

ACT TWO

Scene One

(Scene: Congress Street—the Strip. Thanksgiving night. It is raining. CECE sits on a wooden crate under an awning out of the rain. She has been crying. TUCKER leans against a wall a few feet away. He looks more respectable, with new clothes, and has cleaned himself up. He watches her crying for a moment.)

TUCKER: *(Sings)* Blue eyes crying in the rain.... *(He offers her a handkerchief.)* Take it. It's almost clean.

(CECE takes the handkerchief, wipes her eyes.)

CECE: Thanks. My eyes aren't blue, they're brown.

TUCKER: *(Sings)* Don't it make your brown eyes blue?

CECE: Are you a comedian? You sure ain't a singer.

TUCKER: Do you remember me? Last time we met, I was sorta havin' a bad day, but I'm much better now.

CECE: *(Remembers)* The man with no shoes.

TUCKER: That's right. I felt bad because I had no shoes, until I met a man who had no feet, and I said, "Hey, if you're not usin' your shoes...." *(Laughs)* I got new boots. You like 'em?

CECE: *(A lie)* Real sharp.

TUCKER: They're Tony Lamas. You don't think they look too fruity do ya? 'Cause I don't wanna look like no midnight plowboy. Know what I mean?

CECE: *(Humoring him)* They're very macho.

TUCKER: Good. My name's Tucker. *(He expects a response, but gets none.)* You like a stick of gum?

(She declines. He chews one.)

TUCKER: Your name's Cece. Short for Cecilia.

(CECE looks at him.)

TUCKER: Surprised I know your name, ain't ya? I know a lot about you. I been askin' around about you.

CECE: *(Wary)* Why?

TUCKER: 'Cause I like you.

CECE: You don't know me.

TUCKER: I'd like to. *(Pause)* You remind me of someone I used to know.... Back in Texas. My ex-wife.

CECE: So move to Texas and leave me alone.

TUCKER: Can't. She's dead. Car accident. She and my little boy. Killed 'em both. Really busted me up for a while, but I got over it...You sorta look like her, like she did then, but sorta different too. Shit, this ain't goin' right. Look, what I'm tryin' to say is...I think you and me...we'd get along. You'd like me once you got to know me.

CECE: I already got a boyfriend.

TUCKER: Yeah, I know. *(Pause)* So where is he tonight? It's Thanksgiving, and you're sittin' out here all by your lonesome in the rain. Don't seem right. Seems to me like he don't treat you with any respect. A girl in your predicament, carryin' a baby, lettin' you sit out here...all alone...ain't right. *(Pause)* Yeah, I know about that too. I got eyes and ears, just like radar. You know you look like you ain't had a decent meal in weeks. I think you could use a trip to the salad bar, girl.

CECE: You may the weirdest person I have ever met on this street.

TUCKER: Maybe so, but seein' how it's Thanksgiving and all, I figure you might have dinner with me.

CECE: You are offering to buy me dinner?

TUCKER: That's right. I sure am. I thought we could go to the Sizzler. Surf and Turf...all you can eat, fried shrimp.

CECE: You got money for all this, Mr. Rockefeller?

(TUCKER unfolds a sheaf of stolen credit cards.)

TUCKER: Good ol' American plastic. I figure I got two more days on these cards before I gotta ditch 'em. Can only run hot credit cards so long....

CECE: You're crazy.

TUCKER: Yep, that I am. Well, what do you say? Are you hungry?

CECE: Yeah, I'm hungry. *(She hesitates to think it over.)* If I go...don't expect any favors.

TUCKER: I don't expect nothin', 'cept company. That's my car across the street-the blue Pontiac.

CECE: That's yours?

TUCKER: Yeah, you like it? It's...uh...borrowed too. Don't worry, I'm a safe driver. *(He starts toward the car.)* Well come on. Let's eat.

(MOIRA *appears with a bag of groceries.* CECE *stops. She and her mother regard each other for a moment.*)

MOIRA: Cece... (*Self-consciously, covers a bruise under her eye*)

CECE: What are you doin' here?

MOIRA: I just came out to get some things...I...was gonna cook....

TUCKER: You comin', Cece?

CECE: What happened to your face?

(*She reaches to touch the bruise, but* MOIRA *stops her hand.*)

MOIRA: Don't...

CECE: Did he do that?

MOIRA: No. God, no...I fell on the front steps, that's all.

TUCKER: Are you comin'?

CECE: Yeah, I'm comin'. (*She turns away from* MOIRA, *walks to* TUCKER.)

MOIRA: Cece...

TUCKER: Who's she?

CECE: Somebody I used to know. Let's go.

(CECE *and* TUCKER *exit.* MOIRA *stands in the rain, watching her.*)

(*Blackout*)

Scene Two

(*Scene: a pedestrian shopping mall. A large garbage can sits near some benches.* JACKIE *and* CHARLIE *are panhandling Christmas shoppers.* JACKIE *has his hat on the ground for spare change as he serenades shoppers. It is mid-day.*)

JACKIE: (*Singing*) Well, have a blue Christmas...yes, a blue Christmas. (*Spoken*) That's right folks...only thirty more days. (*Sings*) Chestnuts roasting on an open fire...Jack Frost nipping at your nose...

(CHARLIE *paces on the opposite side of the trash can, trying to score some money.*)

CHARLIE: (*To a person on the street*) Got change for a cup of coffee?

JACKIE: (*To a person*) Yo, brother...you got any coin for a man in need? Have a nice day!

CHARLIE: (*Spots another man*) Sir, you got any spare change? Have a nice day.

JACKIE: That's it, Charlie. You gotta be polite, even if they don't give you nothin', 'cause next time, maybe they will. (*Spots a person*) You, sir...how about helpin' me with the down payment on my condominium? Yessir. Same to you. *(Under his breath)* Motherfucker. *(Spots another man)* Yessir, I play requests. What you want? How about *Stardust*? Thank you. Have a nice day. Only thirty days till Christmas.

CHARLIE: How's it goin'?

JACKIE: Lousy. Biggest shoppin' day of the year, and I ain't made two dollars yet. People got no holiday spirit.

CHARLIE: Gettin' cold early this year.

JACKIE: Amen, brother. *(Sings)* Baby, it's cold outside.

CHARLIE: You got a song for every occasion?

JACKIE: That I do, my man, that I do.

CHARLIE: Wanna rent the front seat of your car tonight?

JACKIE: Thought you had a house party lined up for the weekend.

CHARLIE: Got canceled. They came home.

JACKIE: Life's a bitch.

CHARLIE: It sure is. What about the squat? We need it. Holly's sick.

JACKIE: Sorry. Already got it rented.

CHARLIE: What about the back seat?

JACKIE: That's for me.

CHARLIE: How about just for a few hours tonight? You can sit in the donut shop.

JACKIE: Five bucks.

CHARLIE: Five bucks?...it used to be three.

JACKIE: Times are hard. Ain't you heard, philanthropy is way down this year. Try the shelter.

CHARLIE: They'll be full tonight.

JACKIE: Life's a bitch.

CHARLIE: I'm really tired of hearing that, Jackie.

(JACKIE plays a sad blues line on his sax.)

JACKIE: So, where's your girlfriend?

CHARLIE: She took off yesterday. You seen her?

JACKIE: Maybe I have, and maybe I haven't....

(He plays, Someone To Watch Over Me. *CHARLIE finally tosses a coin in the hat.)*

JACKIE: Thank you. Seems I mighta heard she was with some new guy last night.

CHARLIE: A "date".

JACKIE: Wasn't no date. A guy on the street...goes by the name of Tucker.

CHARLIE: Who is he?

JACKIE: A crazy motherfucker. Been askin' around about her...all week.

CHARLIE: Where'd they go?

JACKIE: *(Shrugs)* You got me.

(Plays his sax. CHARLIE *digs out another coin, throws it in the hat.)*

CHARLIE: That's all I got.

JACKIE: Thank you. They drove away in a nice blue LeMans, but I don't know where. Don't have wings.

CHARLIE: A blue LeMans?

JACKIE: And very hot. Still had the sticker in the window.

CHARLIE: How do you know it was hot?

JACKIE: I know this dude. He never pays his tab. Watch out for him, Charlie. If he decides to "get a line on you"...don't turn your back, brother.

(HOLLY *enters coughing.*)

CHARLIE: Took you long enough.

HOLLY: Give me a break, the store was crawlin' with people, had to wait for a clear shot. (HOLLY *coughs violently.*)

CHARLIE: Jeez, cough all over me, why don't ya?

HOLLY: Oh, fuck...I feel bad.

JACKIE: What's the matter with you?

HOLLY: I got bronchitis or somethin'. Shit. I gotta sit down. I'm dizzy.

JACKIE: Don't get near me with that.

(JACKIE *moves a few feet further away.* HOLLY *sits on the ground, very weak. He puts his head down.*)

CHARLIE: Don't sit on the pavement. People are lookin'.

HOLLY: I don't care. I gotta sit down.

CHARLIE: Did you get it?

HOLLY: I got it. (HOLLY *opens his jacket and removes a cassette tape. The tape is still in its plastic anti-theft device.* HOLLY *hands it to* CHARLIE.)

CHARLIE: *(Looks at the tape)* What the hell is this?

HOLLY: Your stupid tape. That's it.

CHARLIE: Billy Joel? I said I wanted Joan Jett.

HOLLY: Oh, shit. I copped the wrong tape.

CHARLIE: Holly, what the fuck's wrong with your brain? Joan Jett—*I Hate Myself For Lovin' You*. That's what I asked you to get. I don't want Billy Joel, for Crissake!

HOLLY: I'm sorry...next time, steal your own Goddamn tape. I was in the "J" section...I musta got confused. It was real hot and crowded in there, I could barely focus. Man, I almost passed out.

CHARLIE: Fuckin' Billy Joel.

HOLLY: O K, I'll go back.

CHARLIE: No way...then you would look suspicious.

HOLLY: Fuck it, I'll go. Shit...I can't get up. Somethin's wrong with my legs.

(CHARLIE *is oblivious to* HOLLY's *struggle.* CHARLIE *tries in vain to remove the anti-theft device.*)

CHARLIE: *(To* JACKIE*)* Can you believe it? Fuckin' wimpoid Billy Joel.

JACKIE: Still rock and roll to me.

CHARLIE: Very funny. Dammit, how do you get these things open?

HOLLY: Charlie...I can't get up.

CHARLIE: *(Not hearing him)* Come on, open...goddamit! *(He gives up, tosses the tape in the garbage can.)* Bunch of crap...wasn't what I wanted anyway.

(As CHARLIE's *back is turned,* JACKIE *quickly retrieves the tape from the garbage can, and pockets it.*)

CHARLIE: *(To* HOLLY*)* What's the matter with you?

HOLLY: I'm real weak. I don't feel so good.

CHARLIE: Can you stand up?

HOLLY: I don't think so.

JACKIE: Oughta get him to a doctor.

HOLLY: No doctors. Just get me up, I'll be all right.

JACKIE: Police cruiser is coming.

CHARLIE: You have to stand up. If the cops see ya, they'll take you in.

HOLLY: Help me.

(CHARLIE *tries to lift* HOLLY.)

HOLLY: I hurt all over, Charlie. I'm scared.

JACKIE: Better hurry, man...they're comin'.

CHARLIE: Then, help me!

(JACKIE *helps* CHARLIE *get* HOLLY *to his feet.*)

JACKIE: Man, if you're lyin' in the street, they pick you up like garbage, and you are *gone*, baby. Everybody smile and wave. (*Sotto voce*) Yeah... yeah go find a donut, copper.

(*They wave to the passing police car.*)

JACKIE: You better get him outta here. They'll be back.

CHARLIE: Where can I take him? He can't walk.

JACKIE: What's the matter with your legs?

HOLLY: Don't look at my legs, please. They're ugly.

CHARLIE: Jackie, we got no place to go.

JACKIE: (*Thinks*) I might know of a squat on the east side. You hold him up. I'll flag down a jitney.

CHARLIE: We ain't got money.

JACKIE: You can owe me. (*He heads off to flag a cab.*)

HOLLY: I really fucked up, Charlie. I can feel it...I'm gonna die.

CHARLIE: Shut up, Holly.

(*Blackout*)

Scene Three

(*Scene: a cheap motel room, late evening. A TV flickers with the sound off.* TUCKER *in a sleeveless undershirt, shaving with a straight razor.* CECE *sits crosslegged on the floor by the bed.* CECE *has a box of kitchen matches in front of her. She lights a match and stares at the flame.*)

CECE: S-O-C-I-O-P-A-T-H. Sociopath. H-T-A-P-O-I-C-O-S. When I was in the Youth Center, I could spell that word frontways and backwards six times on a match before it burned my fingers. I'm not that fast now.
(*She blows out the match.*)

TUCKER: How long were you in?

CECE: Fourteen months...for arson. You ever do any time?

TUCKER: Two times. Got most of my tattoos in prison.

CECE: What were you in for?

TUCKER: *(After a pause)* It don't matter.

CECE: You don't want to talk about it.

TUCKER: Rather hear about you.

CECE: You ever kill anybody?

(TUCKER *folds the razor closed, wipes his face with a towel. He doesn't answer. He opens a bottle of tequila, takes a swig and lies back on the bed.*)

CECE: Guess it ain't my business.

TUCKER: *(Changing the subject)* Tell me all about the fires.

CECE: *(Sighs, heavily)* Well, I set my first one when I was about nine or ten. The summer my old man left us. Me and Bobby Conroy...we were playin' in his daddy's old milk barn. This was when we still lived up at Rumford. Anyway, we were punchin' holes in the barn wall with a ball-peen hammer. Bobby found a can of paint thinner in the tack room. And I supplied the matches. Went up like the fourth of July. All the neighborin' farmers stood on the hill, watchin' it burn all night long. I was scared, so I was hidin' behind my mama's legs, but I'd peek out from time to time from behind her dress. She was cryin'. I think she knew. She squeezed my hand so hard I got a big bruise, but I didn't care. I couldn't take my eyes offa those colors reachin' up to that black sky-all sorta Christmas red and Florida orange. Bobby Conroy finally broke down and confessed. Got his ass whipped good. I never told. Mama didn't say nothin', but I could tell she knew. *(Pause)* Couple years later, she'd be at work at the paper mill-be gone all day-and I'd be home alone or in school-always thinkin' about those colors. Couldn't get 'em outta my head. That summer, I sorta went wild. I burnt three barns, an old fishin' boat, and a couple of abandoned house trailers. Then I got caught.

(TUCKER *laughs hysterically.*)

CECE: You think that's funny?

TUCKER: Trailers. I love it. There's a certain mobile home park in Houston, I'd like to torch.

CECE: I never did it to hurt people. Just like to watch things burn. I set some brush fires too. Some guy showed me how. He'd catch a big, ol' jack rabbit in a snare, then he'd hold the rabbit by his ears, and dunk his hindquarters in a bucket of kerosene. Light the tail, and set him loose. A jackrabbit will zig-zag two or three miles 'fore he realizes he's dead. I didn't do much of that, 'cause I didn't like the idea of killin' anything, even if it was a pesty rabbit.

(TUCKER *laughs harder.*)

CECE: You got a weird sense of humor. *(She takes a drink from the tequila bottle, and winces.)*

TUCKER: Not too many girls like tequila...straight.

CECE: God, that's awful.

TUCKER: Told ya. *(Takes a drink)* My turn to tell a story.

CECE: Okay. We got any more of those sodas left?

TUCKER: There's some Sprite on the dresser.

(CECE gets up to get a drink. TUCKER makes himself comfortable on the bed)

TUCKER: When I was about your age, I was in the service. I hated the army, so I went AWOL...ended up in New York City-Green-witch Village. I was wanderin' around, nothin' to do...I saw this nightclub, called Cafe Wha? It ain't there now...but, back then I was into psychedelic rock bands, so I went into this place...there was a local group on the stage...long-haired bunch of cocksuckin' rejects...really shitty band...called.... *(Begins to stutter)* Lu...Lo...Loo...Luth... *(He takes out his pill bottle and quickly swallows a couple of pills, washing them down with tequila.)*

CECE: What are those?

TUCKER: Just some thorazine. Settles my stomach. *(Laughs)* Sometimes, I stutter. Words get caught in my head. This band...Lo...Looo...LOTHAR and the Hand People!

(CECE laughs.)

TUCKER: You laugh. That was the name of the band. And Lothar, the lead singer...had a weird instrument-a theremin...ever seen one?

CECE: No.

TUCKER: Looks like a big stainless steel thermometer you use on a horse. It's mounted on a wooden stand, and you plug it into an amp, and then you run your hands up and down in this force field along the metal stick...and it gives out real painful buzz tones...very high frequencies...notes only dogs, and very gifted people can hear.

CECE: People like you.

TUCKER: That's right. Lothar made all these horrible tones...they got caught in my cranium. It put negative ions and excess pressure on my medulla oblongata. You know what that is? The brain stem. Connects with everything...runs down the back of the neck, joins up with the shoulder muscles...feeds right down into the chest cavity...and at the other end it connects to spots where the sound gets stuck....

CECE: You sound like a brain surgeon.

TUCKER: I know a lot about the way the brain works. I know about electrical impulses that charge right through the temples. You have to bite down hard on a rubber gag, or you'll chew through your own tongue. *(Pause)* Sometimes they gotta cut out the harmful parts, so all that's left is the quiet part...otherwise you get blinding migraines, and everything has an aurora.

CECE: What are you talking about?

TUCKER: Music and the effect on the brain. See, sometimes you get sick when you hear certain notes, and I told Lothar if he didn't quit makin' that tone, I was gonna punch his lights out. He wouldn't stop, so I pushed him off the stage, and three huge roadies dragged me out in the alley, and jumped up and down on my head for an hour. *(Pause)* I had a migraine for six days. So, you gotta kill this music, or it'll kill you.

(TUCKER *takes a long swig.* CECE *looks at him, totally confused.*)

TUCKER: *(Changing subject, suddenly)* So, who taught you how to do the brush fires? Charlie?

CECE: Naw, I met him later at the Youth Center.

TUCKER: What was he in for?

CECE: Stealin' stuff. *(Pause)* I guess Charlie was the only good thing that happened to me out there.

TUCKER: Good thing? Don't seem so good to me.

CECE: Well, at the time it was...I guess it was good. I don't know.

TUCKER: You still set fires?

CECE: No. I quit for good.

TUCKER: Why?

CECE: *(After a pause)* It's personal.

TUCKER: Hey, you can trust me. My lips are sealed.

CECE: Everyone who knows makes fun of it. You'd laugh at me.

TUCKER: Honey, I'd never laugh at you. You know why? 'Cause I feel like you and me are soul mates, that's why.

CECE: You hardly know me at all.

TUCKER: But I will...in time. Tell me. Why'd ya stop? Did you hurt somebody? I wanna know everything.

CECE: Gimme a cigarette first.

(TUCKER *lights a cigarette for her.* CECE *sits back, leaning against the bed.*)

CECE: I saw my death in the flames once.

TUCKER: You mean like you saw your own future?

CECE: Yeah, somethin' like that. It happened the summer I got released. I came home to Rumford, and she was gone. The house was empty, she'd moved out. I guess a bunch of 'em got laid off at the mill that year. And the day I came home, it was the same day those Klan assholes came up for that rally.

TUCKER: I remember that. Saw it on T V.

CECE: Yeah, well I was there...all this pushing and shovin' and yellin' about coloreds takin' over all the jobs. All bullshit...there weren't any coloreds even livin' there. I didn't see a black person til I came down here to the city. People up there didn't hate anybody...'except the French Canadians, but, that don't count. Well, the hecklers started throwin' stuff at the Klan...rocks, bottles, and then the guns came out, and it was real serious all of a sudden. The State Police sent everyone back behind the barricades so nobody'd get hurt. They didn't want no shootin' once the main rally started at dusk. After dark, you couldn't get near the place with all the cops around.... But, there's the one place I know-the top of a big old Spruce tree on a side of the hill. I climbed up there so I could see. They were all standin' in a big circle in those white hoods...and I had to see it, 'cause I knew there were gonna be those colors. After a bunch of speeches, this one guy, in white robes, holds a Zippo to a strip of gauze they got wrapped all around a big wooden cross. The gauze was totally soaked in lighter fluid. You could smell the accelerant all the way up where I was. Took him two tries to get it lit, but then, oh, man did it go up! And up...and up...all the way into the night...those reds, and oranges, and blue-green flickers I loved to see...and then suddenly this cold sorta feelin' came over me...and that's when I saw his face...floatin' in the air, right above the cross...and he was lookin' right at me. He wouldn't stop lookin' at me. I could see the cuts in his skin...they were so real. *(Pause)* Thorns were dug into his scalp...and tears and blood caked on his face...and he was lookin' right through me...I never felt so bad in all my life, I felt bad for even lookin' at him. And then, the face went up, into flames shootin' so high you couldn't see the top...if you coulda followed 'em that high you would have been above the clouds...you would have seen the face of God...and you'd be dead. And don't ask me how, but at that moment, I knew how I was gonna die...I would burn myself to death in a fire of my own doing. And suddenly, I felt somethin' go out of me...and I felt somethin' I had never felt in the flames before...forgiveness for all the meanness and wickedness in the world...I don't know what it was...but I had this moment of hope...and a terrible fear of death. Death by fire. *(Pause)* I don't read the Bible, I don't go to church, or confession, like I know I should...I'm not religious. I don't even know if there is a heaven or hell... if there is, I'll probably go to hell, 'cause I've done a lot of bad things...I may be damned for eternity...but I know one thing, I won't burn myself up in no fire. I don't wanna set one, ever again. You know, I tell people that story, they think I'm nuts...but I'm not. It's a true story. *(Long pause)* Well, say somethin'.

(CECE *turns to look at* TUCKER. *He has passed out on the bed, sleeping soundly. She stands up, looks at him, shakes her head.)*

CECE: You son-of-a-bitch! *(She puts on her jacket, and exits the room.)*

(Blackout)

Scene Four

(Scene: the next morning. The outside of an abandoned building. CHARLIE *is practicing his skateboard moves. His boogie box sits nearby, churning out Led Zepplin's* Heartbreaker *at full volume.* CHARLIE *executes tricky skateboard moves and plays "air guitar", as he skates.* TUCKER *enters looking hung over.* TUCKER *watches* CHARLIE *for a moment, then applauds.)*

TUCKER: A star is born. *(He turns off the tape.)*

CHARLIE: *(Wary)* You're Tucker!

TUCKER: That's right, Charlie.

CHARLIE: Where's Cece?

TUCKER: Seems to be the question of the day, huh?

CHARLIE: I heard she was with you.

TUCKER: She was. She took off.

CHARLIE: Yeah. She has a habit of doin' that. Try the strip.

TUCKER: Already been up there. This is your squat?

CHARLIE: It's a friend's place.

TUCKER: Looks like a rat hole. Where's your little pansy friend? Haven't seen him around.

CHARLIE: He's sleepin'. Why? You need a date?

TUCKER: Keep it up, smart boy.

(TUCKER *starts to walk toward the squat,* CHARLIE *blocks his way.)*

CHARLIE: Where the fuck you think you're goin'? I told you, Cece ain't here.

TUCKER: You know Charlie, I don't know what she ever saw in you, man. You're a fuckin' loser. You know that? And seein' how she's carryin' my baby, now, well, somethin's gotta give, Charlie. *(He looks at* CHARLIE *for a long moment, then takes a few steps away from him, and circles back. From his jacket pocket,* TUCKER *takes out a plastic bag partially filled with airplane glue. He opens the bag.)* You huff glue, Charlie?

CHARLIE: What?

TUCKER: Glue...you know...like rubber cement.

CHARLIE: No!

(TUCKER *holds the baggie up to his own face, and inhales the contents deeply. He staggers backwards from the effect, and falls on his butt, laughing.*)

TUCKER: Too bad, don't know what you're missing. You don't even feel the cold after awhile...in fact you don't feel anything, man...(*He lies back laughing hysterically. Suddenly, serious, he sits up and staggers to his feet.*) So, where'd you say Cece had gone to?

CHARLIE: I don't know.

TUCKER: You tell her I was here...and I'll be back. (*Pause*) What's the matter, Charlie. Don't you like me?

CHARLIE: You're fuckin' crazy.

TUCKER: That's right, Charlie. Hazardous to the general health. See ya around.

(TUCKER *strolls off, whistling.* CHARLIE *watches him as the light fades to black.*)

Scene Five

(*Scene:* ELLEN's *squat is an abandoned building. Many plastic bags of* ELLEN's *junk. An old table, chair, and hotplate.* HOLLY *lies under a blanket on a bare mattress behind a blanket on a clothes line in one corner of the room.* ELLEN *is preparing soup in a pot on the hotplate.* CHARLIE *sits in the chair reading an old* Rolling Stone. *It is late at night.*)

ELLEN: He can't stay here any longer.

CHARLIE: Ellen, he's too weak to move.

ELLEN: This is my squat. I found it. It's mine. I live here. I don't have room to spare. I'm the only one who can live here. I own it.

CHARLIE: You don't own the building.

ELLEN: Oh, yeah? (*Shows him a flyer*) I even get mail. See? Letters in my mailbox.

CHARLIE: That's not a letter. It's a flyer.

ELLEN: It's addressed to me.

CHARLIE: "Occupant".

ELLEN: That's me. I'm the occupant...Jackie Blue had no right to bring a sick person in my house. I could get infected. I'm not well.

CHARLIE: Chill out, Ellen. I'll get him out in a few days.

ELLEN: A few days! Where am I gonna sleep? He's on my mattress. I'm not gonna sleep on that mattress now. I could catch something.

CHARLIE: Right...like this place is so clean already. *(He picks up a sack of rotting garbage.)*

ELLEN: Don't touch my things. Leave that alone. It smells bad in there. I know he pissed my bed.

CHARLIE: I'll get you a new mattress.

ELLEN: Where?

CHARLIE: I'll take one off a truck. There's a loading dock right behind Furniture Mart. I'll get you a brand new one, okay?

ELLEN: *(Sulks)* Okay. *(Pause)* But I want a Sealy...not some cheap one.

CHARLIE: All right.

ELLEN: The posturepedic one...for my back.

CHARLIE: Okay.

ELLEN: And the box springs too.

CHARLIE: Okay...okay...

ELLEN: And double bed size...no single. In that shiny material...in pink.

CHARLIE: Jesus!

ELLEN: Connie's bedroom was pink. She had a big four-posted bed with a canopy. All in pink.

(CECE *appears in the doorway, out of breath.*)

CECE: Hi. Jackie said you were down here.

CHARLIE: Nice of you to make it.

ELLEN: Well, what is this? Grand Central Station? Walk right in my house. Night or day...don't knock...

CECE: I just heard what happened.

CHARLIE: Where have you been?

CECE: Around. I didn't know where you were. I was lookin' for you.

CHARLIE: Must not have been lookin' too hard.

CECE: You got a bug in your ass?

CHARLIE: Did you have a nice time with your new friend?

CECE: Oh, is that what this is about. Fuck you-grow up!

ELLEN: I don't allow swearing in my house.

CECE & CHARLIE: Shut up, Ellen!

CECE: How is he?

CHARLIE: Not good.

(CECE *goes to* HOLLY, *kneels by the mattress.*)

CECE: Holly.

HOLLY: Ceec...how ya doin'?

CECE: I'm okay. How do you feel?

HOLLY: Terrible. I can't walk. I keep fallin' down. *(She coughs violently)* Oh, jees...I need some antibiotics. How do I look? Shitty, huh?

CECE: You look sick, Holly.

HOLLY: Couldn't get a ten dollar trick if my life depended on it. I hurt all over.

CECE: We'll take you to a hospital.

HOLLY: No...no hospital.

CECE: Holly, you have to...

HOLLY: No...you go in one of those places, you don't come out again. I know. They killed my mother in one. They took her in and she never came back. (HOLLY *coughs.*)

ELLEN: You have to get him out of my house.

CECE: *(To* CHARLIE*)* We should call an ambulance.

CHARLIE: He'll freak out.

CECE: He could die.

CHARLIE: He's just got a really bad cold. If we let him rest, and give him soup, he'll be okay.

CECE: He's sweatin' bullets, Charlie. It could be pneumonia.

ELLEN: *(After a pause)* Oh, God...it's AIDS.

CHARLIE: Shut up!

ELLEN: I heard...that's how it starts. You get pneumonia...and you can't walk! Look at his legs...he's got sores. *(She is beginning to panic.)*

CHARLIE: Shut the fuck up, Ellen!

ELLEN: You can't talk to me like that! This is my home! All of you-get out! I won't have AIDS in my bed. You take that disease ridden slut out of

Connie's bedroom. You think my daughter wants to sleep in that filth when she visits from Hollywood!

CHARLIE: You don't have a daughter, you old bag!

ELLEN: That's a lie! I've got her picture.

CHARLIE: It's a picture of Brooke Shields! You tore it out of a magazine!

ELLEN: You shut up! You get out of my house! NOW! You can't come in here and say these things to me. I'll call the police on you. You broke in here...you came uninvited. *(She grabs her purse)* I'm going to find a pay phone. I'll call 9-1-1. They'll come get all of you. He had better not be here when I get back. I'll press charges. Breaking and entering is a crime. *(She leaves quickly.)*

CHARLIE: *(After a pause)* We gotta move him.

CECE: Where?

CHARLIE: I don't know.

CECE: He can't walk.

CHARLIE: Then we'll find a way to carry him.

(Blackout)

Scene Six

(Scene: the street. Late night. HOLLY *is seated in a shopping cart from a grocery store.* CHARLIE *and* CECE *push him along.)*

CECE: This is nuts. We're going in a big circle. We can't push him around all night. It's cold. ...Wait! Stop, please.

*(*CHARLIE *stops the cart.)*

HOLLY: Oh, you stopped. The air felt good on my face. Like the tilt-a-whirl.

CHARLIE: Are you okay?

HOLLY: Yeah. I promise I won't puke again, Charlie.

CECE: I can't push him anymore.

CHARLIE: We gotta keep movin'.

CECE: Where are we taking him?

CHARLIE: I don't know...anywhere.

CECE: Anywhere...nowhere. This is bullshit! *(She walks away.)*

CHARLIE: Where you going?

CECE: To find a phone. We're calling an ambulance. Holly is going to the hospital.

(CHARLIE *crosses to her.*)

CHARLIE: No, Ceec...

CECE: Why not? They can help him.

CHARLIE: He's too scared.

CECE: Look at you! You're trembling. You're more scared of the hospital than he is.

CHARLIE: I'm shivering, not trembling. It's cold.

CECE: What are you afraid of? You think he's got it, don't you? And if he's got it, then, maybe you've got it too? I understand Charlie...we're all scared. We can't let him die out here.

CHARLIE: Don't call, please.

(*Sound of tires squealing. A car screeches to a stop.* CECE *and* CHARLIE *are illuminated by headlights.*)

CHARLIE: Who's that? It's a blue LeMans.

CECE: Oh, no...

(TUCKER *enters in an agitated state. He keeps one hand in his pocket, as if he may have a weapon.*)

TUCKER: I have been driving all over this cocksuckin' town looking for you, Cece. You just walked out on me. Nobody walks out on me.

CECE: Go away, will ya?

TUCKER: Come on, baby...I missed you.

CECE: I'm not your baby.

CHARLIE: Why don't you hit on someone else? We're kinda busy right now.

TUCKER: Charlie-boy...why are you still hangin' around my lady? I thought I made myself clear to you. (TUCKER *looks at* HOLLY *in the cart, and kicks it.*) Well, what is this? A basket of fruit?

(CHARLIE *starts toward* TUCKER.)

CHARLIE: Hey, fuck off, asshole!

(TUCKER *pulls a straight-razor from his jacket pocket, holds it in front of* CHARLIE's *face.*)

TUCKER: Come on, Charlie-boy. Make your move, and I'll slice your bag and run your leg through it. Come on, what are you waitin' for? You chicken? Cluck...cluck.

CECE: Leave us alone!

TUCKER: *(To* CECE*)* Honey, I think you better get in the car, 'cause I don't think you really want to see what's gonna happen now....

CECE: You fuckin' creep.

TUCKER: Sweetheart, get in the car!

CECE: NO!

TUCKER: Don't try my patience, sugar. We're goin' down to Texas, and we have to leave tonight. You wanna see Houston, don't ya? So we gotta move...police are lookin' for this car...okay, darlin'?

(CHARLIE *swings the skateboard at* TUCKER's *head. He ducks.*)

TUCKER: GET IN THE CAR NOW!

(Sound of police sirens, accompanied by flashing lights)

TUCKER: Jesus shit...

(TUCKER *sprints off. Sound of a policeman chasing after him. A booming* VOICE *comes over a police bullhorn, as more police cars arrive.*)

VOICE: *(On bullhorn)* EVERYONE...STAY RIGHT WHERE THEY ARE! YOU...MOVE AWAY FROM THE CAR! NOW! HANDS IN THE AIR! EVERYONE-HANDS IN THE AIR!

CECE: They got him.

CHARLIE: Good.

(They stand still with their hands raised. Sirens fill the cool night air. CECE *lifts* HOLLY's *hands up.)*

HOLLY: *(Groggy)* What the fuck is goin' on?

(Blackout)

Scene Seven

(Scene: LINDA's *office.* LINDA *is at her desk.* CECE *is pacing.)*

CECE: I can't believe they're gonna prosecute Charlie for stealin' a fuckin' grocery cart from Shop 'N Save. It's not fair.

LINDA: Any theft is a violation of his parole agreement. Charlie knows the rules...just like you do, Cece.

CECE: Where is he now?

LINDA: Probably on his way back to the Youth Center. If I hadn't intervened on your behalf, you could very easily find yourself back there too.

CECE: At least it would be three hots and a flop.

LINDA: Are you trying to be funny? *(Pause)* Is that what you really want? A return trip?

CECE: No.

LINDA: *(After a pause)* Cece, I don't think you realize just how close you came to a bad end. *(She looks at a file on her desk)* This man you were associating with...Tucker...did you know that he was an escapee from a mental institution?

CECE: I was beginnin' to get that idea. I didn't know him. He was just sorta followin' me around. Lots of guys on the street do that. You don't pay it any attention unless it gets up in your face.

LINDA: He's a convicted murderer. He strangled two girls, about your age.

CECE: What are you trying to do, scare me?

LINDA: I wish I could. I wish something would wake you up. Cece, if you really want to kill yourself there is nothing I can do to stop it....

CECE: Who said I was tryin' to kill myself?

LINDA: You just don't get it, do you? YOU CAN'T HAVE A BABY OUT ON THE STREETS! IT'S NOT A VIABLE OPTION!

CECE: Okay, okay...maybe, I'll get an abortion.

LINDA: Is that what you really want, Cece?

CECE: I don't know. Jesus... *(Long pause)* I'm runnin' out of time, aren't I?

LINDA: *(Quietly)* Yes. *(Pause)* Look, if you decide that you want to have the child, I can set up an appointment for you to talk with someone from Saint Andre's. They have a good facility out there, you'll get good care. But, they have rules, Cece. There's a curfew. You can't be out all night. You gotta do chores, everyone works....

CECE: Jail without bars, huh?

LINDA: Or...you could choose to go back to your family.

CECE: Or...none of the above.

(LINDA *sighs, looks out the window.*)

CECE: There must be somethin' else.

(LINDA *rubs her eyes.*)

LINDA: Cece, when I first started working here, twelve years ago, we had a pretty good social welfare system. We had plenty of good foster homes. We didn't have any need for shelters, not for kids anyway. I had a pretty light caseload then. All the folders would fit in the top drawer of this desk. Now I have three file cabinets with case folders like yours. I got kids from violent homes, kids with drug problems, runaways, throwaways, the sexually abused...you name it...and sometimes I don't know what to do with them all. The shelters are full, the jails are full...the system has broken down. *(Pause)* And sometimes the worst part of my job is having to tell a kid that she's probably better off in her lousy home, than she is sleeping in the park.

CECE: Why are you telling me all this?

LINDA: Your mother came to see me two days ago.

CECE: My mother came here?

LINDA: Yes. She didn't know any other way to get in touch with you. She figured you'd show up here sooner or later.

CECE: What did she want?

LINDA: I think she just wants to talk to you. *(Pause)* It's a first step, Cece. *(She looks at* CECE *as the lights fade)*

Scene Eight

(Scene: the roof of a hospital. HOLLY *and* CHARLIE *sit on the edge with their legs dangling over. A wheelchair sits behind them.* HOLLY *wears a hospital issue bathrobe, and his wig is now gone. His hair has been cut quite short.* CHARLIE *sits alongside. They share a bottle of vodka as they stare out at the night.)*

CHARLIE: Nice night. Man, you can see all the way to the lighthouse.

HOLLY: Yeah. Who woulda thought the best view of the city would be from the roof of the med center. Fuckin' amazing. In my next lifetime, I'm gonna buy this place, and build a huge penthouse right here. Have big windows all around, and maybe a hot tub.

*(*HOLLY *laughs, starts coughing.* CHARLIE *takes off his jacket, and drapes it around* HOLLY'S *shoulders.)*

HOLLY: Thanks. Now, you'll be cold.

CHARLIE: I'm okay.

HOLLY: Oh, don't look at my hair.

CHARLIE: I wasn't.

HOLLY: It's for a for-shit haircut. Hospital barbers are such butchers.

CHARLIE: Looks kinda punk.

HOLLY: More like Pee-Wee Herman. They took away my wig. Said it had lice. *(Pause)* The night nurse should be making her rounds about now. She's gonna flip when she can't find me.

CHARLIE: She'll never think to look up here. And by the time they find us...it'll be too late anyway.

HOLLY: Yeah. *(Pause)* Are you sure it's the right thing to do?

CHARLIE: What else is there? I ain't goin' back to jail.

HOLLY: I can't believe you just walked away from the bus.

CHARLIE: It was so easy. They were doin' a head count...I said I had to piss...they didn't send anyone to watch me, so I climbed out the window in the john.

HOLLY: You talk to Cece?

CHARLIE: No. *(Pause)* What would I say?

HOLLY: Yeah, I know what you mean. I was gonna write a letter to my old man, I couldn't think of anything to say except, goodbye—eat shit and die!

(CHARLIE *takes a baggie filled with barbiturates from a pocket in his jacket.*)

CHARLIE: We better get started. *(He shows* HOLLY *a handful of pills.)*

HOLLY: Yellow subs. What are the other ones?

CHARLIE: Seconals or phenobarb...I dunno. *(Pause)* Should be enough.

HOLLY: And then some. What did it cost ya?

CHARLIE: I traded my boogie box.

HOLLY: That was a nice box.

CHARLIE: You ready?

HOLLY: *(Looks at the pills)* In a minute. I'm scared, Charlie.

CHARLIE: You won't feel nothin'. You just go to sleep. Deep peaceful sleep.

HOLLY: I wish we'd gone to a movie.

CHARLIE: Nothin' good playin.

(HOLLY *is terrified.* CHARLIE *puts his arm around* HOLLY *to comfort him.* CHARLIE's *hand rests on* HOLLY's *shoulder, a fistful of pills in his grip.)*

CHARLIE: It'll be okay. *(Pause)* Just close your eyes. Think about somethin' good.

(HOLLY *closes his eyes.*)

CHARLIE: Somethin' you always wanted....

HOLLY: A black Trans-Am.

CHARLIE: Yeah, man. Think about that...all shiny, with a gold-flaked firebird on the hood, and underneath...four-hundred-and-fifty monster cubes...

HOLLY: I can see it.

CHARLIE: It's warm outside...it's summer...we got the windows down...wind is whippin' our hair...we're goin' like a bat outta hell on Interstate 90...headin' west...the Velvets are blastin' on the car stereo...

HOLLY: *White Light/White Heat*..."Sister Ray"...

CHARLIE: We're loaded, man...we got cash...a quart of vodka...a handful of ludes...

HOLLY: *(Singing)* Just like my Sister Ray says...

CHARLIE: ...We're doin' a hundred and thirty, and we still ain't hit top end...

HOLLY: *(Singing)* Just like my Sister Ray says...

CHARLIE: Nothin' can catch us, man...we're goin' out in a blaze of glory...right into the sun...we just burn up...

HOLLY: Warp nine!

CHARLIE: Right...

HOLLY: Just like my Sister Ray says...

(*Suddenly,* CHARLIE *pops his handful of pills into* HOLLY's *mouth.* HOLLY *sits still, eyes still closed, not daring to swallow the pills.* CHARLIE *takes several handfuls of pills and washes them down with the vodka.* CHARLIE *looks at* HOLLY, *offers him the bottle. Slowly,* HOLLY *takes the bottle, and drinks, swallowing the pills, opens his eyes. They sit side by side staring out,* CHARLIE *looks at the empty plastic bag, lets it slip from his hands and flutter down to the street below.* CHARLIE *looks out. For the first time, the enormity of the situation hits him.* CHARLIE *is stunned with grief and his own helplessness.* CHARLIE *opens his mouth, no sound, but a sob comes forth.* CHARLIE *weeps.* HOLLY *has been looking at him.* HOLLY *puts his arm around* CHARLIE, *who leans in to be comforted.* CHARLIE *sobs quietly for several seconds.* HOLLY *holds him, looking out at the harbor in the distance.*) Look...the Scotia Prince is out in the harbor. (*Pause*) That's a beautiful ship...all those lights. I hear they got a casino on board...and a disco. I always wanted to take the overnight cruise to Halifax. I hear Nova Scotia's real nice.

(*Silence:* HOLLY *holds* CHARLIE *in his arms.* CHARLIE *sniffles. Lights fade slowly to black.*)

Scene Nine

(*Scene:* MOIRA's *house.* CECE *is standing in the hallway.* MOIRA *sits on the couch. It is morning.*)

CECE: I tried to call you Monday night. You musta been out.

MOIRA: Monday nights I go candlepin bowling now.

CECE: Bowling? You?

MOIRA: Yeah. We got a league...at work. I ain't much good, but it's fun... and I like some of the ladies I met there.

CECE: The house smells different.

MOIRA: Yeah, I did the hall...and your bedroom. They were havin' a paint sale, and I get it at discount so....

(CECE *goes to her room, then returns.*)

CECE: I like the color. What is it, peach?

MOIRA: Yeah. It's brighter in there now.

CECE: What happened to his stuff. He move out?

MOIRA: I threw it out. Put all his crap in the yard. Found out he was still seein' her while he was livin' with me. I called him on it, and he knocked me around. I finally up and said—"Get out!" Same shit I went through with your father. And what did that get me? My front teeth knocked out, that's what! *(Pause)* Seems like I always get hooked up with the same kind of man. Why is that?

CECE: I dunno.

MOIRA: So, you like the bedroom, huh? Good. I didn't know whether to do it up in pink or blue, so I thought peach would be a nice compromise. Baby can't tell what color it is anyway.

(CECE *starts to cry.*)

MOIRA: Why are you cryin'?

(*The full impact of her situation hits* CECE *for the first time.*)

CECE: I'm too young to be a mother.

MOIRA: You? What about me? I'm not old enough to be anybody's grandmother. How do you think I feel? Don't wanna be called, "Grandma". But, what can you do?

(CECE *breaks down.*)

CECE: I wanna come home.

(MOIRA *puts her arms around* CECE.)

MOIRA: It just tears me up, thinking' about you out there. As much as I hated you when I put you out...you're still my baby. My own flesh and blood...*(Pause)* Sometimes, I think maybe everything's gonna be okay. We'll have a new person to take care of. Somebody so small and helpless. They depend on you for everything. I remember when you were born... I was afraid of you.

CECE: Afraid of me?

MOIRA: Yeah, I was. Imagine that. I didn't know how to hold you. I didn't know what to do. What if I dropped you? You were this tiny little thing... and you needed somethin' so bad...you had little balled-up hands and feet...and your face...oh, you looked just like an angry turnip.

(CECE *laughs through her tears.* MOIRA *holds her close.*)

MOIRA: I was so young then. I didn't know anything.

(*Slow fade to black*)

Scene Ten

SCENE: (*The Strip. A few months later. A cold winter day.* JACKIE *is warming his hands over an oil drum with a fire. A few yards away,* CHARLIE *stands on crutches, panhandling with a paper cup.*)

CHARLIE: Please sir...could you spare some change for a disabled Gulf War vet, so I can get a decent meal? Thank you. (*To another person*) Please ma'am, some spare change. I'm a victim of chemical weapons, and I need a place to live. Can you spare a dollar? Thank you. (*He counts the money in his cup.*)

JACKIE: How you makin' out?

CHARLIE: Twelve bucks today.

JACKIE: Not bad. That disabled vet stuff works pretty good. You oughta try to look more emaciated. Such in your chest some...yeah, like that. And try to cough when you say...chemical weapons.

(CHARLIE *coughs, tries to look pathetic.*)

JACKIE: Yeah, that's cool. With them crutches, you're a heartbreaker.

(CECE *enters,* JACKIE *spots her.*)

JACKIE: Well, well...lookee here. A blast from the past. (*To* CHARLIE) Friend of yours.

(CECE *smiles at* JACKIE. *He looks at her pregnant stomach, now very visible.*)

JACKIE: How ya doin' little mama?

CECE: Not too bad, Jackie.

JACKIE: Ain't seen you in this part of town in a long time. Where you been hangin'?

CECE: I went home.

JACKIE: My, my...some people got all the luck. You got any spare change for a starvin' artist like myself?

(CECE *gives him a dollar bill.*)

JACKIE: A whole dollar. God bless you. You wanna hear a tune for that? You name it, and if I know it, I'll play it. Got me some new teeth. I can play again. God bless, Medicaid, huh? *(Laughs)*

CECE: Maybe later, Jackie.

(CECE *crosses over to* CHARLIE, *who avoids looking at her.*)

CECE: Hi, Charlie. I...uh...heard you got released, so I came by....

CHARLIE: Yeah, I'm out. They felt sorry for me, so they let me go. *(Bitter)* Guess I found the perfect way to beat a rap...try to kill yourself, and they drop all charges. Ain't that a bitch? *(Pause)* Like the crutches?

CECE: Pretty good scam.

(CHARLIE *limps a few steps.*)

CHARLIE: Yeah, 'cept it ain't a scam. They're for real. I got dead nerves in my right leg.

CECE: I'm sorry...

CHARLIE: I really fucked up, huh? Typical. We O D together...Holly pulls it off, and I don't. When I passed out, I musta been lyin' on my side in a weird way...my leg was twisted, or somethin'...a blood vessel got cut off. They found us on the roof, and I was still breathin', so they rushed me to emergency, pumped my stomach, and what do you know?—I wake up a cripple. Fuckin' life, huh? You got a smoke?

CECE: I quit...for the baby, you know.

CHARLIE: Yeah, right. *(Pause)* So...how's home life?

CECE: It's not perfect.

CHARLIE: Hey, what is? So, what are you gonna name the kid?

CECE: If it's a girl...Holly.

CHARLIE: That's nice. He woulda liked that. *(Pause)* What if it's a boy?

CECE: I'm hopin' for a girl.

CHARLIE: No little Charlie junior, huh?

CECE: No.

CHARLIE: *(After a pause)* So what brings you down here? Come to laugh at the cripples? Toss 'em some pennies?

CECE: Why'd you do it, Charlie? It doesn't make any sense.

CHARLIE: Who are you? My caseworker? Take a hike.

CECE: You had no right to do that to Holly.

CHARLIE: He wanted it.

CECE: After you talked him into it, right?

CHARLIE: I did it for him.

CECE: No, you didn't. *(Pause)* I don't think I can ever forgive you, Charlie.

CHARLIE: Hey, what gives you the right to pass judgment on me? Huh? You think because you got a permanent squat, you can look down on me now. You should be grateful to me. I took care of you. I kept your ass alive out here.

CECE: No, you didn't. I did.

CHARLIE: Yeah, well...we'll see, won't we? 'Cause you'll be back. Maybe in a few months...maybe a year...you'll leave the kid with your old lady, or she'll throw you out again. You'll be right back on this corner, flaggin' down a carload of navy boys. Nothin' ever changes, Ceec.

CECE: No...no... things have to change, or we don't learn nothin'.

CHARLIE: Learnin' is for school. Out here, you just ride with the tide.

CECE: No...

CHARLIE: *(After a pause)* Yeah, well...you're gonna have to excuse me, Ceec. Some of us still gotta work for our supper. See ya around sometime. Take care of yourself.

CECE: Yeah...you too, Charlie.

(CHARLIE *limps away on his crutches.* CECE *watches him, sadly. She pulls her coat closed against the cold wind. She stands for a moment near* JACKIE.)

JACKIE: Do yourself a favor...don't come back down here. *Ain't Nothin' Goin' On, But The Rent.* You know that song? You got some spare change, I'll sing it for ya.

CECE: No...play me a slow one. Slow and sad. *(She tosses some coins in his hat.)* Take care of yourself, Jackie.

JACKIE: Always do. *(He plays his saxophone—a slow, aching version of* Someone To Watch Over Me, *as lights fade to black.)*

END OF PLAY

DARK RIVER

DARK RIVER premiered at the Mad Horse Theater Company of Portland Maine, on 3 April 1993. The cast and creative contributors were:

GORDON WALKER	Tony Owen
CARL WALKER	Walt Dunlap
IRENE WALKER	Cynthia Barnett
MAGGIE WALKER	Deborah Hall
JACK PRUDHOE	Dale Simonton
NAN POLLARD	Terry Drew
Director	Michael Rafkin
Set design	Charles S Kading
Lighting design	Tom Rodman
Costume design	Susan E. Picinich
Sound design	Tom Faux
Stage manager	Lisa Bragdon
Production manager	Joan Sand

CHARACTERS

GORDON WALKER, *(44) a lawyer from New York*
CARL WALKER, *(42) owner of Walker Pipe Company.* GORDON's *brother*
IRENE WALKER, *(40)* CARL's *wife*
JACK PRUDHOE, *(30) a part-time truck driver*
MAGGIE WALKER, *(38) a schoolteacher. Sister of* CARL *and* GORDON
NAN POLLARD, *(31) an environmental analyst for a State Office of Environmental Protection*

Time: late summer 1992

Setting: the backyard and boat dock of CARL WALKER's *summer house on the shore of Little Minot Lake in Minot Falls, Maine.*

for the citizens of Gray, Maine...who have endured.

ACT ONE

Scene One

(Time: early morning. Late summer. 1992)

(Scene: the backyard and boat dock of a summer cottage on the shore of Little Minot Lake [pronounced "my-not"] in a small town in central Maine. The set consists of a grassy area near the edge of the lake. A wooden boat dock on pilings extends out toward the audience. Upstage, the screened porch of the summer cottage is visible. There is a large picnic table with attached benches near a barbecue grill. Various trees or shrubs fill the background, making the road in front of the house invisible.)

(At rise: GORDIE WALKER *sits on one of the picnic table benches. A styrofoam cooler and a pile of fishing gear are nearby.* GORDIE *is dressed in casual summer wear-chinos, short sleeve shirt, topsiders.* GORDIE *has a thermos filled with screwdrivers. As the play begins, He pours a drink into the cup on top of his thermos. He sips the drink and stares out at the lake. He wipes sweat from his brow with a handkerchief.)*

*(*CARL WALKER *enters from the screened porch area.* CARL *is also dressed casually.* CARL *is carrying a mug of coffee and a fishing rod. He lets the screen door bang closed behind him, and crosses down to* GORDIE *at the picnic table.)*

CARL: Goddamn this ozone! Can you believe this weather? Nine o'clock and it's already pushing eighty-five degrees.

*(*CARL *crosses down to where* GORDIE *sits on the picnic table.)*

GORDIE: You should have been in Manhattan on Friday. You could slice the air like cream cheese. Saw a guy on Seventh Avenue scalping window fans for three hundred bucks.

CARL: Never been a summer like this up here.

GORDIE: The end of life as we know it.

CARL: The weather is screwed up, that's for sure...but, I guarantee it'll be a lot cooler out on the lake.

GORDIE: Forget it, I'm not schlepping your old Evinrude to the dock.

CARL: Oh, I junked that old monster last year. Got a new thirty-five horse, and you don't have to carry it. It's already on the boat.

GORDIE: Where's the boat?

CARL: At the marina...all gassed up and waiting. What do you say we get the hell out of here before the phone starts ringing. Catch a few fish, tip a few cold ones...I got two sixes of "Nasties" in the cooler...should be plenty. You wanna fly cast or troll?

GORDIE: Carl, you know I hate going out on the water.

CARL: I got some Dramamine. Come on, it'll be fun. I'll even let you use the old man's rod and reel.

GORDIE: Even when we were kids, I never liked fishing. Put me in a boat, and I puke.

CARL: It's all in your head, Gordie. *(Dumps out his coffee)* Too hot to drink coffee. I'm sweatin' already.

(GORDIE *pours himself another drink.* CARL *notices.*)

CARL: We have orange juice in the fridge. You don't have to bring your own.

GORDIE: It's not just OJ.

CARL: Startin' a little early, aren't you?

GORDIE: Want one?

CARL: No, thanks. *(He opens his tackle box, removes some lures, begins assembling a rod and reel.)*

GORDIE: The great outdoorsman, huh?

CARL: Yep...every Saturday....even in the winter. Last two seasons, we put an ice shack out there...got a little propane heater inside...

(GORDIE *chuckles.*)

CARL: Why are you laughing? It's fun...we got fresh fish all year round. You used to play ice hockey on this lake, remember.

GORDIE: Yeah...back when my knees would bend without cracking.

CARL: Pick a lure.

GORDIE: I wouldn't know the difference.

CARL: Come on...pick one.

GORDIE: Okay, that one.

CARL: That's for salt water fishing....

GORDIE: See, I'm no good at this.

(CARL *selects a lure, attaches it to the line.*)

CARL: I think you'll like this one...bass really go for it...trust me.

GORDIE: We'll see if I get on the boat.

CARL: Well, I'm going out for sure....because by ten o'clock, that Pollard woman will start calling here, and if I'm not near a phone, then I don't have to deal with her for one day.

GORDIE: You realize....sooner or later, you're gonna have to let her in to inspect the plant. And, the longer you hold out, the worse it looks...like you have something to hide.

CARL: I'm not hiding anything. I just don't like her whole approach.

GORDIE: If she gets a court order, then you've got no choice.

CARL: Arrogant, self-righteous bitch....

GORDIE: So, you let her inside...she'll nose around, and then she'll go away. What's the worst she can come up with?

CARL: Damn little! We passed two OSHA inspections with superior ratings. All we make is pipe sleeves and joints...it's not like we've got pesticides, or anything dangerous.... *(Pause)* I wish I knew who the hell called her in.

GORDIE: What about the shop steward...what's his name...? The one you never got along with?

CARL: DiFazio? Naw, he's too unimaginative. Not his style. Besides, what would he gain? He's too scared for his own job. It's somebody inside. But who?

GORDIE: Someone you laid off....trying to get back at you.

CARL: Maybe.

GORDIE: So, she just shows up two weeks ago...outta nowhere, huh?

CARL: Yeah, she works in the lab at the D E P in Augusta, and I guess she teaches part-time at some college in the area. Three times, she tried to walk in the front gates of the plant. I had Security throw her out each time. I told her...until I see some official documents, or until I know exactly what she's looking for...she doesn't get in. Then, I find out she goes behind my back, talkin' to some of the guys I laid off....questions about what kind of "substances" we work with. I already told the woman, every solvent we use is sealed in a container and shipped out of state when we're finished with it. There are no spills here, no long-term storage. But, that explanation just doesn't seem to be good enough for her.

GORDIE: It's definitely connected to the layoffs. Only thing that makes sense. How many people you got in the factory now?

CARL: Forty-nine...not counting the security guards.

GORDIE: There used to be a hundred and twenty people on that floor.

CARL: Maybe you haven't noticed, but we happen to be in the middle of a fucking recession!

GORDIE: Tell me something. Why'd you ask for my input? You haven't solicited my advice on the business in years.

CARL: There's nobody local I can trust to keep their damn mouth shut! I've heard enough rumors about the troubles we're in.

GORDIE: Walker Pipe has been in trouble for years, Carl. I doubt anyone would be surprised.

CARL: So what are you implying? It's my fault the whole damn economy is in the crapper? Nobody is buying pipe like they used to. Building trades have been in recession for years. That's a fact.

GORDIE: And it's a fact that when the old man was running it, there was a depression. Forty-nine jobs...Carl...it's hardly worth it anymore....

CARL: *(Slow burn)* And of course, with your great expertise, you could have run things a whole lot better, right?

GORDIE: I didn't say that. *(Pause)* I probably would have done the same things, Carl...made the same mistakes you did....

CARL: To this day....it still pisses you off, doesn't it?

GORDIE: It was his decision. I'm perfectly happy with what I'm doing. I don't want the problems you have here. I'm sorry, I know times have been bad.

CARL: It's a disaster. Six factories went under in the county in four years. It's a wonder anybody is holding on. I'm the only manufacturer left in the valley, and people are damn scared, and they've got every right to be.... *(Pause)* I go to Shop 'N Save, I see guys who used to work for me-bagging groceries in the checkout line. I can't look them in the eye. You know how many times I catch myself saying..."Oh, things will get better soon. In a few months we'll be expanding again." Bullshit! Those jobs are finished. And in their hearts, they know it, but we go on pretending. Nobody wants to be the first to acknowledge the truth...it's over. People don't have dreams anymore, they can't afford them.

GORDIE: *(After a pause)* Four years ago, you had the perfect opportunity to unload, and just walk away....

CARL: The developers in Boston....

GORDIE: Yep.

CARL: You think I should have taken their offer?

GORDIE: It was a fair price...

CARL: And if I had taken it....

GORDIE: You and Irene could be sitting in the sun in Barbados, or somewhere....not a care in the world.

CARL: The foresight of hindsight, huh? *(Pause)* You think they'd still be interested? You still have contacts with them?

GORDIE: I suppose I could. *(Pause)* If that's what you really want.

CARL: I don't know....Christ, what would the old man say?

GORDIE: Forget him. What do you want? *(Pause)* Listen, if I were to contact them again, you understand, there's no guarantee you'd get anywhere near the original offer. A run-down factory that's losing money doesn't exactly excite that many investors.

CARL: All the machinery is in perfect working order!

GORDIE: You're missing the point, Carl. The Boston Group isn't interested in manufacturing. They're developers. They're gonna change it all anyway. You know what I'm saying.

CARL: This is the same group that bought the old Pejepscot mill?

GORDIE: The same guys. They also did the mill conversions over in Manchester.

CARL: I've seen 'em...a bunch of over-priced condos, sittin' empty...little ski boutiques, and gourmet food emporiums...all ducks and baskets. *(Sarcastic)* Instant New England charm.

GORDIE: If there's gonna be any future up here, that's what it's gonna be. Get used to it.

CARL: And what happens to my employees? Where do they go?

GORDIE: There would be construction jobs for lots of people.

CARL: And when it's finished, then what? Do they trim the grass on the putting greens?

GORDIE: What do you expect? A lifetime guarantee?

CARL: We're talking about people's lives. Three generations of Walkers worked in that business, Gord!

GORDIE: Forgive me if I don't get sentimental.

(CARL walks away from him.)

GORDIE: Who's gonna run it when you're gone? You and Irene don't have any kids, and if you do...well, it'll be over before they even start school... you know it...it's inevitable...it's gonna happen. Are you listening to me? *(Pause)* Look, do you want me to put in a call to these guys, or not?

CARL: I don't know.

GORDIE: Well, if and when you make up your mind, you'd better be sure this time. I'm not gonna jerk these guys off a second time. Understand? I'm tellin' you Carl, don't leave me hangin' out to dry again.

CARL: You could broker quite a deal for yourself, couldn't you, Gord? What would your commission be?...twenty percent? Twenty-five? What is the going rate on a family business these days?

GORDIE: Aw, grow up! I try to talk some business with you like an adult, and you pull this shit! Fuck you, I'm trying to help you, schmuck! *(Pause)* How many times have we gone around and around about this kinda stuff?

CARL: Our whole lives.

(GORDIE *wipes sweat from his face.*)

GORDIE: Christ, it's hot! Let's go find someplace cool and dark...and get drunk.

CARL: The bars aren't open yet.

GORDIE: You got any ice?

CARL: In the cooler.

(GORDIE *finds ice in the cooler, rubs it on the back of his neck.*)

CARL: I'll give you an answer about the developers...by the end of next week...okay?

GORDIE: Fine.

CARL: How long can you stay?

GORDIE: Just the weekend.

CARL: You're welcome to stay at the house. Still got the extra bed on the sunporch. If you want, I'll help you get your bags out of the car. Irene will fix some breakfast if you want.

GORDIE: I already had breakfast in town...at the new motel. I took a room there.

CARL: When? This morning?

GORDIE: Last night.

CARL: I thought you just drove up this morning.

GORDIE: No.

CARL: I see. Well, you should have dropped by last night. We were all up until one-thirty playing cards.

GORDIE: It was late. I was tired.

CARL: You know you are welcome to stay with us, Gord.

GORDIE: The motel will be fine. *(Pause)* How's Irene?

CARL: She's fine. And, she's expecting you for dinner tonight. Will you come?

GORDIE: Of course. I'll be there.

CARL: *(After a pause)* After all this time, you're still uncomfortable with the whole situation, aren't you?

GORDIE: I just think it would be better if I stayed in town, that's all.

CARL: Suit yourself.

(IRENE *appears at the screen door of the cottage.*)

IRENE: Carl, you've got a phone call. Good morning, Gordon.

GORDIE: 'Morning, Irene.

(IRENE *steps off the porch, and crosses down to them.*)

IRENE: We missed you last night. We played canasta.

GORDIE: Sorry, I got in late.

CARL: Who's on the phone?

IRENE: Your favorite headache, Nan Pollard.

CARL: My one day off. What does she want?

IRENE: I didn't ask.

(CARL *trudges slowly toward the house.*)

CARL: You should have told her I was out on the lake fishing.

IRENE: She'll just call back later. You're looking well Gordon.

(They embrace.)

GORDIE: You too. Nice to see you again.

IRENE: I'm setting a place for you at dinner tonight. And I accept no excuses.

GORDIE: I'll be there. I promise.

IRENE: Good. Do you like fish?

GORDIE: Sure.

IRENE: Great...that's what we're having, providing of course, you and Carl get busy and catch some. Otherwise, you only get potato salad.

GORDIE: I'm a terrible fisherman. I'd put a hook in my hand.

IRENE: Don't worry, we have Iodine and Band-Aids.

GORDIE: I really hate fishing....you have no idea....

IRENE: Aw, loosen up, it'll be good for you. You're in Maine—Vacationland! And it's going to be one hot day! You could use some sun.

GORDIE: Yes. You look good. I missed you.

IRENE: Well, then stop making yourself so scarce. Get out of that crazy city more often.

GORDIE: I wish I could....

IRENE: We're glad you finally came up. Maggie's been talking about it all week. She's really excited. Seeing you again is gonna lift her spirits about two dozen miles.

GORDIE: How is she?

IRENE: Well, she's still alive...that's what counts, I suppose.

GORDIE: Irene!

IRENE: What? I shouldn't make jokes? Hah! We've all done enough crying, Gordon. A healthy sense of humor is the best coping device I've found.

GORDIE: Is she okay now?

IRENE: Yeah, well, her doctor says it's in remission...but you never know... she has her good days, and her bad ones...she doesn't complain much... that's Maggie. I think she's a lot stronger since the last surgery. She was well enough to go back to her classes this spring...they let her finish teaching the last half of the semester. It was good for her to be active again....at least it took her mind off it. She's even making lesson plans for next fall, so at least she's optimistic. *(Pause)* Seeing you again is what she really needs.

(GORDIE *walks to the end of the dock, stares out at the lake.*)

GORDIE: I should have come up sooner.

IRENE: It's not worth kicking yourself about it, Gord. There was nothing you could do. Just be with her now. *(Pause)* How are you and Carl getting on?

GORDIE: The usual. We can talk like civilized people for about, oh, four minutes before we're at each other's throats. Same old, same old.

IRENE: I made up the extra bed on the sun porch....

GORDIE: I thought it might be better for me to stay in town this trip.

IRENE: Okay. *(Pause)* If you change your mind, you know where the towels are.

(GORDIE *nods, looks at the lake and sighs. A man approaches from the side of the house*—JACK PRUDHOE, *thirty-two, a local truck driver. He is lanky, with long, straggly hair, a soiled baseball cap, jeans, boots, and an open flannel shirt.* JACK *nods sheepishly at* IRENE.)

IRENE: Can I help you with something? Are you lost?

JACK: Mornin', Mrs. Walker.

IRENE: Good morning.

JACK: I'm lookin' for your husband. They told me at the plant that he's down here on weekends.

IRENE: Carl's not here right now.

JACK: I gotta find him. It's real important.

IRENE: He's in the house, on the phone. You're welcome to wait for him. Should just be a minute or two.

JACK: I'll...uh...just wait for him out by my truck....

IRENE: I know you from somewhere. What's your name?

JACK: *(Reluctant)* Uh...Jack...Jack Prudhoe.

IRENE: *(Shaking hands.)* I'm Irene Walker...this is my brother-in-law, Gordon Walker.

JACK: *(Waves to* GORDIE.*)* How ya' doin'?

IRENE: Prudhoe? I know that name...Prudhoe.

GORDIE: *(Crossing to* JACK.*)* I remember. All-state halfback, right?

IRENE: That's it. You're the football star! Jack Prudhoe. Of course.

JACK: No, ma'am. That was my older brother, Calvin....

IRENE: Right. Calvin Prudhoe.

GORDIE: He must have broken every record on the books. What a running back! Your brother, huh?

JACK: Yes, sir.

GORDIE: I saw him play a lot of great games...must have been years ago.

IRENE: Carl played on that same team with your brother in high school.

GORDIE: "Gallopin' Calvin", that's what they called him. I remember.

JACK: Yeah, he was real fast all right.

GORDIE: I haven't heard of him in years. Where's your brother now? Playing pro ball?

JACK: No, sir. He's dead now. He got blowed up in Viet Nam...in '72.

IRENE: Oh, that's terrible.

JACK: Yep.

IRENE: I'm sorry...

(They are silent. JACK *shifts uncomfortably.)*

GORDIE: Prudhoe...that's a shame. He was a great one. Too bad. What about you, Jack? You play football?

JACK: No, sir....never did.

IRENE: I knowkI've seen you before. Where do I know you from?

JACK: I used to work for your husband...over at "Pipe"...in the shipping department.

IRENE: Oh, yes....Now I remember. The loading dock...

JACK: I worked there about three years...then I got laid off.

IRENE: *(After a pause.)* Well, I'm sorry we had to do that, Jack, but my husband will be hiring people back, just as soon as things get better, I can promise you. Now, if you haven't applied already, you know, you should be getting some benefits coming to you....

JACK: That's okay, I got another job.

IRENE: Oh, that's good. Where are you working?

JACK: *(Hesitates)* Well...I...uh, drive a truck now. Part-time.

IRENE: Independent?

JACK: Uh, yeah...independent.

GORDIE: From shipping to deliveries, huh?

(JACK *is getting twitchy, and does not want to answer more questions. He looks at his watch.*)

JACK: Yeah, I guess. Well, I'm gonna hafta go now.

IRENE: Carl is coming right back.

JACK: I can't stay.

IRENE: Do you want me to give him a message?

JACK: No, that's all right. I gotta talk to him personal. I gotta go... my little girl is bad sick. You tell him I was here, O K?

IRENE: Your little girl is sick? What's the matter?

JACK: I dunno for sure. They got her over at Memorial. She got into somethin' in the creek. The doctors don't know what it is. They can't seem to do nothin' for her, and they don't listen to me. They think she found somethin' in the house, under the sink, but I told 'em, it's in the water...she got it in the water....

(JACK *turns to go.* IRENE *stops him.*)

IRENE: Wait! Just wait a minute, Jack! What water? Where's this water you're talking about?

JACK: Biddeford Creek, that's where!

IRENE: Wait a minute!

JACK: I gotta go now.

IRENE: No...please...tell me about the water. What's in the water?

JACK: I don't know what it is, but it ain't right. We live over in North Minot. I got a trailer on some farm land near the creek. You know where I mean?

IRENE: Yes, I know where it is.

JACK: I got well water for my trailer, and lately seems like the well's gone bad...smells awful when it comes outta the tap.

IRENE: What's it smell like?

JACK: Like rotten eggs or somethin'...so I got me some bottled water to drink and bathe with...hell, you can't use the shower no more. *(Rolls up his sleeve.)* I got a rash the last time. I figured that one of them ol' underground gas storage tanks mighta leaked, and it went in the well, but, damn, it don't act like no gasoline I ever seen...don't smell like it either. Ate a hole round the enamel in the drain of my tub. *(Pause)* And then, day before yesterday, my girl Cindy, she's playin' down at the creek, and she started havin' a convulsion or somethin'. Couldn't stop coughin'. I don't know what she got into. I went down to the creek, and that smell was real powerful, worse than in the trailer, so I grabbed her up, and took her over to the emergency room...and they don't know what to do for her. I'm scared she's gonna die...'cause somebody poisoned her.

IRENE: If there's anything I can do....

GORDIE: *(Warning)* Irene!

JACK: Thanks, Mrs Walker....I just gotta get back now....

IRENE: I'm real sorry about your daughter.

GORDIE: IRENE*!*

IRENE: And, don't you worry, Jack. I'm sure they're gonna do everything they can for her. They've got some very fine doctors at Memorial. They took good care of my sister-in-law when she had cancer, so don't worry. You go on over there, and if there's any way the company can help out...you give us a call...anything...

GORDIE: IRENE*!*

IRENE: What do you want, Gordon?

(GORDIE pulls her aside.)

GORDIE: *(Quietly)* Will you be careful? Liability....!!! *(To JACK)* We hope she's feeling better, Jack.

JACK: Yeah. So, tell your husband, I'll be at the hospital. Tell him to call me today. Okay...?

(CARL *enters from the porch area, carrying more fishing gear.*)

CARL: That Pollard woman will talk your ear off. Jack Prudhoe? What are you doing out here?

JACK: I been looking for you, Mr Walker. I been all over town.

CARL: You've, uh...met my wife, Irene? My brother, Gordie? Gord, you remember Prudhoe's brother, Calvin. We played football in high school...year we won the state championship. Remember that?

GORDIE: I remember.

CARL: I hope you didn't bring me any problems today, Jack. 'Cause we're about to go fishing. I would like to have one day in the week to spend with my family, without having to worry about business. So, I'd appreciate it if you'd save it for regular working hours, okay?

IRENE: Carl, this man says tha....

JACK: *(Cuts her off.)* That's okay, maybe it can wait. I think I better go. Maybe I came at a bad time.

CARL: What's going on?

(JACK *is silent.*)

CARL: What's the problem? Jack?

JACK: *(Blurts out.)* I...I can't work for you no more, Mr. Walker. That's what!

(JACK *turns and walks away.* CARL *watches him go.* IRENE *and* GORDIE *stare at* CARL.)

CARL: What's got into him? What are you two looking at? What?

IRENE: I want a straight answer. Is he, or is he not on the payroll?

CARL: Not officially.

IRENE: Meaning?

CARL: I hired him to do some driving for me. Part-time.

IRENE: I thought you laid him off.

CARL: I did, but I felt sorry for the guy. He's had a hard time of it. His unemployment ran out. He's got a five year old kid. I just tried to help him out. I had a driver quit on me, so I hired Jack. Twice a month, I let him do the run to North Conway.

IRENE: And what exactly is he moving to North Conway?

CARL: Just some barrels of solvent. Some junk we get rid of every two weeks.

GORDIE: You let this loser dump chemicals for you?

CARL: The load goes over the state line, Gordie! There's a regional dump site in New Hampshire, and I send over a couple of truck loads every month. It's a straight deal with the Highway Patrol. They let us cross over and dump if we pay a fee. It's perfectly legal. Check it out if you don't believe me! Look, I pay fifteen hundred every month for the privilege. So what's the big problem?

GORDIE: Someone may be dumping it on this side.

CARL: Well, it's not my company. I personally supervise those shipments.

IRENE: He's not accusing you, Carl.

GORDIE: How do you know Jack's taking it where he's supposed to?

CARL: I know because I get the signed receipts back every month. So, what's the point here?

IRENE: Jack's daughter is in the hospital. It sounds like chemical poisoning.

(CARL's *attitude darkens as he considers the implications. In a rage, he throws his tackle box on the ground, and kicks the picnic table in frustration.*)

CARL: GODDAMMIT! THIS IS NOT MY FAULT!!!

(*They are silent a long moment.* GORDIE *pus the top on his thermos bottle.*)

GORDIE: Baby brother, when you step in it....you go all the way under, right to the bottom.

CARL: What do I do? Help me. What should I do? Gord, I need advice.

GORDIE: I'm way out of my league here, Carl. Call the guys in Boston. Take whatever they offer, and be grateful.

(GORDIE *staggers away bit unsteady.*)

CARL: Where are you going?

GORDIE: Anywhere out of this hot sun... (*Holds up the thermos.*) And... for reinforcements.

CARL: You miserable lush.

GORDIE: Yes, an avocation I can proudly say I am suited for. What's your excuse?

(GORDIE *walks away.* CARL *looks at* IRENE. *Her face is full of concern.* CARL *sits heavily on the bench by the table. He looks out at the lake, terror in his eyes.*)

(*Blackout*)

Scene Two

(Time: early afternoon, the same day. Bright sunshine)

(Setting: the same)

(At rise: IRENE *and* MAGGIE *[35] are reclining on chaise-lounges on the boat dock.* IRENE *wears a swimming suit and sunglasses. She rubs sun tan oil on her legs.* MAGGIE *also wears a swimming suit, but mostly, she is covered up with a terry-cloth robe.* MAGGIE *scans the horizon with binoculars. A pitcher of iced tea with styrofoam cups sit nearby on a small table.)*

IRENE: Do you see the boat?

MAGGIE: No, not yet.

IRENE *(Points)* What about over there? By the cove.

MAGGIE: Where are you pointing?

IRENE: Find the A-frame on the other side...

MAGGIE: Okay, found it.

IRENE: Now, look to the right....about three o'clock.

MAGGIE: Nope. That's the Crawfords' boat. Maybe Carl didn't go out after all.

IRENE: *(Disappointed)* And I wanted fish tonight.

MAGGIE: Maybe he's at the other end of the lake.

IRENE: *(Reclines)* Well, I hope he brings something back. I don't have anything thawed for the barbecue. *(Pause)* Warm day, huh?

MAGGIE: Yes, isn't it.

IRENE: The sun feels great.

MAGGIE: Warm. Very warm.

IRENE: Do you want me to rub some of that cocoa butter on your back?

MAGGIE: No, thanks. I'm fine.

IRENE: If you stay all covered up, you'll never get any sun.

MAGGIE: I'd just burn up. I'm so pale.

(Silence. MAGGIE *sips her tea.)*

IRENE: You can take off the robe. There's nobody around.

*(*MAGGIE *sighs. Slowly she removes the robe, and sits with her arms folded tightly across her chest.)*

IRENE: Believe me, it doesn't show.

(MAGGIE *lowers her arms. She looks at her bosom, adjusts her straps.*)

MAGGIE: I hate this damn falsie.

IRENE: It looks fine.

MAGGIE: It's too pointy.

IRENE: You can't tell a thing. Really.

(MAGGIE *sulks.* IRENE *pats* MAGGIE's *arm, removes her sun glasses and lies back with her eyes closed. Silence.* MAGGIE *starts to cry, stops herself.* IRENE *looks at her.*)

IRENE: It's okay, honey. *(Pause)* You want to talk about it?

MAGGIE: What's to say. I look like shit.

IRENE: No, you don't. Your hair looks fine, I told you it would grow back.

(*MAGGIE touches strands of her hair.*)

MAGGIE: Some of it still falls out.

IRENE: Look on the bright side, at least you got rid of the split ends.

MAGGIE: *(Laughs)* That's true...and at least I don't have to wear that horrible turban anymore. I hated that. All the kids would make jokes behind my back.

IRENE: Oh, they did not. They were glad to have you back.

MAGGIE: And the vice-principal, Mr Roder, he was the worst. Every time I'd go into the office, or the teachers' lounge, he'd suddenly be leaving. Whenever he would have to talk to me, he'd never look me in the face...always staring at the floor, or some spot on the wall....

IRENE: People are just skittish about illness. They don't know how to deal with it...you'll see, it'll all be back to normal when you start the fall semester.

MAGGIE: If I'm still around then....

IRENE: MAGGIE!

MAGGIE: Okay. I won't be morose. *(Pause)* Cliff Everling never asked me out again...after I went in the hospital the first time. Can't say I really blamed him, though. If I were a man, I wouldn't ask me out either.

IRENE: Oh, stop. Cliff Everling was a jerk...in any case.

MAGGIE: Yeah. He was probably lousy in bed, too. Never got to find out. We only went out two times.

IRENE: There will be other chances.

MAGGIE: *(Skeptical)* Sure. *(Pause)* Oh, well, I guess I've had a pretty full life regardless. I don't have any regrets.

IRENE: Will you stop talking like that? What's the matter with you, today?

MAGGIE: I dunno. I'm restless. Time is passing, I'm not doing anything. Waiting to get better.

IRENE: You have plenty of time.

MAGGIE: You really think so?

IRENE: Of course. There's time for anything you want to do.

MAGGIE: You know what I'd like? I wanna go on one of those Carnival Cruises that Kathie Lee Gifford is always singing about on T V. You know, like the Caribbean...meet some handsome stranger, we fall madly in love, we have a whirlwind tour of exotic ports of call, and then quite suddenly, I succumb to a tropical fever, and die in his arms like some nineteenth century heroine, like Camille.

IRENE: Sounds like Victor Hugo.

MAGGIE: More like Zola. Very corny, huh? *(Pause)* Actually, I lied when I said I had no regrets. I wish I had lived more when I had a chance. I would have been much more promiscuous.

IRENE: Maggie!

MAGGIE: I would have. I mean it...why not?

IRENE: Well, there's still time for that too.

MAGGIE: *(Not believing it.)* Sure. All the time in the world.

(MAGGIE *becomes emotional, then stops herself.* IRENE *touches her arm in a reassuring manner.*)

MAGGIE: I'm going to die. It's really true, isn't it?

IRENE: Eventually...yes...

MAGGIE: No...soon. I can feel it. I'm not really getting any stronger. I'm the same as I was. We're just pretending it's not happening.

(IRENE *sighs.*)

MAGGIE: Especially Gordon....Did you see him?

(IRENE *nods.*)

MAGGIE: How is he?

IRENE: His usual ornery self. He'll be here tonight. He promised.

MAGGIE: If he's sober. *(Long pause.)* You should be glad you didn't marry him.

IRENE: We both know that it would never have worked out.

MAGGIE: He still loves you.

IRENE: I doubt that. It was too many years ago. We were kids....

MAGGIE: You may have written it off, but not Gordon. He hates to lose.

IRENE: It wasn't a contest, Maggie.

MAGGIE: Don't kid yourself. Between Gordie and Carl, everything is a battle royal...listen, I grew up with it....

(NAN POLLARD, *[31] enters the back yard. She spots the women on the dock, and crosses down to them. NAN is a thin, attractive woman, in a somewhat mannish way. She wears khaki shorts, topsiders, a knit Lacoste shirt. NAN carries two jars of water samples, a small knapsack, and clipboard.*)

NAN: Hi, there!

(MAGGIE *and* IRENE *turn at the sound of her voice.*)

IRENE: Hello.

NAN: Nice hot morning, isn't it?

IRENE: It's afternoon.

NAN: Hot afternoon, then.

(NAN *steps onto the dock.* MAGGIE *looks at* IRENE.)

MAGGIE: Who is she?

(IRENE *shrugs.*)

NAN: Lovely place you've got here. Is all this yours?

IRENE: Yes. We live here in summers.

NAN: *(Looks around)* Great view. Very beautiful. I bet you're Irene Walker. Right? I'm Nan Pollard. I'm with the state D E P....

IRENE: *(Cool)* I know who you are. My husband has mentioned you on several occasions.

NAN: All very complimentary, I hope.

IRENE: Naturally. This is my sister-in-law, Maggie Walker.

NAN: Nice to meet you.

MAGGIE: Yes...

(IRENE *sips her tea. Awkward silence.*)

IRENE: *(Sounding official)* My husband isn't here right now. He's out fishing. I don't know when to expect him back.

NAN: Oh, that's all right. I wasn't really looking for him. Just out for a walk. *(She shields her eyes from the glare on the water.)* Very bright sun today. I've been hiking around the shoreline. I started way down there, by the public beach. It's quite a trek up to this end.

IRENE: Ten miles around the perimeter.

NAN: All of it privately owned?

IRENE: Most of it. *(Pause)* Are you looking to purchase some land, Ms Pollard? There are some available lots on the other side.

NAN: Not in my price range, I'm sure.

IRENE: Probably not.

(NAN *sits on the edge of the dock, removes a shoe and sock.*)

NAN: Whew...it feels good to sit down. I wore the wrong shoes for hiking. I'm getting a blister. Do you mind? Just need to rest a bit.

IRENE: No, I don't mind.

MAGGIE: Would you like some iced tea, Ms Pollard?

NAN: Yes, please. I was hoping I could find a cool drink.

IRENE: Help yourself.

(NAN *pours a glass of iced tea, and drains it quickly.*)

IRENE: Go ahead, have another. You look hot.

NAN: *(Pours another)* Thanks. I was getting dehydrated. *(Looks out at the lake)* Pretty good fishing here? What do they catch?

IRENE: Bass...some blue-gill...

NAN: Nice. Beautiful lake.

IRENE: Yes.

MAGGIE: What do you have in those jars?

NAN: Oh...just some water samples from the lake.

IRENE: Find anything interesting?

NAN: Don't know yet. Have to run some tests at the lab in Augusta.

(IRENE *holds up one of the jars, looks at it closely.*)

IRENE: Looks like clear water to me.

NAN: Well, you can't really tell anything by looking at a jar. You have to see it under a microscope, to see if there are micro-organisms in it....

MAGGIE: Micro-organisms...is that good or bad?

NAN: Depends on what kind they are. You'd be amazed at the kinds of things that are swimming around in our drinking water.

IRENE: No, I wouldn't actually. I'm sure it's teeming with poisonous little enzymes.

NAN: Well, I doubt you would find "swimming enzymes"...they don't swim...they....

IRENE: All right, tadpoles, whatever you call them. So, what do you do if you find some toxic little bugger in our lake? What happens then? See, I want to stay informed, in case I spot one crawling out of the lake, I want to know whether or not I should smash it with my shoe.

NAN: They don't crawl either.

IRENE: I know...I was making a joke. So what would your advice be? Don't drink the water? What if I boil it first? Yes? No?

(NAN *doesn't like being baited. She looks away, annoyed, not answering her.* MAGGIE *rises slowly.*)

MAGGIE: I'm going in.

IRENE: Not feeling well?

MAGGIE: I'm too hot. I'll see if I can take a nap.

IRENE: You need anything?

MAGGIE: *(Suddenly snappish)* Stop babying me! I'm not helpless! *(Pause)* I'm sorry, Irene. I'm tired.

IRENE: I know.

MAGGIE: You'll have to excuse me, Ms Pollard. It was nice meeting you.

NAN: Yes...

(MAGGIE *exists up the dock toward the house.* NAN *stares at her as she goes.* IRENE *stares glumly at the lake.*)

NAN: Is she all right?

IRENE: No, she's not.

(IRENE *does not elaborate, so* NAN *lets it drop.* NAN *picks up the binoculars.*)

NAN: May I?

(IRENE *nods.* NAN *scans the horizon with the binoculars.*)

NAN: That looks like your husband out there in that boat.

(IRENE *takes the binoculars, and looks.*)

IRENE: So, he did go out after all.

NAN: Is he catching anything?

IRENE: Hopefully, our dinner. *(Pause)* Or should we refrain from eating the fish too? What's your expert opinion on that?

NAN: Is there some particular reason why everything you say to me has this condescending, and sarcastic tone?

IRENE: Does it? I hardly know you, Ms Pollard....

NAN: Seems like everybody I meet in this town has an attitude problem. You know, personally, I don't care what any of you people think of me. I'm here to do a job, and no amount of intimidation is gonna make me leave until it's finished. I think it would make all our lives a bit easier if all you people would get off my back, and just let me get on with my work!!

IRENE: You needn't raise your voice.

NAN: You people don't like me very much, well, let me tell you something-the feeling is mutual!

IRENE: Ms Pollard, contrary to what you may have heard around this town, some of us don't really have much opinion one way or the other about your little science project...but, we do recognize rudeness when we see it.

NAN: You've been mocking me ever since I got here.

IRENE: Uninvited, I might add!

NAN: All right, I'll be leaving. Thank you for the ice tea, Mrs Walker. Have a nice day. *(She starts up the dock.)*

IRENE: *(Stops her)* Ms Pollard...please...I apologize.

(NAN *stops, turns back.*)

IRENE: I wasn't being fair. You'll have to forgive me, this hasn't been the best day...we're under some pressure, and...uh...I took it out on you. I'm sorry.

NAN: Apology accepted. I'm sorry I got a little worked up too. It's a hot day....

IRENE: Yes. I hear you've had a difficult two weeks here already.

(NAN *nods.*)

IRENE: Please don't judge us too harshly. There are good people here... but they're all scared...scared for their jobs.... their way of life....and maybe frightened of what kind of news you may bring them....

NAN: I'm just trying to find answers.

IRENE: Yes, I know. *(Pause)* Not everyone is against what you're trying to do. I think everyone wants to do the right thing, but there are limits, very real limits. We want to know the truth, just like you, we're willing to face it, no matter how unpleasant...but you have to keep one thing in mind...when you finish, and you leave...the rest of us have to go on living here.

NAN: I realize that.

IRENE: Do you? You're not from a small town in Maine, are you?

NAN: No, I grew up in California...suburbs...San Jose....

IRENE: How did you end up here?

NAN: My husband works with the Oceanography Institute in Woods Hole. We decided to try living in the East....we like it here....it's a good place to raise a family.

IRENE: Yes...you have children?

NAN: Not yet...we plan to. How about you? Kids?

IRENE: *(Sore spot)* No....not yet... *(Pause)* As I was saying...uh, it's difficult in a small town...old allegiances run deep...and when someone...an *outsider* is about to bring us...perhaps unsettling news, well, then....

NAN: *(Pause)* Maine is my home now too, what happens here affects us all. I'm just looking for evidence. Scientific truth. *(Long pause)* I could use an ally....maybe even a friend.

IRENE: You can't ask me to go against my husband.

NAN: No, I wouldn't ask that. I just thought perhaps...as another woman...you would see tha....

IRENE: I don't think this is a feminist issue, Ms Pollard.

NAN: I was just hoping you had some influence, that maybe he'd listen to you....

IRENE: Just leave me out of it, please. We all have to look out for our own now...you understand that?

NAN: Well, if you won't intercede with your husband, then perhaps you can help me with the missing part of my puzzle—the anonymous whistle-blower. The person who called the agency to get me down here. I've been here two weeks and no one has come forward yet to identify himself. Without my witness, I'm gonna have a hard time moving forward.

IRENE: I can't help you with that.

NAN: Can't or won't?

IRENE: Either way. *(She looks out at the lake.)*

NAN: But, you know who he is, don't you?

IRENE: No.

NAN: Putting your head in the sand isn't gonna save you any pain.

IRENE: Oh, you'd be surprised what pain you can avoid if you choose not to see it.

NAN: Oh, really?

IRENE: Yes. You saw my sister-in-law, hmm?

NAN: Maggie.

IRENE: Yes...and what did you see? Tell me.

NAN: A young woman...possibly very sick...

IRENE: Yes, in fact, she's dying. But, nobody really wants to see that, so nobody does. Like one of your little micro-organisms. It's invisible to the naked eye, but it's there. And what we can't see, won't hurt us, right?

NAN: No.

IRENE: *(Agreeing)* No. *(She picks up one of the water sample jars, looks at it.)* What do you think you're going to find in here?

NAN: I don't like to make predictions.

IRENE: What do you know already?

NAN: Well, yesterday, I was at the hospital, and I was talking to an old man who used to work at Walker Pipe. He's in there quite regularly, for radiation treatments...it seems his liver is shot...so, we're talking... when they brought in this little girl to the emergency room. She was in bad shape. Toxic poisoning.

IRENE: Yes, the Prudhoe girl...we heard about it this morning. Terrible...

NAN: Her father carried her into the hospital. She was comatose, and he looked almost as bad. The man was scared to death. And do you know what the grieving father does for a living? He removes barrels of toxic waste solvent from your husband's factory. That's very ironic, and very sad. *(Pause)* Do you know what substance is in those barrels?

IRENE: No.

NAN: T C A. Tri-chloro-thylane.

IRENE: What is it?

NAN: It's a fairly common industrial solvent. Your husband's company uses it to thin the resins that bond vinyl coating onto pieces of pipe. They used to use it in Silicon Valley in the computer chips, then they began to find heavy traces in the ground water. Then, they began to link exposure to T C A with abnormal levels of leukemia, nerve damage, and liver cancer.

IRENE: Why didn't someone warn manufacturers about these solvents?

NAN: Like who?

IRENE: The scientists like yourself.

NAN: And who's going to pay for all these tests? The taxpayers? *(She sighs, finishes a last sip from the styrofoam cup she has been drinking tea from. She looks at the cup.)* Two hundred years from now, when we're long dead, and turned to dust, this cup will still be here. Nobody knew that when they invented styrofoam. Who knew that it wouldn't decompose? And we've invented some fifty thousand chemical substances this century. You know how many different pesticides there are?

(IRENE *shakes her head.*)

NAN: More than four hundred...and less than seven percent have even been tested. I don't know how we'll ever catch up.

IRENE: But, you do know about this T C A stuff?

NAN: Enough to know if improperly handled, it's very dangerous.

IRENE: Could it be in our water?

NAN: I hope not. *(Pause)* I shouldn't even speculate.

(IRENE *holds up one of the jars.*)

IRENE: The water looks so clear.

NAN: Yes. *(Pause)* Sometimes I hate going to the lab. Today's one of those days. I really hope my suspicions are wrong.

(IRENE *hands the jar back to* NAN. *She rises and gathers her things.*)

IRENE: Sometimes there's no comfort in being right.

NAN: No...none at all.

IRENE: God help us all. (IRENE *crosses up the dock to the house.* NAN *remains seated on the dock. She holds up one of the sample jars, examines it.* NAN *sets the jar aside, rests her chin on her knee, and stars at the lake as the lights fade to black.*)

Scene Three

(Time: later that evening. Dusk)

(Setting: the same)

(At rise: Sound of music coming from a record player in the house—Edith Piaf's Greatest Hits. IRENE *sits on the picnic table, looking out at the lake, listening to the faint music. She wears jeans, running shoes, and an old college sweatshirt with "Colby" on the front. Behind her on the picnic table, are the remains of dinner— paper plates, cups, empty beer cans, corn cobs, and the remains of a cookout.* IRENE *is lost in her thoughts. She slaps a mosquito on her arm. She finds a can of insect repellant, and sprays her arms and legs.* CARL *appears at the screen door of the porch, upstage. He comes up behind* IRENE. *She notices him, smiles, looks*

back to the lake again. CARL *sets down the bag, puts his arms around her, kisses the back of her neck. She takes one of his hands in her own.* CARL *offers his beer.* IRENE *takes a sip, hands it back. He sits next to her at the picnic table.)*

CARL: How ya doin'?

IRENE: Fine.

CARL: I got lonesome. Wondered where you were. You want come inside?

IRENE: Not right now. It's a nice sunset.

CARL: *(Looks at the lake)* Best time of the day.

IRENE: Yes.

(Sound of crickets, and in the distance, the sounds of Canada geese.)

IRENE: Listen...you hear that?

CARL: Crickets.

IRENE: No, listen again. Over there.

CARL: Geese. Winter's on the way.

IRENE: Such a forlorn sound.

CARL: I don't think so. They sound happy to me.

IRENE: You're an optimist.

*(*CARL *smiles, slaps a mosquito.)*

CARL: Mosquitoes will carry you away this summer.

IRENE: Not me. *(Holds up a can of bug repellant)* I got Deep Woods Off. You want some.

CARL: No, I'm okay. *(He slaps a mosquito, changes his mind, and sprays repellant on his arms.)*

IRENE: I love it when it's this light, so late in the evening. Almost makes the rest of the year seem bearable.

CARL: *(Down East accent)* Well, ya' can't take the winter, then ya' don't deserve the summer. Ayuh!

IRENE: *(Same accent)* Yessuh!

(They laugh, then lapse into silence. Sound of MAGGIE *singing in the house, harmonizing along with the record.* CARL *and* IRENE *laugh.)*

IRENE: Maggie's gonna wear out that record.

CARL: She told me, in her next lifetime, she plans to come back as a "chanteuse".

IRENE: What's Maggie doing?

CARL: Finishing up the dishes.

IRENE: Poor Maggie. She really wanted to see Gordie.

CARL: *(Looks at the table.)* She barely touched her dinner.

IRENE: None of us ate much. It was a nice fish, though.

(CARL *begins to clean the mess from the table, putting trash in the garbage bag.*)

CARL: There's still a lot of bass left. You wanna save it?

IRENE: No, throw it out! He's not coming, and I don't want it smelling up my icebox. (CARL *dumps the fish into the garbage bag.*) You don't have to do that now.

CARL: Can't leave it, we'll have raccoons again.

IRENE: I'll take care of it later.

CARL: Just sit. You cooked, I'm in charge of clean-up.

(IRENE *broods while he works.*)

IRENE: So where is he?

CARL: *(Slaps a mosquito)* Passed out in a ditch for all I care. I've given up trying to figure out Gordie. It's been eight months or so since his last disastrous visit, I thought maybe enough time has passed, maybe we can get along, maybe we....why do I keep wasting my time?

IRENE: Because he's your brother.

CARL: And nothing ever changes. So we'd all better accept that fact and get on with our lives.

IRENE: I guess we can thank ol' Joe Walker for that. Putting you two against each other...it wasn't fair.

CARL: Fair? I don't think that word was in the old man's vocabulary. Just ask Maggie.

IRENE: Maggie's tough. She got through it.

CARL: Well, according to him she didn't have that many options anyway, having "the misfortune to have been born female"—(his words!) She didn't fit the overall scheme. As far as he was concerned she could either get married, become a teacher, or leave home. It didn't matter to him.

IRENE: You had other options too.

CARL: Would it have made you happier if he'd chosen Gordie?

IRENE: No, but it might have made *you* happier. If you didn't want the responsibility you shouldn't have taken it.

CARL: Back then I was too scared to say no. I didn't want to disappoint him. He was very intimidating. I know he didn't cut much of an imposing figure when you knew him...he was weak, and dying then, but oh, you should have seen him in his prime. Even in those last years when he was sick... he was still running everything from a make-shift office in his bedroom... barking orders down the stairs...cussing out distributors on the phone... never let up for a second. He was so good at it...and in a way you couldn't help admiring the man. His tenacity was awe-inspiring. Of course few people outside the immediate family knew that he ran his own household with the same mean spirited, take-no-prisoners approach. Joe Walker was one tough little son of a bitch, and somehow he always got people to do exactly what he wanted.

IRENE: He was the most intense, angry man I ever met.

CARL: Yeah, well, dying hadn't been part of his plan....irritating inconvenience.

IRENE: I never could figure out if he liked me or not.

CARL: Who knows? I don't recall him saying much positive about anyone, except our mother. Once, after she'd been dead about five or six years, he said that she had been, "basically a decent, but weak woman." I think he meant it as a compliment. *(Pause)* I'm glad he's gone, but at the same time, sometimes I wish he was still here, running things again. He'd know exactly what to do. Know what he'd say?

IRENE: "Break their balls."

CARL: Something like that.

IRENE: Good ol' Joe...always the enlightened approach.

CARL: *(After a pause)* I'm thinking about doing something.

(IRENE *looks at him.*)

CARL: On Monday, I'm gonna let Nan Pollard in to inspect the plant.

IRENE: What made you change your mind?

CARL: According To Gordie I'm already up against the wall. Maybe there's no point in fighting what's inevitable. I want to do the right thing, only problem, how will I know if it's right?

IRENE: Any way you choose we risk everything.

CARL: Well, if we're forced to close, I could sell out to those developers in Boston. We cash out, move to Aruba...

IRENE: Aruba? What would we do there?

CARL: Rot in the sun.

IRENE: What about Maggie?

CARL: I don't know. I'm scared, Irene.

IRENE: You know I'll be with you, no matter what happens.

(CARL *rises, stands looking out at the lake for a long moment. He sighs.*)

CARL: After I brought the boat back this afternoon, I went by the hospital. I saw the little Prudhoe girl...in intensive care. She's got tubes running down her throat, out her arms. I saw her, and I broke down, right there... I couldn't help it. A nurse had to help me out of the room. I just ran out of that building, sprinting across the parking lot to the car. I got inside and I was shaking so hard, I couldn't drive. I had such a tightness in my chest....

IRENE: No one is blaming you for what happened to that little girl.

CARL: Not yet, but you wait and see...it'll be my mistake in the end.

IRENE: No one person is responsible.

CARL: I wish I could believe that. Somebody in the town wants to nail my ass to a wall...somebody wants to get me, so bad, destroy everything I've built. Only one person I know hates me that much.

IRENE: Who?

CARL: Who do you think? Who has the most to gain, if I go under? Gordie could make a real killing here, and he knows it.

IRENE: Gordie? That's ridiculous.

CARL: Is it? I don't think so. The last thing he said to me-I'm not fit for this job. You heard him.

IRENE: He was drunk and mouthing off.

CARL: Yeah, sure. Fucking Judas! It's just his style.

IRENE: Oh, stop it! Your brother is not out to ruin you.

CARL: What if I'm not fit for this job? Huh? What if it's true? A big joke, huh? But nobody's laughing. And the joke is on Joe Walker....'cause he made the big mistake.

IRENE: Carl, stop it!

CARL: Why didn't he pick Gordie? Why? It doesn't make any sense. Gordie should have been the one, he's older, he's more clever. I'm just a plodder. I don't have that instinct for the jugular...that thing, whatever it takes... a gut for business...whatever you wanna call it....I don't have it. I never did.

(CARL *moves away from her.* IRENE *stops herself from going to him*).

IRENE: Did it ever occur to you, that just maybe there was a logic to your father's choice? Perhaps he knew exactly what he was doing. Did you ever think that maybe he picked you because...he knew....he knew that you would do things differently. Just maybe, he passed over Gordon, because

Gordie was too much like himself. Joe Walker may have been a lot smarter than you think.

(CARL *looks at her for a moment. His internal anguish transforms itself to giddy laughter.*)

CARL: I don't know whether to laugh or cry.

IRENE: Well, you're laughing.

CARL: Did you just make that up?

IRENE: Yes. It's the best theory I can muster. Do you have a better one?

CARL: No...I don't.

IRENE: Then, it will have to do, 'cause we'll never know for sure.

CARL: *(After a pause)* You know...if that was true...Gordie would really be pissed off!

IRENE: Maybe that's why he did it!

(*They laugh together.* CARL *smiles at her, puts his arms around her.*)

CARL: You're something...here we are going to hell...and we're laughing....

IRENE: Why not?

(CARL *slaps a mosquito.*)

CARL: These mosquitoes are too much for me. Let's go in.

IRENE: Not yet. I'm going to watch the sunset.

CARL: Well, I'm going in....

IRENE: Okay, I'll be there soon....promise.

CARL: I love you.

(CARL *kisses her forehead. He goes up to the house.* IRENE *sits on the picnic table, watches the sun sinking. In the bushes upstage,* GORDIE *appears. He walks down toward where she sits.* GORDIE *appears rumpled, a bit tipsy. She turns and sees him.*)

GORDIE: Hi, there!

(IRENE *turns away, faces the lake.*)

IRENE: Oh, it's you.

GORDIE: I...uh, was over there in the bushes. *(He sits wearily at the picnic table.)* I guess I missed dinner.

IRENE: *(Cool)* Yes, you did.

GORDIE: I'm sorry, Irene.

IRENE: Save your apologies for Maggie. She's the one who's upset.

GORDIE: And what about you?

IRENE: I've learned not to expect anything from you.

GORDIE: I lost track of the time. I fell asleep. I just woke up about twenty minutes ago. *(He rubs his face with his hands.)*

IRENE: How long have you been lurking in the bushes?

GORDIE: Not long. I waited until Carl left. *(Pause)* I've got a headache. What time is it?

IRENE: About eight fifteen.

GORDIE: I went back to the motel. I had a few drinks in the bar. I went back to my room to lie down for a nap. Must have dozed off for hours. I had a wake-up call. I must have slept right through it.

IRENE: You don't have to make up stories, Gordon. You weren't here, because you didn't want to come.

GORDIE: *(After a pause)* The part about the drinks was true.

IRENE: You had more than a few.

GORDIE: Yeah. Do you have any aspirin?

IRENE: Up at the house.

(GORDIE looks toward the house, decides it's not worth the effort.)

GORDIE: I'll suffer.

IRENE: Why did you come back?

GORDIE: You invited me to dinner. I came to apologize for not showing up.

IRENE: What is it that's tearing away at you, Gordie? Every time you come back home, we all go through hell with you. Why?

GORDIE: I don't know.

IRENE: That's not good enough.

GORDIE: Well, that's the only answer I got.

IRENE: You didn't used to get blotto every time I saw you. It only happens here, when you come home. Why is that?

GORDIE: Maybe, when I look around, I don't see anything but, old pain. Then, I realize for the umpteenth million time, I don't really fit into this picture...I oughta just let things be...learn to accept people with all their frailties, and just walk away...but I can't let go...I try...but....

IRENE: What do you want from us? We all care about you, Gord. Isn't that enough?

(GORDIE looks at her longingly, then looks away.)

GORDIE: What does it matter? I'm going back to New York soon enough.

IRENE: When are you leaving?

GORDIE: Maybe tomorrow.

IRENE: Before you go, I want you to do me a favor.

GORDIE: See Maggie.

IRENE: Yes.

GORDIE: And what do I say to her?

IRENE: Just tell her that you love her.

(GORDIE *looks away, full of pain and guilt.*)

IRENE: That's so hard for you, isn't it? Gordie...Gordie...what's happened to you? You can't even express affection.

GORDIE: I could once...a long time ago. *(He looks at her.)* I have never felt as good since that time....

IRENE: Please, don't start....

GORDIE: It's the truth. What we had was real....

IRENE: I don't feel like reminiscing right now.

GORDIE: It might have worked, if you'd given it half a chance...had some patience....

IRENE: You were the one who left! You went to law school...then on to New York. What was I supposed to do? Spend my whole life waiting for you? What was I supposed to do?

GORDIE: You didn't have to fuck my brother!!

(IRENE *stares at him.* GORDIE *immediately regrets what he has said.*)

IRENE: Good night, Gordon.

(*As she turns to go, he grabs her hand tightly.*)

GORDIE: I didn't mean that! *(He holds her hand to his face.)*

IRENE: Let go of my hand.

GORDIE: Do you know how many times I've wanted to call you up in the middle of the night?

IRENE: *(Jerks her hand away)* Stop, dammit!

GORDIE: Please, Irene.

IRENE: You can't touch me that way again...ever!

(CARL *appears at the screen door.*)

GORDIE: Just let me put my arms around you. That's all.... Just let me hold you for a moment...

(IRENE *shoves him back, and slaps him hard.*)

IRENE: NO!

(GORDIE *sits on the bench rubbing his face.*)

IRENE: What's the matter with you? It's over...it's been over for years, Gordie.

(CARL *opens the door and crosses down to them.*)

CARL: What's going on?

GORDIE: We're just talking over old times.

IRENE: Shut up, Gordon!

GORDIE: I'm sorry...I had too much to drink...and...

CARL: I don't know about you folks, but I've had enough excitement for one day.

IRENE: I'm going in. *(She starts for the house.)*

GORDIE: *(Sings quietly)* Goodnight, Irene...Goodnight, Irene...

CARL: I think you've caused enough turmoil for one visit. Maybe you should head back tonight.

(IRENE *stands on the screen porch, looking at them.*)

GORDIE: I haven't seen Maggie yet.

CARL: O K. Tomorrow, then. I want you out of here by noon.

GORDIE: If that's the way you want it....

CARL: That's exactly the way I want it. And on your way, why don't you take your little friend from the D E P with you.

GORDIE: What the hell are you talking about?

CARL: You and Nan Pollard. I know you're the one...and what I saw out here tonight, just confirms it...don't give me that fuckin' look! I know what you're trying to do. It's not enough for you to destroy me, is it? You gotta go after Irene too. Gotta hurt everyone around you...never satisfied till you draw more blood.

GORDIE: You are the most paranoid lunatic I ever met. If you think I called in that investigator, you are...you're FUCKING NUTS!!! What is it with you, and this obsession you have about me wanting your job? I don't want this! None of it! I'm happy with what I am....happy as a pig in shit!

(IRENE *comes down to them, exasperated.*)

IRENE: Both of you stop fighting! Now!

CARL: Oh, no...he's gonna admit that he's got it in for me...always has... he'll wreck our marriage....nothing's sacred with him....just like the old man...he loves to hurt people...

GORDIE: Compared to him we're all amateurs.

CARL: Go on, tell her...why you blew the whistle. Huh? Go on...tell her about the sweet deal you can make, if I sell out...SAY IT!

GORDIE: YOU'RE CRAZY!!

IRENE: STOP IT! STOP IT! GODDAMNIT! He didn't do it, Carl.

CARL: Bullshit! I know him....

IRENE: NO! I did!

(CARL *and* GORDIE *stare at her, dumbfounded.*)

IRENE: I'm the one who called the state office...

CARL: You? Why?

IRENE: Oh, God...this is so hard...please, just listen to me. I know what you must be feeling...that I betrayed you, but no...I just had to do something. That last time, when Maggie was in the hospital...I just couldn't look in her face anymore...the pain in her eyes....just like your father had when he was dying. I can't go through that again with Maggie. Not again, Carl. I'm scared. Who's next? You? Me?...and then, I started thinking about those two times I miscarried....

CARL: That has no connection. The doctor said....

IRENE: I DON'T CARE WHAT HE SAID! DOCTORS DON'T KNOW EVERYTHING! *(Pause)* Carl, something very wrong is happening here, and I can't tolerate not having control over my life! I want to know the truth! If Nan Pollard finds nothing, then she'll go away, but if she does find something, I want to know about it. I want to know what's killing us. I want to know why I can't carry a child...something as simple as that... I have to know....

(IRENE *chokes up.* CARL *shakes his head in disbelief.*)

IRENE: Please...forgive me....

CARL: *(Looks at* GORDIE.*)* Sorry, Gord... *(Looks at* IRENE*)* I think I need a little space right now.

(CARL *is shattered. He walks away, toward the front of the house. He cannot deal with her at this moment.*)

IRENE: Carl...talk to me...Carl...Are you coming back? Carl?

(CARL *is gone.*)

(GORDIE *slowly extends his handkerchief to* IRENE. *He is touched by her bravery and honesty. He stares at her as the lights fade to black.*)

END OF ACT ONE

ACT TWO

(*Time: later that night. After midnight*)

(*Setting: the same*)

(*At rise: bright moonlight floods the area near the dock and picnic table. A solitary figure can be seen standing on the dock*—JACK. *He lights a cigarette.* JACK *wears a baseball cap, T-shirt, jeans, boots and a denim jacket. He looks at the lake, and spits in the water. He removes a pint of whiskey from his back pocket and takes a swig. He recaps the pint, puts it in his pocket, turns and goes up the dock, out of sight. Sound of a heavy object being moved toward the dock.* JACK *reappears with a sixty gallon oil drum on a hand truck. He maneuvers the truck and barrel down the ramp to the end of the dock, and sets it down carefully. He wipes his face with a bandana.* JACK *ties the bandana over his mouth and nose to shield himself from fumes from the oil drum. He slides the drum off the dolly. He removes a hammer and chisel from his belt, and begins to pry open the spout on the oil drum. When he gets it open, he sets the tools on the dock.* JACK *lifts the back edge of the barrel so the contents will begin to spill into the lake.* CARL *appears at the ramp leading down the dock.* CARL *wears jeans, a T-shirt and windbreaker. He carries a flashlight and a baseball bat.* CARL *creeps up behind* JACK, *touches him on the shoulder with the bat.* JACK *freezes.*)

CARL: Don't move, or I'll take your Goddamn head off! Now, set the barrel down slowly. Don't spill anything! Now, move away from that oil drum... real slow....and turn around.

(JACK *does as he is told.* CARL *shines the light on his face.* JACK *lowers the bandana.*)

CARL: I shoulda known it would be you, Jack. (*He looks at the oil drum*) Where'd you get this?

JACK: Where do you think I got it?

CARL: Did you go in the plant?

JACK: Yeah.

CARL: What's it doin' here?

JACK: I'm bringin' it back where it belongs. To the Walkers!

CARL: You're crazy. You know what this stuff is?

JACK: Yeah, I know; And now, somebody's gonna get theirs. Time to pay back the fuckers who hurt my girl.

CARL: I never hurt you, Jack.

JACK: Bullshit! You're all in it! All you Walkers!

CARL: Keep your voice down. People are sleeping.

JACK: Good. Let's get 'em up.

CARL: Don't press your luck.

(CARL *extends the bat.* JACK *sticks his own chin right to the end of the bat.*)

JACK: Go ahead. Do it, man...'cause I don't give a shit anymore.

(CARL *holds the bat steady for a moment.* JACK *waits, not backing down.* CARL *lowers the bat, slowly.*)

CARL: If I didn't have so much respect for your brother's memory....

JACK: Aw, screw you and my brother! All you people act like he was a fuckin' saint. He played football. So what? Big fuckin' deal. Hey, Calvin is gone! You're talkin' to me now! You pay attention to me. Calvin is nothing'...and I'm glad he's fuckin' dead.

(CARL *slugs* JACK *in the stomach with the end of the bat.* JACK *falls back on the dock, hitting his head.*)

CARL: Don't ever say that to me. Your brother was my best friend. You show him some respect. All right, get up. Get on your feet.

JACK: I can't.

CARL: I didn't hit you that hard.

JACK: I'm bleedin'.

CARL: Where?

JACK: Back of my head. It's runnin' down my shirt.

(CARL *kneels, looks at* JACK's *injury.*)

CARL: Well, sit still...let me look at it. You musta hit your head on a nail. I just pushed you down...that's all.

JACK: OW!

CARL: Dammit? Hold still. Put your head up so I can see. Yeah, you got a little-bitty cut. You'll live.

JACK: I'm gonna be sick.

CARL: Put your head down between your knees.

(CARL *pulls a bandana from* JACK's *pocket.* CARL *holds the bandana on the wound.*)

CARL: Here, hold this up there...real tight. It'll stop the bleeding. You okay?

JACK: Yeah, I was just sorta dizzy for a minute.

CARL: It's just a scratch. Can you get up now?

JACK: In a minute, okay?

(JACK *pulls out his pint of whiskey, takes a long swig, hands it to* CARL, *who declines.*)

CARL: I didn't mean to hurt you, Jack.

JACK: *(Sitting and drinking)* I know. *(Pause)* I just get fed up with people always tellin' me how great Calvin was. Nowadays, I don't even like tellin' folks my last name, 'cause when they recognize it, I gotta listen to a lecture on all of his wonderful accomplishments...they talk like I ain't even standin' there. I get tired of bein' invisible, you know?

CARL: Well, folks just admired him a lot.

JACK: Yeah, well, I done some things too. I just never got on the six o'clock news....but, I done stuff too.

CARL: I know you have.

JACK: People don't wanna know about me. There ain't nobody comin' to take your picture at the loadin' dock at Walker Pipe. *(Pause)* After he got killed, I thought maybe it would get easier...but it didn't...it got worse. Remember that Veterans' Day Parade....some years back.

(CARL *nods.*)

JACK: The whole town declared it was "Calvin Prudhoe Day." I had to go up on the bandstand, and shake hands with the Mayor and the Governor. High School retired his number...they gave me his old football jersey, and a commemorative plaque. The Army sent a whole drawer full of medals. Yessir, they gave him the Silver Star...just 'cause a fuckin' Claymore blew up in his face. *(He takes another long swig.)* Yessir...that was some day. And, the Homecoming Queen, Marie, presented me the plaque, then kissed me on the cheek...right there. *(He points to his face.)* I got my picture in the paper that day. Front page. Me and Marie got married the next June. *(Pause)* You know what I did with Calvin's football jersey? I washed my car with it every Saturday, 'til it wore out. Yep.

(JACK *hands the pint to* CARL, *who doesn't take a drink.*)

JACK: *(Rises)* For awhile there, folks was givin' me just about everything I wanted. Is that why you gave me a job, Mr. Walker? You thought I'd be a hero too?

(CARL *looks at him with sadness.*)

CARL: I loved your brother.

JACK: Yeah, everybody did. Maybe I should write one of them tell-all books, huh? Get famous... *(He crosses to the oil drum.)* ...Or, maybe I should push this into the fuckin' lake.

CARL: I can't let you do that, Jack.

JACK: Oh, yeah...how you plannin' to stop me? You gonna kill me...? Hey, I'd get in the papers again?

CARL: You don't really want to hurt people, Jack.

(JACK *considers this for a moment, then turns and walks up the dock.*)

CARL: Hey, where are you going?

JACK: Home.

CARL: What about this oil drum?

JACK: Keep it. It's yours.

CARL: You can't leave it here.

JACK: Sure I can. It ain't my problem no more. I quit.

CARL: Wait a minute!

JACK: I'm goin' to California...my wife and me...we're gonna take Cindy outta that hospital tomorrow...pack my ol' truck...and we're outta here. You'd be smart to get out too, 'cause there's crazy people poisonin' each other around here. Better run while you can. *(He suddenly freezes, looks off to one direction.)*

JACK: Somebody's watchin' us.

CARL: Where?

JACK: Over there...in them bushes. I can see him standin' there.

(CARL *shines the flashlight toward the bushes.*)

CARL: I can see you. Who's there?

(After a few seconds, GORDIE *steps from the shadows.)*

JACK: I told you there was somebody *(to* GORDIE*)*. Evenin', Mr Walker.

GORDIE: What's up? You guys doing some night fishing?

CARL: Gordie, what are you doing out here? It's late.

GORDIE: Had insomnia...took a little drive...thought I'd stop by. What about you? Couldn't sleep, huh? Guilty conscience? *(He walks to the oil drum.)* Well, well....what have we here?

JACK: See you guys around. I'm takin' off now.

GORDIE: Stick around, Jack. I've got some information you might want to hear.

JACK: Oh, like what?

GORDIE: I think I have a pretty good idea how your daughter got poisoned.

(JACK *moves quickly to* GORDIE.)

JACK: Who did it? I'll kill the fucker.

GORDIE: I don't think you're getting the whole picture.

JACK: *(Grabs* GORDIE*)* Who was it? You tell me!

GORDIE: Take your hands off me!

CARL: Jack!

JACK: Who put the poison in my creek? You better tell me.

GORDIE: I'm getting to that, but first, we gotta back track a bit... Earlier this evening...oh, around ten-thirty...I was on my way over to your trailer....

JACK: My place? Why?

GORDIE: Well, before things start to escalate, thought we should have a talk.

JACK: About what?

GORDIE: I thought maybe if we talked some, off the record...you might be willing to settle this matter of your daughter's...uh, sickness...outside of a courtroom...less publicity and all that....

CARL: Who asked you to stick your nose in?

GORDIE: I'm trying to save your miserable ass.

JACK: Look, I ain't interested in no lawsuit, but I do expect some justice!

GORDIE: Good....so, I dropped by your house....

JACK: I was out this evening.

GORDIE: Oh, I know. As I was driving up...you went tearing out of your driveway in your pick-up truck...so I followed you. I thought I might be able to catch up with you, but you were in quite a hurry. I followed you out of town...up Route 26...about ten miles, then, you turned on a dirt road that leads over to the old Buckfield Quarry.

JACK: Yeah, I went over there. So what?

GORDIE: I watched you haul a sixty gallon oil drum out of the pit, and then put it on your truck...and what do you know? Here it is, that same oil drum...sitting in my brother's back yard.

CARL: Buckfield Quarry? I thought you got it from the plant.

JACK: Well, it came from the plant...originally.

CARL: Did you go to the plant tonight? I want the truth!

JACK: No, sir, I didn't. *(Pause)* That barrel come from the quarry, like he said.

CARL: And how the hell did it get up there?

JACK: It was one of them I dumped last month. Now, let me explain something...see, I was gonna...

CARL: You mean you didn't take it across the state line? Why didn't you do like I said?

JACK: I tried, Mr Walker, but they kept givin' me a hassle every time I took a load over.

GORDIE: Who gave you a hassle?

JACK: Highway Patrol.

CARL: Didn't you show them the agreement?

JACK: Yes sir, I had it with me every time, but they said it ain't no good no more since the elections last time...said they didn't care about the agreement...then they told me it wasn't enough money. They kept jackin' up the fee, every load I took across. I was runnin' out of money. I just couldn't pay 'em no more.

CARL: You should have come to me.

JACK: Shit, I was scared. They told me if I told anyone what they was doin'...*anyone* at all...they'd bust me next time I set foot in New Hampshire. They said if I didn't like their new "Privilege Tariff", then go somewhere else. So, I didn't go back no more.

CARL: Goddamn cops on the take.

JACK: What choice did I have? They woulda tossed me in jail if I didn't pay up.

CARL: What did you do with all that money I gave you every month? That was a company budget for disposal purposes only. What did you do with it?

(JACK *hesitates before answering.*)

JACK: I still owe a lot of mortgage on my trailer...times is hard...my wife's been sick...she can't work, and...I'll pay it back, I swear. I still got some left...not much... if you want it, it's in the bank.

(CARL *walks a few steps away, fraught with concern.*)

GORDIE: The money is the least of the problem, Jack.

JACK: I SAID I'D PAY IT BACK!

(JACK *looks from one to the other for any sign of understanding. They are silent.*)

JACK: At least I used my head, I did find an alternate spot to get rid of them barrels. It's perfect. The mills used to dump stuff up there all the time...for years, man. And besides, it's a hell of a lot closer. *(He still receives no encouraging response.)* And, I've been real careful. I always go late at night. None of them barrels got any markings from the plant. I made sure of that. Anybody finds 'em, they can't be traced. It's perfect. I'm tellin' ya, I done it right! *(Pause)* It's just an old granite pit. Ain't nothin' hurtin' nobody up there. Everyone in the valley used to dump shit there, and nobody ever gave a hoot.

GORDIE: Buckfield Quarry was closed over twenty yeas ago, Jack.

JACK: Yeah, so? It's safe. It's solid granite, man.

CARL: How long have you been dumping up there?

JACK: Goin' on two years now *(Pause)* So, what's wrong with it? The place is over ten miles away for Crissake!

CARL: Why do you think they closed the pit? Huh? How come nobody is supposed to use it now? Did you ever think about that? Did you? I'll tell you why....there just happens to be an underground spring...not two hundred years from that pit....and that spring feeds into Biddeford Creek.... it flows right past your trailer, right through the west side of town, and eventually empties into this lake. Right here. They knew that twenty years ago. That's why they closed the pit. They got signs posted everywhere— NO DUMPING! CAN'T YOU READ THE FUCKING SIGNS? They're written in English and French.... What's the matter with you? THE PIT IS OFF LIMITS!

JACK: Nobody every told me about it. How was I supposed to know?

GORDIE: *(To* CARL*)* A real class act, Carl.

CARL: He's the one who dumped them. Not me!

GORDIE: And who hired him? *(Pause)* You were supposed to supervise this. Ultimately, it's your responsibility. You told me you saw the receipts...every month...records he gave to you...you told me you saw them. Where are they?

*(*CARL *doesn't answer.)*

GORDIE: I'll tell you where they are. There are no receipts. Right?

CARL: I had some receipts...I saw them....

GORDIE: All of them?

CARL: No. *(Long pause)* I...I only have the ones from the first six months.

GORDIE: The first six months?

CARL: I...I thought that would be enough...I guess I got distracted with other...I THOUGHT EVERYTHING WOULD BE O K...all right, I admit it... I screwed up...does that make you happy? I DON'T HAVE ALL THE GODDAMN RECEIPTS!! He stopped giving them to me.

GORDIE: And you stopped asking for them.

(CARL *sits on the dock in shame. Silence.* JACK *looks at them, tries to cover his panic, by making some half-baked suggestions.*)

JACK: Look, we can get those barrels out of there. There's less than fifty of 'em. I'll call some guys. We could get a truck out there tomorrow night.

GORDIE: It's too late.

JACK: All right, tonight, then! The three of us...we'll do it! We'll work all night if we have to.

CARL: And where would we take them?

JACK: I DON'T KNOW! ANYWHERE! What do you want from me?

GORDIE: Jack, it's too late.

JACK: Stop sayin' that. We can do it. Nobody has to know...

GORDIE: It won't work.

JACK: Why not?

GORDIE: Because I told someone about it.

(*Stunned silence. They stare at* GORDIE.)

GORDIE: (*After a pause.*) I called Nan Pollard. I told her where she could find what she's looking for.

CARL: When?

GORDIE: About an hour ago. She's probably on her way up there now.

JACK: Why did you do that?

GORDIE: It just seemed the right thing to do.

CARL: First, Irene...and now, you...Christ, are you trying to put us all in jail?

JACK: Oh, no, man...they're gonna arrest me.

GORDIE: Irene's right...you gotta know...one way or the other.

JACK: How can he do this? Your own brother? He told on us. FUCK! I ain't goin' to jail. Hey, Mr. Walker...if I go down the tubes, you're goin' with me.

CARL: Jack, shut the hell up!

(JACK *starts to leave.* GORDIE *grabs his arm.*)

GORDIE: I don't think you'd better leave.

JACK: Fuck you, man! I'm gettin' out. There's a crazy bastard in this town, and he's trying to poison my family. Let go of me. I gotta get my kid outta the hospital.

GORDIE: She's in intensive care. They won't let you take her.

JACK: She's my kid. I'll kill 'em if they try to stop me. Don't you guys see it? Huh? It's a conspiracy...it's the Army, man. They got these little nerve gas pills, and they're droppin' 'em in our water. They're gonna get everyone in the valley. We gotta stop 'em.

(CARL *grabs* JACK *and swings him around violently.*)

CARL: You crazy fool! Listen to me....

JACK: Naw, you're one of 'em. They got you brainwashed.

(CARL *grabs him by the collar, screams in his face.*)

CARL: LISTEN TO ME! There is no conspiracy. There are no poison pills. It's you—JACK PRUDHOE!!

GORDIE: Let go of him, Carl.

CARL: YOU PUT THE POISON IN THE CREEK!!! YOU'RE THE ONE! YOU DID IT!!!

(JACK *collapses on the dock, sobbing and babbling incoherently.*)

CARL: You miserable shit!

GORDIE: Did you hurt him?

CARL: No...I don't know what the hell's wrong with him. Look at him. He's totally flipped out. Jack...get up...Jack...

(CARL *and* GORDIE *watch him. Slowly,* JACK *sits up, leaning back against the barrel.* JACK *holds the baseball bat in his lap.* JACK *wipes his face, regains composure. His grip tightens on the bat.*)

GORDIE: Are you all right? You want us to call you a doctor? Jack?

JACK: *(Matter-of-fact.)* I'm gonna have to kill you, Mr. Walker...'cause of what you done to my girl.

CARL: Don't be stupid. Give me the bat.

JACK: Yes, sir...you got it! *(He rises, and lunges after* CARL, *swinging wildly, missing.*)

CARL: Jack...stop it!

(JACK *swings and misses again.* GORDIE *ties to step in,* JACK *turns on him also.*)

JACK: Come on...*(To* GORDIE*)* This is between him and me, but if you get in the way...I'll kill you too.

CARL: Give me the bat!

JACK: Why don't you come and take it from me, Mr. Walker? Come on, put out your hand...

(JACK *swings at* CARL's *hand, misses.* CARL *lunges for* JACK, *but* JACK *sidesteps him, hitting* CARL *in the leg.*)

CARL: OW!

JACK: Hey, you're not as fast as when you played with Calvin, huh?

GORDIE: Put it down, before you get hurt....

CARL: *(Slowly circling)* Come on, hand it over...real nice.

JACK: I'll kill both of you. Come on....

(JACK *swings at* GORDIE, *misses.* CARL *gets behind* JACK *and grabs him in a bear hug. THEY tumble to the dock, struggling.* JACK *wrestles himself free, and jumps up. As* CARL *starts to rise,* JACK *brings the bat down full force on* CARL's *hand.* CARL *screams.)*

CARL: OW! My wrist....you broke my wrist! Damn!

(Porch light comes on. IRENE *and* MAGGIE *visible at the back door in nightgowns.)*

IRENE: What is all this noise?

GORDIE: Call the police! Hurry up!

*(*IRENE *goes into the house.* MAGGIE *stands at the door watching, then follows* IRENE *inside.)*

*(*GORDIE *moves toward* JACK, *who threatens him with the bat.)*

JACK: You better stay back.

(Unseen by JACK, CARL *rises from the dock, with the chisel in his good hand.* CARL *holds the chisel like a thrusting knife blade.* GORDIE *sees the chisel in* CARL's *hand.)*

GORDIE: No, Carl....don't....

*(*JACK *turns around suddenly, swinging wildly. As the bat swings, the momentum carries* JACK *into* CARL. *In a sudden, instinctual move,* CARL *plunges the sharp chisel into* JACK's *mid-section.* JACK *gasps, staggers forward, and falls to his knees on the dock.)*

GORDIE: Oh, God...No!

JACK: Oh, no...I can't breathe....

*(*JACK *falls backward into a sitting position against the barrel.* CARL *and* GORDIE *stare at him, unable to move.* JACK *looks at the blood on his hands and the front of his shirt.* CARL *kneels beside him.)*

CARL: Don't try to move, Jack. Please....

JACK: Oh, God...don't let me die...help me....

*(*JACK *looks at them, dazed, as lights fade quickly to black.)*

Scene Two

(Time: the next day. Noon. A grey day)

(Setting: the same)

(At rise: the oil drum sits on the dock. It has been wrapped in a protective, plastic covering. NAN seals the barrel's covering with duct tape. NAN wears a protective suit and face visor, worn for handling hazardous waste materials. Once she finishes securing the tape, she places the barrel on a hand-dolly to transport it up the dock. IRENE sits on the picnic table some distance away. She sips a cup of coffee, watches NAN move the barrel. MAGGIE stands by a tree, nervously biting a fingernail, also watching NAN.)

IRENE: Are you sure you can move that thing by yourself?

NAN: No problem.

IRENE: Well, don't throw out your back or anything.

(NAN maneuvers the dolly, slowly.)

NAN: Don't worry. I've got it under control. Just stay back. You don't have protective gear, so please keep your distance.

IRENE: Don't worry. I'm not moving.

(MAGGIE looks at IRENE with concern.)

MAGGIE: What if she spills it?

IRENE: Think positive, Maggie.

(NAN skillfully wheels the dolly up the dock and off stage. MAGGIE breathes a sigh of relief.)

MAGGIE: It's gone...thank, God...

IRENE: Everything's gonna by okay.

(IRENE calls off to NAN.)

IRENE: Ms Pollard, make sure you don't spill any of that near my garden. I'd like to keep the tomatoes.

NAN: *(Off)* Don't worry. I won't.

MAGGIE: Where is she going to take that stuff?

IRENE: I don't care as long as she gets it away from here.

(Sound—a car door slamming)

IRENE: Sounds like Gordie's back.

MAGGIE: *(Looks off)* Yes, it's him.

GORDIE: *(Off)* Where are you taking it?

NAN: *(Off)* To the lab.

(GORDIE *enters looking disheveled, and exhausted.* MAGGIE *runs to meet him.*)

MAGGIE: Where have you been so long? We were so worried. What happened?

GORDIE: *(Moves to the bench)* Whoa, let me sit down first...I'm beat.

IRENE: Where's Carl? Why didn't he come with you? Is something wrong?

GORDIE: Carl's still at the hospital...said he wanted to check on Prudhoe again. He'll be along soon. One of the Deputies is with him, so I brought the car home. What a night!

IRENE: And how's the wrist?

GORDIE: Broken in two places. They set it and put it in a cast. He'll be okay.

MAGGIE: Where have you two been all night? We called the hospital a dozen times. They said you left in a police car.

GORDIE: Yeah. After the emergency room, they took us over to the sheriff's office, where we've been since about...*(He looks at his watch.)*...four A M. Took hours to get our statements down. Then, they finally let us go. *(Pause)* What happened to Prudhoe? We didn't hear anything after they wheeled him into surgery. I called the hospital, but they couldn't tell us anything.

IRENE: He was on the operating table for three hours. The blade punctured his lower intestine. He could have died from peritonitis. It was close, but he's gonna pull through.

GORDIE: Anything on the daughter?

IRENE: Last we heard, still the same...stabilized.

MAGGIE: That poor girl. I can't believe all this is happening.

(IRENE *heads toward the house.*)

IRENE: Well, at least it's not another dull summer!

MAGGIE: Irene!

IRENE: There's still some breakfast coffee left. Anyone want a cup?

GORDIE: Yes, please...and an aspirin if you can find one.

IRENE: Coming right up. *(She exits into the house.)*

MAGGIE: What an awful day.

GORDIE: Yes.

MAGGIE: Irene said you're going back to New York today. Is that true? I've hardly seen you at all.

GORDIE: I have to stay over now. On Tuesday, Carl and I have to give a deposition to a judge about what happened to Prudhoe. So, I guess you won't be getting rid of me that soon.

MAGGIE: Good. I'm glad you're here...in spite of all this mess. I missed you, Gord. I was afraid you'd end up in jail after last night. Tell me the truth. What did happen out here last night?

GORDIE: Well, we caught Prudhoe trying to dump that barrel into the lake. When we tried to stop him, he attacked us with a baseball bat, and somehow in the scuffle, Jack fell on the blade of the chisel, stabbed himself. It was an accident.

(MAGGIE *looks at him skeptically, then laughs.*)

MAGGIE: Oh, Gord...you are such a lousy liar. You can't con me...you never could...

GORDIE: Well, it better work in court on Tuesday, or I just perjured myself when I gave my statement to the sheriff. I'm really that bad, huh?

MAGGIE: Awful. How do you ever win a case in court?

GORDIE: We always settle before it gets that far. Really, that obvious, huh? I'm gonna have to work on that.

(MAGGIE *hugs him.*)

MAGGIE: It's really good to see you. Come on, loosen up...I won't hurt you...cancer's not contagious. Just hug me, huh?

(GORDIE *hugs her, uncomfortably.*)

GORDIE: I'm sorry....I wish I had come up sooner.

MAGGIE: It's all right...I'm okay now....

GORDIE: I guess I didn't know how to deal with it...I....

MAGGIE: Nobody does...not even me, and I *have* to live with it.

GORDIE: So, you're gonna start school in the fall again.

MAGGIE: That's what they tell me...we'll see....

GORDIE: You will, you're a fighter...you'll be there.

MAGGIE: I hope so. I miss the kids...even if they are idiots.

GORDIE: Oh, they can't be that bad.

MAGGIE: Hah...what they don't know would fill volumes.... Last semester I had one class that thought Corsica was in Greece, therefore Napoleon must be Greek, right? They're sweet, but oh, so dumb.

GORDIE: Worse than us, huh?

MAGGIE: Incredible... *(Pause)* Tell me something.... Is all this...awful calamity with Prudhoe...is it...I guess, what I'm asking is Carl involved? Is it his fault?

GORDIE: It's not his fault...he could have done some things differently, but no...I wouldn't blame it all on him.

(MAGGIE *looks at him for a long moment.* GORDIE *looks at the ground.*)

MAGGIE: Before I die...

GORDIE: You're not going to die....

MAGGIE: Let me finish...please...if I die soon, there's one thing I want you to do for me. Make peace with your brother. Would you?

GORDIE: It's not just up to me, Maggie.

MAGGIE: Look at me, Gord. Don't look at the ground. Look me in the face. Don't do like everyone else, Gord. It hurts worse when you deny it exists.

(GORDIE *looks at her.*)

MAGGIE: I love you and Carl...more than anything in the world...I don't want to think that we all ended up just like our father...full of bitterness and resentment....

(GORDIE *takes her hand.*)

GORDIE: I'll try....

(MAGGIE *kisses him on the forehead, as* IRENE *re-enters from the porch, carrying a coffee mug and a bottle of aspirin.*)

IRENE: Here it is...the perfect remedy for a sleepless night, and a hangover.

GORDIE: *(Takes the mug)* Thanks.

IRENE: Black, right?

GORDIE: Right.

IRENE: *(Opens the aspirin bottle.)* How many? Twelve? Thirteen?

GORDIE: Two will be fine.

(GORDIE *washes down the aspirin with the coffee.* NAN *enters, removing her gloves and rubber boots.*)

NAN: I got the barrel all squared away. No spills, no leaks. I need to keep it a few days to run some tests.

IRENE: As far as I'm concerned, it's yours. Thanks.

(NAN *crosses to* GORDIE.)

NAN: I'm sorry we didn't get to meet formally. I'm Nan Pollard.

GORDIE: *(Shaking hands)* Gordie Walker.

NAN: Nice to meet you, finally.

GORDIE: Yeah...

NAN: Look, I just wanna say, I appreciate what you did last night....calling me. What you did took a lot of courage. Most people just don't want to get involved. Thanks.

GORDIE: I didn't do it for you.

NAN: Well, for whatever reason you did it...it was the right thing.

GORDIE: Was it?

NAN: Yes it was. *(To* IRENE*)* Could I use your phone for a local call?

IRENE: Sure. It's in the kitchen. Maggie, show her where it is, will you?

MAGGIE: Sure. Follow me.

(MAGGIE *leads* NAN *to the house.* NAN *deposits the boots and gloves outside the door.)*

IRENE: *(After a pause)* So, why did you stick your neck out?

GORDIE: You inspired me last night...the way you told Carl...I may actually have learned something important.

IRENE: Oh, what was that?

GORDIE: The past doesn't matter...it's what we do now...that's what counts.

IRENE: I hope that turns out to be true.

GORDIE: You're a strong person, Irene.

IRENE: Or, a very stupid one...what I did may end up costing me my marriage as well as our livelihood.

GORDIE: Carl won't let you go...no matter how much he hurts right now. He knows what he'd lose...he's not that foolish.

IRENE: I wanna say something. I'm sorry the way I acted with you last night.

GORDIE: I should be apologizing to you. I'm the one who behaved badly.

IRENE: You were drunk.

GORDIE: Doesn't excuse it.

IRENE: We never resolved it very well, did we?

GORDIE: No.

IRENE: It was messy, and I regret the way I handled it back then.

GORDIE: It was a long time ago.

IRENE: I know it's no consolation, but I'm glad you're here this weekend. I do miss you.

(IRENE *hugs him.* MAGGIE *enters from the screened porch.*)

MAGGIE: Carl's back.

(MAGGIE *goes offstage to meet him.* IRENE *sighs heavily, dreading seeing* CARL.)

GORDIE: Keep your chin up. You'll do fine.

(CARL *enters with* MAGGIE.)

IRENE: Welcome back. There's donuts and coffee. How's the arm?

(CARL *has his arm in a cast and in a sling. He looks at* IRENE *with sadness in his eyes before he answers. They are both wary.*)

CARL: It's numb right now. They gave me some Darvon at the hospital.

IRENE: You should have called. I would have come to get you.

CARL: That's okay...the Deputy dropped me off.

(CARL *sits heavily on the bench near* GORDIE.)

GORDIE: Gonna be a while before you do any fly casting with that arm.

CARL: Yeah. I saw the barrel out on the truck. Where's Nan Pollard?

GORDIE: On the phone.

CARL: How are you holding up?

GORDIE: I could use a few hours sleep.

IRENE: Can't we all. What did they say about Jack Prudhoe?

CARL: He's gonna live.

GORDIE: What about his kid?

CARL: No change.

GORDIE: If you want I could recommend somebody in my firm for a consultation.

CARL: What's it going to cost me?

GORDIE: They don't come cheap.

CARL: What about you?

GORDIE: It's not my area of expertise...besides, conflict of interest. I gotta testify about Prudhoe.

IRENE: Carl, I wanna say something about...Pollard...and why I...

CARL: I really don't feel like talking about that right now. Okay?

IRENE: Okay. *(Clears the air)* Well, does anyone want anything to eat? 'Cause I'm starved.

GORDIE: What's easy to fix?

IRENE: Sandwiches?

GORDIE: Fine. Carl, you hungry?

(CARL *shrugs, looks at* IRENE.)

IRENE: Maggie, you wanna help?

MAGGIE: Coming.

(MAGGIE *and* IRENE *head toward the porch and into the house.*)

CARL: You need some help?

IRENE: *(Entering the house)* No, just rest your arm.

GORDIE: Do yourself a favor...don't make her feel any worse than she already does.

CARL: You freelancing as a marriage counselor now?

GORDIE: And don't bait me either! You got more important stuff in front of you.

CARL: Okay...*(Pause)* Thanks for standing up for me at the sheriff's office.

GORDIE: Just make sure the details of your story match mine on Tuesday.

CARL: I came this close to killing a man. How am I gonna live with that? Maybe we should change our testimony on Tuesday. Tell the truth...say what really happened.

GORDIE: You stabbed him in self-defense. He assaulted you. Besides, it'll never get as far as a courtroom. Prudhoe's not gonna press charges.

CARL: Who knows what he might do. The guy's very unstable.

GORDIE: He may be a lunatic, but he's not stupid. He won't take a chance on implicating himself. A good trial lawyer would tear him to shreds. Prudhoe cuts his own throat if he testifies. And, who's gonna believe him anyway...he's crazy. Trust me on this one.

CARL: And what happens if his daughter dies? I'll end up taking the rap.

GORDIE: No way. He still ends up implicating himself. He drove the truck. He dumped the barrels, not you. And if you play it right, and the receipts happen to disappear...then, they never existed. Prudhoe can take the fall. That's why I think you should talk to someone in my firm. If we're lucky, we can shift all the blame.

(MAGGIE *appears on the porch carrying a try of food. She stops, listens to them.*)

CARL: You're asking me to set up that poor bastard.

GORDIE: Yes, I am. It's the only way, Carl. You gotta destroy the receipts. Then it's his word against yours. Who they gonna believe? Some dead-beat truck driver with a third grade education? Come on, think, man...you gotta do it.

CARL: That's evidence tampering...we could go to jail.

GORDIE: We could go to jail anyway...we already perjured ourselves.

(MAGGIE walks down to them, sets the plate on the table. She stares at them.)

MAGGIE: I don't like what I'm hearing.

CARL: Maggie, stay out of it. Go back in the house.

MAGGIE: No, I will not. Don't tell me what to do, Carl.

CARL: MAGGIE!

MAGGIE: NO! Don't you dare treat me like our father did. Look at you.... both of you...do you hear yourselves? *(Pause)* Out here plotting like a couple of cheap Mafiosi. I am sick to death of this kind of talk...didn't we have enough of it when we were growing up? *(To* CARL*)* You break my heart when you act like him.

CARL: I'm sorry...I'm not sure it concerns you.

MAGGIE: Oh, yes it does. I know what's going on. Don't try to hide it from me. I don't need protecting. As long as I'm still breathing, I hold one-third of the stock in Walker Pipe, and I'll be damned if I'll sit by quietly while you play fast and loose with people's lives. *(Pause)* If one of us is responsible for the misery in this town, then we're gonna pay whatever price has to be paid.

GORDIE: That's all very fine and noble, Maggie, but are you prepared to spend whatever time you've got left sitting in jail with us?

MAGGIE: If that's what it comes to...yes. I have to live with myself, Gordie.

GORDIE: Fine...you go live with your clear conscience.

(GORDIE walks away, angry and disgusted. He sits on the end of the dock. MAGGIE looks at CARL.)

MAGGIE: Which side are you on, Carl?

(CARL doesn't answer. NAN *enters from the porch, walks toward* CARL.*)*

NAN: Oh, good...you're back. We need to talk.

CARL: Okay.

NAN: I need to get in the plant as soon as possible.

CARL: All right. Tomorrow morning.

NAN: Actually, today would be better. I want to run tests on a long list of substances. I want to be sure you don't have anything else besides the T C A we've already identified. And these tests do take some time.

CARL: Okay. We can go over after we eat. You anticipate some new problem?

NAN: Possibly. I just got off the phone with a lab technician at the hospital. Last night, I asked him to run a series of tests on a blood sample from Jack Prudhoe. They did, and it doesn't look so good. The guy has abnormal readings of Mercury and lead. I think I can trace the lead. I went over to his trailer, and discovered he's got old metal plumbing pipes. See, when T C A gets in metal pipes, it creates a chemical change. It releases lead into the water, and that's what he's been drinking. *(Pause)* But, the Mercury... that's what worries me. In fact, I can't believe he's still functioning. He's got high enough Mercury levels in his blood to blow his brains out three times over. I gotta find where the Mercury is coming from.

CARL: It's probably in the pit...bottom of the quarry.

NAN: Are you sure of that?

CARL: That's why they closed the pit.

NAN: Were there ever any woolen mills around here?

CARL: Used to be several of them. They all moved south to the Carolinas, or over to Taiwan. We used to have a carpet mill on the west side. Closed in the sixties.

NAN: *(Whistles)* Azio and hydroquinone dyes...terrible stuff...all major carcinogens.

(IRENE *enters from the house carrying a tray with more sandwiches, and drinks.*)

NAN: Did your father ever talk about what kind of solvents he used before the T C A?

CARL: Are you kidding...twenty-five years ago...nobody even talked about that kind of thing. What's your point?

NAN: The point is, I don't have any idea what kind of chemical mixture is festering at the bottom of that old quarry. They may have closed it down twenty years ago, but nobody went to the trouble to remove what was already in there. *(Pause)* This morning, when I drove up there, I saw barrels, some of them yours, some of them, from who knows where...but all were dumped a lot more recently than twenty years ago. And that worries me. Because I don't know what happens when you mix these new synthetics like T C A with compounds that are already in the pit. Maybe they create new compounds...I don't know.

(*Everyone is silent.*)

MAGGIE: Is...is it in the water? Our drinking water?

NAN: I would say that there is strong evidence that the entire west side of town may be contaminated...especially the area near the creek. *(Pause)* I hate to bring you people news like this. I just have one last thing to say. I think it would be wise for all of you to have a blood test. It might also be a good idea to test everyone who works in the plant.

CARL: I'll post a notice tomorrow.

IRENE: Are you going to shut us down?

NAN: That's not my decision.

MAGGIE: Well, whose decision is it?

NAN: I only present my report to the state committee. They make policy recommendations.

MAGGIE: Well, I think your policy sucks!

IRENE: Maggie, calm down.

MAGGIE: No I will not. *(To* NAN*)* If you know it's up there, then go get it. Move it out of our town! Get it out!

NAN: It's not that simple.

IRENE: Maggie...

MAGGIE: No, I want an answer! Why isn't it simple? Why can't you do anything? People are dying down here, and you say you can't help?

NAN: It's not up to me. We're dealing with a state agency...a bureaucracy.

CARL: What would a cleanup cost?

NAN: Who knows? To get the E P A Superfund...it takes time, and I don't know if it's even feasible. There would have to be more studies made...

MAGGIE: *(Furious)* STUDIES! WHAT THE HELL FOR? DON'T YOU HAVE ENOUGH EVIDENCE? It's up there! Get rid of it, now! *(She looks at all of them.)* Why are you staring at me? All of you...you're gonna do nothin'. A big fat zero...just like my father. You'll let it sit around for another twenty years!

IRENE: MAGGIE! STOP IT!

MAGGIE: You want evidence? I'll show you evidence....

(MAGGIE *starts to unbutton her blouse.* IRENE *steps in to stop her.)*

IRENE: Maggie, don't...

(IRENE *turns MAGGIE away from the others just as she is about to open her blouse.)*

IRENE: Please...don't...

(MAGGIE *stands, blouse open in front of* IRENE.)

MAGGIE: Look at me, Irene!

(CARL *moves to help* IRENE *with* MAGGIE. MAGGIE *pulls away from* IRENE, *turns and opens her blouse to her brother,* CARL.)

MAGGIE: LOOK AT ME, CARL! LOOK! This is what I look like...this is what your negligence has done...look at it...this is what you did to me...

CARL: Oh, God...no....

(CARL *retreats, turning away, unable to look any longer.* IRENE *and* GORDIE *are devastated by* MAGGIE's *accusation against* CARL. MAGGIE *sobs, and sinks down to the ground.* IRENE *kneels, holding her.*)

IRENE: Oh, Maggie...Maggie...

(MAGGIE *sits on the ground like a bewildered child looking at her hands.*)

MAGGIE: I used to have such pretty hands. Everyone said they were my best feature. Look at them now...they're almost transparent. What's happened to me?

IRENE: Maggie, we should go inside now.

MAGGIE: I don't want to die...looking like this....

(IRENE *helps* MAGGIE *to her feet, and gently guides her toward the porch.*)

IRENE: Come on, honey...let's go inside, okay? You're gonna be all right. You're just overly tired. Come on...

(*They exit into the house.*)

GORDIE: *(To* NAN*)* She's...uh...she's not well.

NAN: Maybe I should go now.

GORDIE: Yes.

(NAN *turns to* CARL, *who sits on the bench, filled with anguish.*)

NAN: I know it's not much consolation, but when I file my report, I'll make sure the state office is aware that your company is not the only one cited...pending further investigation, etcetera....

CARL: Fine.

NAN: I think...uh, maybe we better postpone the plant inspection for another day.

CARL: Yes, that would be better.

NAN: Please say goodbye to your wife for me. I wish we could have met under better circumstances. Good-bye.

(CARL *sits staring at the ground.* GORDIE *nods to* NAN, *who leaves toward the driveway side of the house.* GORDIE *crosses slowly to the cooler near the porch, he finds a beer inside, opens it, takes a long swallow. He crosses down to the picnic table, sits, slowly peels the label from the bottle. Both men lost in their own thoughts.* IRENE *enters from the screened porch.*)

IRENE: She's resting now. Poor Maggie. *(Pause)* Well, now we know, don't we?

CARL: I never meant to hurt her...I didn't want to hurt anyone...but ultimately...I did....she's right...I killed her....

(CARL *starts to break down.* IRENE *goes to him, puts her arms around him.*)

CARL: Can you ever forgive me?

IRENE: You didn't kill anyone, Carl. Not Maggie, not your father...these events were in motion long before us...no one person is totally responsible.

(CARL *recovers, wipes his eyes.*)

CARL: I should leave town.

GORDIE: *(Distant)* You leave now, they'll nail you for every barrel in that quarry. Twenty years worth.

IRENE: *(Irritated at his smugness)* Do you have a better suggestion, Gordon?

GORDIE: No...and, from now on, I would prefer to remain on the sidelines if you don't mind.

IRENE: Yes, I do mind. I would like your input!

GORDIE: Next week I'm back in New York. I can't solve this problem for you.

IRENE: We could use your emotional support.

(GORDIE *gets another beer.*)

GORDIE: To what purpose? It's finished! Why beat a dead horse?

IRENE: Tell that to Maggie! Go on...go in the house and tell your sister, that you just don't give a damn.

GORDIE: *(Exploding)* WHAT DO YOU WANT FROM ME! I called Pollard... I lied to the Sheriff...that's all I can do.

IRENE: You think because you've done your one good deed, now you're excused to run back to New York. Not this time. You are a member of the Walker family and a shareholder in the company, and it's about time you started acting like one. *(Pause)* This time next year, Maggie is not going to be here, and you owe her some of your time...now, damnit!

(GORDIE *chokes up.*)

GORDIE: I'm not strong enough to save anyone.

IRENE: None of us are strong, Gordie. We're just people trying to get by... the best we can. We're afraid too...but we want to love you Gordie, we do....

(GORDIE *breaks down and sobs.* IRENE *goes to him, stands behind where he sits, puts her hands on his shoulders very gently.* GORDIE *touches one of her hand with his own.* CARL *watches them from where he is sitting.*)

IRENE: Oh, God...we're all so fragile...

(*They all look out at the lake. They sit still, mesmerized by the water, staring transfixed on some distant point.*)

IRENE: The water is so still....

CARL: It's like sleep...you're sinking down.

GORDIE: And you never touch the bottom.

IRENE: No...never...

(*Tableaux freeze. Lights fade to black.*)

END OF PLAY

OLD SOLDIERS

OLD SOLDIERS was originally produced by Southern Illinois University in Carbondale for the American College Theater Festival. Directed by Christian H Moe, the play won the regional new play competition, and was ranked second in the national playwriting competition in 1975.

The play was later produced by the Academy Theater of Atlanta, Georgia, in 1977, and had its professional premiere in Chicago at the Performance Community in 1980.

OLD SOLDIERS premiered at the Performance Community in Chicago, 22 January 1980. The cast and creative contributors were:

McMurty . . . . Jerry R Hicks
Tom . . . . .R G Clayton
Dick . . . . .Charles Karil
Lucille Sammons . . . . Susan Boettcher

Director . . . . Byron Schaffer, Jr
Scene & lighting design . . . . Alexander Adducci
Costume designer . . . . Kevin Seligman
Sound designer . . . . John Cone
Associate director . . . . Jeff Barker

CHARACTERS & SETTING

McMURTY, *sixties, a retired veteran of the Spanish Civil War*
TOM, *seventies, a retired W W I veteran*
DICK, *seventies, TOM's friend, also a W W I veteran. A widower*
LUCILLE SAMMONS, *forties, a waitress in a tavern, McMURTY's girlfriend*

Time: November 11, 1962, 9:45 P M

for my grandfather, Barney Monroe Martin (1894-1980)

(Scene: the interior of the lobby of the St James Hotel in Chicago. The St James is one of those once elegant hotels that has lost business to motels. The clientele is now made up of old men who prefer its security to the horrors of an old folks' home.)

(It has been raining lightly for some time. A wet American flag has been hung near the doorway to dry. A banner reading "Welcome Harry!" hangs over the banister of the staircase.)

(An old record player sits on an end table near the fireplace. As the play begins, I'm Just Wild About Harry concludes on the record player. The needle on the record player fails to reject.)

(MCMURTY, a man in his late sixties, is practicing golf at an indoor putting green. The wall clock strikes the quarter hour and MCMURTY misses his putt.)

MCMURTY: Damn! Bogey five!

(He retrieves his ball and pulls several more from his pocket and drops them on the floor. He pulls out his watch and checks the time with the wall clock and sets the time on his watch. MCMURTY lines up for another putt. TOM, a man in his seventies, enters from the dining room, wiping his mouth on a napkin. He stops upstage near the end of the register desk. TOM puts the napkin in his pocket and removes a Benzedrine inhaler from another pocket and inhales deeply.)

MCMURTY: Evening, Tom.

TOM: Evening. Any calls?

MCMURTY: *(Returning to his putting.)* No.

(TOM *crosses to the record player, drawn by the sound of the needle scratching. He removes the record carefully, inspecting it closely for damage.*)

TOM: If you're going to play this record...please be careful about the needle...we can't afford to damage it anymore...this thing's an antique...been in the hotel for as long as I can remember...

MCMURTY: Sorry...I'll be more careful, Tom...

(TOM *places the record on a shelf behind the desk where it will be safe.* TOM *looks at the wall clock.*)

TOM: Is that the correct time?

MCMURTY: *(Checks his watch)* Yes. Did you have a good dinner?

TOM: *(Setting his watch)* Fine...just fine... *(Moves downstage to observe the putting)* Better score tonight?

McMurty: Forty-three on the back nine...two bogeys and a birdie so far this round. *(He moves the cup to a new position.)*

Tom: That should make it about par.

McMurty: About. *(He misses a putt.)*

Tom: One over.

McMurty: Hmph! *(He lines up for another putt.)*

Tom: Have dinner?

McMurty: No...how was it?

Tom: Potatoes were cold.

McMurty: No?

Tom: And the fish sticks were hard.

McMurty: Hard?

Tom: Overcooked.

McMurty: Sorry to hear that.

Tom: *(Sits on ottoman)* Everything they make is overcooked. Must be part of their culture. Overcook everything.

McMurty: I wouldn't know...Not as good as old Hester used to do, eh?

Tom: Not quite. I've seen many cooks come and go here...but Hester, now there was a cook. *(He uses inhaler.)*

McMurty: Shouldn't do that, bad for the nose.

Tom: Really?

McMurty: Destroys the blood vessels, hard on the liver, and can damage the brain cells. Habit forming, too.

Tom: *(Looks at inhaler)* I didn't know that.

McMurty: Benzedrine...terrible stuff. Fellows in my outfit used to chew on the cotton stuffing to get at the juice. Kept them out of their heads for hours. Give it up-you'll never make eighty if you don't.

Tom: I've already outlived you.

McMurty: Ten years.

Tom: *(Puts inhaler in ashtray)* Maybe you're right. Don't need a habit at my age.

McMurty: Of course I'm right. Worse than smoking.

(Pause)

Tom: Have you seen Dick tonight?

MCMURTY: No. *(Pause)* Didn't he have dinner with you?

TOM: Not tonight...He went up to his room after the parade, to change his clothes. I haven't seen him since...I thought maybe you had.

MCMURTY: No, sorry...perhaps, he's still in his room. Have you checked to see?

TOM: No? I'll have to do that. I'll buzz his room.

(TOM *crosses to house phone, lifts receiver.*)

MCMURTY: Heard anything from your missing friend?

TOM: Harry?... No, but he'll be in tonight. *(He replaces phone on hook.)*

MCMURTY: A damn shame he missed the parade. Very impressive. Pity there was such a small turnout.

TOM: Small! It was a disgrace. I would be ashamed to be called an American after that piddlin' display of patriotism...No, I'm almost glad Harry wasn't here to see it, he would have been ashamed.

MCMURTY: Dick could've used some help with those flags. *(Points to flags)* I think they were heavy for him. He was really draggin' when he came in here.

TOM: His heart was broken. *(Pause)* The American Legion wasn't even there!

MCMURTY: It *was* raining.

TOM: Macy's and Gimbel's never call off a parade for a sprinkle. Half of the drum section of that junior high band didn't show. Three snares, two trumpets, and a miserable piccolo!! A disgrace to the boys who served their country!

MCMURTY: There have been other wars since yours, Tom.

TOM: Only a few.

MCMURTY: Not many people around remember Armistice Day.

TOM: What do you mean? Everyone I know remembers Armistice Day. *(Proclamation)* The eleventh hour of the eleventh day of the eleventh month...

MCMURTY: How many people do you know, Tom?...Who are still alive?

TOM: I remember, Dick remembers, Harry remembers...

MCMURTY: *(Laughs)* Harry must have forgotten! Or maybe, he got too old for it, eh, Tom?

TOM: Harry'll be here! You'll see!! The three of us have made every Armistice Day reunion for forty-three years! No club, lodge, or organization in the world has an attendance record like ours.

MCMURTY: *(Laughs)* Oh, I believe you, Tom. I'm impressed.

TOM: We'll see, Mr. Bigmouth!

MCMURTY: Relax, Tom, I'm only kidding you.

TOM: Kidding!! The Armistice of the Great War is nothing to laugh about.

MCMURTY: I never said that, Tom. Aren't you being just a bit extreme?

TOM: You're damn right, we're extreme! A true patriot is always extreme.

MCMURTY: Don't take it so serious, Tom. You'll give yourself a coronary.

TOM: *(Trembling)* I've never been healthier. *(Silence)* I'll be a pallbearer at your funeral.

MCMURTY: *(Yawns)* If you say so, Tom.

TOM: *(Sneezes, goes to ashtray and retrieves inhaler, inhales deeply and sniffs.)* Harry's never been late before. *(Pause)* He's been held up or he'd be here. Prob'ly the damn trains! You miss one and you might as well pitch a tent. They don't run regular anymore. One thing you can say for Mussolini, he made the trains run on time.

(TOM *looks out the window.* MCMURTY *picks up a newspaper and ignores him.)*

TOM: With all this rain...no tellin' where he's stranded. *(Pause, then suddenly)* You don't think he's had an accident, do you?

MCMURTY: Was he driving?

TOM: No, he hates automobiles, doesn't trust the damn things.

MCMURTY: Maybe he got on the wrong train.

TOM: Harry's not blind. He's made this trip so many times, he could find his way here in the dark.

MCMURTY: *(Looks at his watch)* He's going to have to this time. It's almost ten.

TOM: *(Dials on house phone)* Dick doesn't answer.

MCMURTY: Must be asleep.

TOM: He was very tired.

MCMURTY: Why don't you leave a message in his mailbox?

TOM: No, it's not necessary. I'll let him sleep. I'll wake him when Harry arrives.

MCMURTY: Could I interest you in an after-dinner drink?

TOM: None for me. *(Sneezes. Pause)* Mr Giacconni said no drinking in the lobby.

MCCURTY: What Mr Giacconni doesn't know won't hurt him. *(Goes to the mailboxes. Removes a bottle and two glasses from one of the mail slots behind the hotel desk.)*

TOM: I don't want any. *(He sneezes.)*

MCMURTY: Of course you do. It will take care of that cold you're getting.

TOM: I don't need any liquor.

MCMURTY: Of course you do. We'll have a toast! *(Pours a drink for both of them)*

TOM: Where's Giacconni tonight?

MCMURTY: Took the night off.

TOM: What a nerve...leaving a bunch of kids in charge of this hotel. I don't like all this part-time help he brings in here. Foreigners. They steal all the silver.

MCMURTY: They're harmless.

TOM: Arabs!

MCMURTY: *(Correcting)* Iran.

TOM: He what?

MCMURTY: *(Laughs)* Iran, it's a country.

TOM: Never heard of it.

MCMURTY: It's near Saudi Arabia.

TOM: I thought so...I can always tell an Arab. They smell...like olive oil or something. *(Uses inhaler)*

MCMURTY: How can you tell what anyone smells like, you've always got Benzedrine rammed up your nose.

(TOM sneezes.)

MCMURTY: You've caught a cold marching up and down in the rain, like a fool.

TOM: *(Sneezes)* I didn't see you out there today.

MCMURTY: It wasn't my war. Go ahead, destroy your nose.

TOM: *(Using inhaler again.)* It's my nose...mind your own business! *(He steps on golf ball and almost falls.)* Would you mind picking up your damned golf balls. I could've broken my neck.

MCMURTY: *(Rolls back carpet into place and picks up golf balls.)* You know something, Tom?

TOM: What?

MCMURTY: You've become a sour old fart, lately.

(Silence)

TOM: At least I can say that I'm proud of the army I served in.

MCMURTY: What was that supposed to mean?

TOM: Exactly what I said.

MCMURTY: *(Picks up the putter threateningly.)* If you make another lousy crack about the Abraham Lincoln Brigade, I swear to God, I'll....

TOM: You'll what? You'd strike a defenseless old veteran...wouldn't you? Hit him with a club, eh?

MCMURTY: This is a putter, not a club. Don't you know anything?

TOM: Don't you dare threaten me with that *thing*...you...you...

MCMURTY: If you say communist...I'll crack your head. I warned you before Tom, the Lincoln Brigade was the finest regiment ever to fight for the cause of freedom. *(Pause)* And I wasn't drafted.

TOM: *(Snorts)* The *American* army wouldn't have had you!

MCMURTY: Always looking for a fight, aren't you?

TOM: I refuse to discuss this matter any further, Mr McMurty, act your age.

MCMURTY: *You* grow up. *(Long pause)*

TOM: I don't believe in bickering. *(Gestures toward kitchen)* It leads to disrespect. The service industries are in bad enough shape as it is.

MCMURTY: *(Pours a drink)* You make my liver inflame when you start in on that...

TOM: Sorry, I won't bring it up again.

MCMURTY: *(Hands a drink to* TOM*)* Here's to your health.

TOM: *(Reluctantly)* And yours. *(Silence. He crosses over and picks up the putter, examines it.)* Very nice. I'd like to have one like this someday.

MCMURTY: There's an interesting story behind that putter.

TOM: I know, you've told me before.

MCMURTY: It was given to me by the greatest golfer of them all, Bobby Jones...

TOM: Is that a fact?

MCMURTY: Yes, Sir! Beat him by two strokes, back in '26. Did I ever tell you about how it happened?

TOM: Yeah, several times.

MCMURTY: Hmm? Several times? I'll have to watch that.

(Silence. TOM *crosses to the window and looks to the street.)*

TOM: *(Finally, sighing.)* It's rained all day. *(Rubs leg.)* Terrible on my arthritis.

(McMURTY *pulls out watch, discovers it has stopped, squints at wall clock, but cannot see it.*)

McMURTY: What time do you have? My watch seems to have stopped.

TOM: *(Producing his watch.)* Nine fifty-five. Harry gave me this watch. Solid silver! Keeps perfect time...Even has an inscription on the back. La Belle Epoque...that's French...means "the good old days".

(McMURTY *pays no attention to* TOM. McMURTY *sets his watch*)

TOM: What did you think of dinner tonight?

McMURTY: I didn't eat.... *(Thinks)* Didn't you ask me that before?

TOM: I...I don't think so.

McMURTY: Yes...I remember...you said the potatoes were cold. *(Chuckles)* You're getting senile.

TOM: *(Irritated by his mistake)* No, it's the weather. When it rains...arthritis...acts up and...

McMURTY: *(Under his breath.)* In the brain.

TOM: *(To himself.)* I can't seem to keep my thoughts...*(Trailing off. Pause. Then, vindictive.)* Well, you'll just have to do without...they stopped serving at nine.

McMURTY: I'm having a late dinner in my room.

TOM: Are you?

McMURTY: Yes.

TOM: Alone?

McMURTY: Of course not. Mrs Sammons is joining me for dinner.

TOM: O, my God, she's not coming here tonight?

McMURTY: Yes, she is, Tom. Tuesdays and Thursdays.

TOM: You cannot have a woman in your room tonight!

McMURTY: Why not?

TOM: Because...because Harry wouldn't like it!

McMURTY: Harry isn't here.

TOM: He'll be here. And when he comes and finds out that you've got a...a...woman, up for the night...Harry will be furious...I just don't know what he might do.

McMURTY: Harry will never know. We won't make any noise.

TOM: No, I'm afraid I cannot allow it. Any other time, but not tonight. Not on our reunion.

MCMURTY: It's too late, Tom. Everything's arranged. Be reasonable.

TOM: You be reasonable. This is not going to be suitable, not one bit.

MCMURTY: Tough shit, Tom.

TOM: What?!!?

MCMURTY: You heard what I said.

TOM: You're disgusting.

MCMURTY: No, just enjoying my retirement.

(DICK *appears on the landing at the bottom of the stairs dressed in a W W I uniform with gas mask on his face and wearing a steel helmet. He stomps to attention and salutes* TOM *and* MCMURTY. DICK *mumbles something that is garbled by the mask.*)

MCMURTY: *(Laughing)* Is it another gas attack, Mr Weaver?

(DICK *crosses downstage, speech still unintelligible.*)

TOM: Take off that ridiculous gas mask. I can't understand a word you're saying.

DICK: *(Takes off mask and is without his glasses.)* Harry?

TOM: No, it's Mr McMurty.

MCMURTY: Put on your glasses, Dick.

DICK: *(He fumbles in tunic, looking for glasses.)* I heard voices, I thought maybe Harry was here.

TOM: Not yet.

MCMURTY: Tom and I were having a drink. Care to join us?

DICK: Yes, I would, thank you. You know, I fell asleep right after the parade. I thought I might lie down for a few minutes before dinner...I must have dozed off.... *(Yawns)* I suppose I missed dinner?

MCMURTY: Yes, it's after ten.

TOM: Dinner wasn't very good tonight.

DICK: Is it ever?

MCMURTY: *(Rises)* I'll see if I can find you some leftovers in the kitchen. *(Exits)*

DICK: *(Calls after him)* Bring another glass, will ya? *(Crosses over to examine flag which is drying by door)* Do you think it's dry enough to fold?

TOM: I suppose.

(TOM *crosses to* DICK. *They begin folding the flag.*)

TOM: Your uniform is wet.

DICK: I know and I slept in it, too. Hope I don't catch a cold.

TOM: I'll loan you a Benzedrine.

DICK: That would be nice.

TOM: Mrs Sammons is coming to visit McMurty again.

DICK: Really, what a pleasant surprise. I haven't seen her for some time now. Let's see...how long has it been?

TOM: Tuesday.

DICK: *(Folding the flag)* That recent?

TOM: Don't let it touch the floor.

DICK: Sorry.... You know, I like Mrs Sammons, she knows so many fine stories.

TOM: What about Harry?

DICK: Oh, dear, I forgot. He won't like it, will he?

TOM: Not at all.

DICK: What will he do?

TOM: I don't know.

(TOM *notices* MCMURTY *coming.*)

TOM: Ahem!

(MCMURTY *enters from dining room with a glass and a box of crackers.*)

MCMURTY: This was all I could find. *(Hands the crackers to* DICK.*)* The cooks said they would make you an egg.

DICK: No, thanks, crackers will be fine.

MCMURTY: Well, let me pour you a drink. *(Pours the drink and sniffs the air)* Do you smell something peculiar?

TOM: *(Points to* DICK*)* It's his uniform.

DICK: *(Sniffs his sleeve and extends it to* MCMURTY.*)* Yes, it smells like horsehair when it's damp.

MCMURTY: Whew, that's terrible! You ought to change out of those clothes before you catch pneumonia.

DICK: *(Chewing on a cracker.)* I have to be in uniform when Harry gets here.

MCMURTY: Says who?

TOM: Harry says.

DICK: It's a tradition.

MCMURTY: *(To* TOM*)* Where's your uniform?

TOM: At the cleaners.

DICK: He means they lost it at the cleaners...six years ago!

MCMURTY: Oh, that's too bad. Perhaps, you can get another one at the Army-Navy surplus store.

TOM: It wouldn't be the same thing.

DICK: Harry would never approve.

MCMURTY: *(Pause)* I'd be interested in meeting Harry. What does this Harry look like? Perhaps I've met him before. Another city maybe?

DICK: Oh, no. You've never met Harry before.

MCMURTY: How do you know?

DICK: If you had met Harry, we'd know. Harry would have told us.

MCMURTY: Oh. *(Pause)* Suppose I ran into him in the past year, before I moved here. It is possible. Maybe we sat together on a train, shared a table in a cafeteria...who knows?

TOM: It's not likely. He lives very far from here.

MCMURTY: So did I. Last year.

DICK: But you would remember if you had seen him.

TOM: Harry is the type of man you don't forget.

MCMURTY: I knew a Harry about six months ago. I was in a hospital in Kansas City...minor gallstone ailment, nothing serous. There was a fellow in the same room, the next bed, actually-undergoing exploratory surgery of... the colon, I believe. We hit if off pretty well...trading war stories and the like. He said he was in the artillery during the First World War. Served in France, somewhere around Nancy—1918.

TOM: *(Unimpressed)* Lots of people served in France.

DICK: What outfit was he in?

MCMURTY: 301st Field Artillery, I believe.

DICK: *(Sigh of relief.)* No...that's not our Harry, different regiment.

MCMURTY: Now, I could be wrong about the number of the regiment, it's been a long time. My memory isn't what it used to be. It could have been the 103rd, I'm not sure anymore.

DICK: 103rd! That's our outfit.

TOM: Easy, Dick. What did this Harry of yours look like?

MCMURTY: He was about your height, Tom.

DICK: Our Harry was much taller.

MCMURTY: Practically bald, brown eyes...medium build.

TOM: Harry has blue eyes.

DICK: And a full head of bushy blond hair.

MCMURTY: Said he was a captain in the gunnery.

DICK: A lieutenant. *(Pause)* Nope, you've got the wrong man.

MCMURTY: I guess so.

TOM: *(After a pause)* Besides, Harry has never been to Kansas City.

(Pause)

MCMURTY: Funny coincidence. *(Pause)* No matter, the wrong Harry.

DICK: What else did this Harry have to say?

MCMURTY: Nothing...Only knew him for a day or two. He died on the operating table. Never saw him again after they wheeled him into surgery.

(Long pause. TOM looks out the window, takes a large sip of his drink. DICK picks lint off the flag. DICK finally breaks the silence.)

DICK: How...how old was he?

MCMURTY: In his sixties, I imagine.

(TOM rises and crosses to window. MCMURTY tries to smooth things over.)

MCMURTY: No need to worry...There must have been hundreds of men named Harry in your outfit.

DICK: *(Pouring a drink.)* Yes...hundreds. *(Pause)* Tom tells me that your lady friend is coming this evening.

MCMURTY: *(Consults his watch)* Yes, she should be here directly.

DICK: Tom's worried about...about Harry, and how it would look with a woman here and....

MCMURTY: Doesn't like females, eh?

DICK: Who?

MCMURTY: Harry.

DICK: No, Tom. Harry was always a ladies' man.

MCMURTY: Oh.

TOM: *(Looks out the window)* Miserable weather!

McMurty: Been raining for hours...I remember a night like this in Spain.

(Tom *looks upward and shakes his head.*)

McMurty: We'd been camped in this little town for days, don't have nothin' to eat but hardtack. There was about two hundred of us and we were all hungrier than hell. There wasn't a thing to eat in all of Spain. Then, I'll be damned if a big white duck didn't fly out of the bell tower of the little church. I threw my sub-machine gun up and let'er rip. I must have been lucky cause he caught the whole damn clip. Ripped 'em from eyehole to asshole. Feathers all over the square. Before all the feathers could light, I had him plucked, spitted, and over a fire. Before I knew what was happening, there was about a hundred and fifty guys standing around watching me cook that duck. I'll never forget the hungry look on these guys' faces, you shoulda' heard the begging and pleading. And one guys said, "Listen, McMurty, if I had a duck, I'd give you half"...

Tom: *(Has had enough.)* What in the hell are you talking about?

McMurty: HMM? Huh? Oh, I'm sorry, I thought it was funny.

(Long pause)

Dick: It was raining like this the night I married my first wife...

Tom: Oh, Jesus...

Dick: Schenectady...or was it Columbus? I don't know. I spent my honeymoon in one of them.

McMurty: Which one?

Dick: My first wife.

McMurty: I know that. Which town?

Dick: I don't know. I can't remember.

Tom: Do you remember her name?

Dick: *(Slight hesitation)* Edith...Edith was my first wife. Dorothy was my second.

McMurty: Are you sure, Dick?

Dick: Of course. How could I forget something like that?

Tom: I could.

Dick: That's because you never married.

Tom: Possibly.

Dick: Were you ever married, Mr McMurty? I can't recall you mentioning anything about a wife.

McMurty: No...sorry to say I never met the right woman.

DICK: Too bad.

TOM: I don't think I'd have the patience to put up with a woman's qualms. Always sick and complaining. No. I don't think I'd enjoy that prospect. Friends are better than wives.

MCMURTY: Well...now that might be debatable.

DICK: Friends don't complain as often as wives. Believe me, I know.

TOM: I've heard you bellyache enough.

DICK: Who said I was your friend? *(Pause)* My best friend is Harry.

MCMURTY: And who is Harry's best friend?

TOM: Me, of course.

DICK: I am. Harry said he liked me the best...on several occasions.

TOM: Don't be absurd. You're a crybaby. Nobody likes crybabies.

DICK: *(Infantile)* I am not a crybaby!

TOM: Yes, you are.

DICK: I am not! I have never cried in my entire life.

(MMMURTY *finds this very amusing.*)

TOM: Yes, you have. I've seen it.

DICK: When?

TOM: St Remy. November the 11th, 1918, at eleven o'clock in the morning. You cried at your post. Standing next to a howitzer with a shell cradled in your arms...tears were streamin down your face. You looked like a pathetic puppy.

DICK: *(Protesting)* THE WAR WAS OVER!

TOM: You looked ridiculous. Holding a shell like it was a loaf of bread... it was weak.

DICK: Everybody cries when a war is over!

TOM: I didn't.

DICK: Well...you have no feelings. You're...you're...malignant!

TOM: What's that supposed to mean?

DICK: *(Laughing)* Ha. Ha. Really caught you with that one.

(TOM *looks to* MCMURTY *to see if a joke has passsed that all but* DICK *have missed.* MCMURTY *shrugs.*)

TOM: *(To* MCMURTY*)* What does he mean?

McMURTY: Dunno. It was a rather strange choice of words, I must say. *(He chuckles. To* DICK*)* Haven't heard that one in a long time.

(Long pause)

TOM: *(Confused)* Well...at least I'm not a namby-pamby!

DICK: Namby-pamby! *(Howls)* Oh, that's good! Baby talk! Ha. Ha.

TOM: That wasn't funny. *(Turns to* MCMURTY*)* Did I say something funny?

McMURTY: *(Laughs)* No.

TOM: *(To* DICK*)* You're getting drunk. He gets like this every time he drinks...makes an incredible ass of himself. *(Agitated)* Where's Harry? *(Pause. Pours a drink)* It's getting late.

DICK: Maybe he's not coming this year.

TOM: *(Gives* DICK *an icy stare)* We'll see.

(Long pause)

DICK: I saw Tom cry once.

TOM: You never! When?

DICK: At Coetquidan. *(To* MCMURTY*)* It was during a gas attack. *(To* TOM*)* You didn't get your mask on in time.

TOM: It was the gas...I didn't cry.

DICK: Tears were in your eyes.

TOM: My eyes were watering from the gas.

DICK: They were tears...all the same.

TOM: Doesn't count. Only cowards cry...people who are afraid of life.

DICK: Something they're ashamed of?

TOM: What are you getting at?

DICK: Oh, nothing, Tom.

TOM: *(To* DICK.*)* Don't say anything you'll regret later.

DICK: *(Nervously changes the subject. To* MCMURTY*)* What about you? Do you cry?

McMURTY: Not often...on certain occasions...if something moves me... a sad movie, a lost love...

TOM: I never knew you were in love.

McMURTY: Oh, yes...many times when I was young. *(Pause)* There was a girl in Pittsburgh during the war...

DICK: Which war?

MCMURTY: The second.

DICK: *(Disappointed)* Oh.

MCMURTY: Her name was Katherine, a dancer. She worked in a canteen for the U S O...one of those dime-a-dance places. She wanted to be a famous ballerina someday...*(Pause)* She was very beautiful, long gorgeous legs. *(Sighs)* A wonderful girl...I never knew anyone who enjoyed life so much. We used to visit museums when she wasn't working...museums and of course, the ballet. We were very happy and very much in love. Three months later she met a sailor. He promised to take her to New York... bright lights, Broadway...they were married within a week. Shortly afterwards her sailor was shipped out. Guadalcanal. He never returned. Katherine left Chicago...moved to California. We used to write to each other for a while. Then one day there were no more letters. I never saw her again. *(Pause)* C'est la vie!

DICK: *(Visibly moved)* That is such a sad story. You never tried to find her again?

MCMURTY: No.

TOM: Too bad. What about Mrs. Sammons? Do you love her?

DICK: What a terrible thing to ask!

TOM: *(Gleeful malice)* If you got married, you would have to move out of the hotel. Mr Giacconni doesn't rent to couples.

(Phone rings. TOM *and* DICK *rise.)*

TOM: Harry!

DICK: *(Moves quickly toward the phone)* I'll get it.

TOM: *(Beats* DICK *to the phone)* I've got it. *(Lifts receiver)* Hello, Harry? *(Pause)* Who?

DICK: Is it Harry?

TOM: *(Shoos* DICK *away)* Yes, he is. Just a moment, please. *(To* MCMURTY*)* It's for you.

DICK: *(Disappointed)* It wasn't Harry.

MCMURTY: *(Crosses to phone and takes receiver.)* Thank you. Hello? Yes. I've been worried. You said an hour ago. I see. Of course, dear.

(MCMURTY *turns his back so that the rest of the conversation cannot be heard.* TOM *and* DICK *move away.)*

TOM: It's that damn woman.

DICK: Mrs Sammons?

TOM: *(Nods. Pours another drink)* When that woman gets here...don't mention anything about Harry.

(MMMURTY *hangs up the phone and crosses back to them.*)

TOM: You keep your mouth shut in front of Mrs Sammons, understand?

DICK: All right.

MCMURTY: I'm afraid you gentlemen will have to excuse me. *(Picks up the putter)* I must change into something more suitable for dinner.

DICK: Mrs Sammons is coming?

MCMURTY: Yes, and I must get changed...she'll be here shortly. Seems they're having some kind of trouble at the club tonight.

TOM: Is that so?

DICK: What kind of trouble?

MCMURTY: I dunno. She didn't say. Well, gentlemen, talking with you has been a pleasure...it's been stimulating as usual. *(Picks up the whiskey bottle)* If you don't mind, we'll be needing this. I'm sure you can find another bottle in the kitchen. I hope your friend Harry arrives. Look forward to meeting him.

DICK: Yes, in the morning, Mr McMurty. You can count on it.

MCMURTY: Yes...well, until morning...good evening!

TOM: Evening.

DICK: Have a jolly time.

MCMURTY: You, too. *(Pause. Confidential)* Oh, say listen, when Mrs Sammons arrives, you'll send her up to my room, O K?

DICK: We'll do that. Good night.

MCMURTY: Have a nice reunion. 'Night. *(Exits up the stairs)*

DICK: Well, that was abrupt.

TOM: *(Sulking)* Ignoramus!

DICK: Who? McMurty?

TOM: Yes, that stupid Irish mick, McMurty!

DICK: SSSH! He'll hear you.

TOM: Who cares? *(Pause, then contemptuously)* A ballerina! I bet he's never even been to Pittsburgh. *(Pause)* I'll bet he never met Bobby Jones, either.

DICK: I wouldn't be surprised. *(Pause)* Who is Bobby Jones?

TOM: A baseball player.

DICK: Oh. Never heard of him. I think I'll have another whiskey.

TOM: He took the bottle with him.

DICK: *(Notices TOM's full glass)* Where did you get that?

TOM: I refilled before he left. You've got to look out for yourself when an Irishman is near a bottle of whiskey.

DICK: *(Starts for the dining room)* I'll see if there's another bottle in the pantry.

(DICK *exits.* TOM *takes out inhaler again. He paces around the room and sits in an easy chair. He rises and pulls a golf ball out of the cushion, tosses the ball behind the sofa. He rises and crosses to the desk. He goes behind register and looks through the contents of the various mailboxes. He finds an apple, puts it in his coat pocket.* TOM *reads a postcard. He hears steps approaching.* TOM *pockets the postcard. He crosses back to the easy chair sipping his drink.* DICK *enters carrying a bottle of cooking sherry.)*

DICK: *(Looking at wall clock. Shakes his head)* It's getting late.

TOM: What have you got in that bottle?

DICK: Cooking sherry.

TOM: Ugh! You're not going to drink it?

DICK: All there was...cupboard's bare.

TOM: There was a bottle of Scotch in there three days ago.

DICK: *(Pours a drink)* Perhaps McMurty drank it.

TOM: Scotch isn't his drink. I wonder what could have happened to it?

DICK: *(Sits on couch, pulls out a golf ball)* Is this yours?

TOM: No. I've been sitting on them all night.

(DICK *pockets the ball.)*

TOM: I bet those Arabs know what happened to that fifth of Scotch I placed in the pantry last week.

DICK: I'll go ask them...

TOM: Don't bother...they'll lie to you...There was a full bottle in there three days ago. One of those miserable bastards unlocked the cabinet for me... He was standing right next to me when I locked it up. *(Mutters)* Every time trouble comes their way, they put on the dumb show...pretend they can't understand English.

DICK: You think one of the kitchen staff drank it?

TOM: Who else?

DICK: Not me.

TOM: Can't trust immigrants for a minute. Everything disappears around here now. *(Pause)* I left my razor on the sink one morning. When I came back twenty minutes later, it was gone. Now who would steal someone else's razor? It's unsanitary. It's like wearing someone else's underwear.

DICK: I don't know. Who would?

TOM: What were they doing when you went into the kitchen?

DICK: Washing dishes.

TOM: Probably loading up their pockets with silverware and salt shakers. Believe me, I've seen it happen. When I was down in Miami a few years ago, when they started to let Cubans in-those greasers took all the jobs away from the coloreds. Cubans the reason we got so many coloreds on welfare.

DICK: Is that so?

TOM: And all the time those Cubans were stealing anything they could get their hands on. You had to nail everything down. I've seen 'em taking the plumbing out of a men's room.

DICK: It's a dirty shame.

TOM: You damn well better believe it. Foreigners are the death of the service industries. *(He runs his hand along the top of the fireplace mantle.)* You don't have to look far to see that.

DICK: Used to be a man took pride in his job...not anymore, nope.

TOM: They're having a terrible time with 'em over in England.

DICK: Who?

TOM: Those Pakis, that's who.

DICK: Pakis?

TOM: Pakistanis...They got 'em all over the place in England.

DICK: Coming out of the woodwork, eh?

TOM: By the thousands...every day! Most of them can't read or write... can't get decent work...rapists, killers, all sorts. None of them speak a word of English, they say. Dirtiest people in the world. Never take a bath.

DICK: I thought that was the Chinese.

TOM: The what?

DICK: Chinese! It's the Chinks that never bathe.

TOM: *(Guffaws)* Shows how much you know.

DICK: It's true. I read it somewhere...I know I did.

TOM: Where?...Where did you read such nonsense?

(Pause)

DICK: I can't remember.... But, I did read it. It said the Chinese were the dirtiest people on earth!

TOM: Bull!

DICK: Maybe it was the Japanese...

TOM: You didn't read that. You made it up. Ask Harry when he gets here. He'll know. *(Pause)* Next you'll be telling me that some Chinaman invented gunpowder.

DICK: I read that, too...the same article.

TOM: *(Swings at DICK)* You idiot! That's a myth. Everyone knows the English invented gunpowder...1066, I believe. *(Long silence)* Look it up if you don't believe me.

DICK: I believe you.

(The front door opens. LUCILLE SAMMONS enters. She is a heavy-set, middle-aged woman with frosted hair-do. She wears a plastic raincoat, galoshes, and carries a bucket of Kentucky Fried Chicken.)

LUCILLE: *(Shaking her raincoat.)* Ooh! That weather...it's miserable. How are you boys, tonight?

DICK: Just fine, Mrs. Sammons. How are you?

TOM: Fine.

LUCILLE: *(Removing galoshes.)* What a night! I thought I'd never get out.

DICK: Exciting night at the club?

LUCILLE: You'll never believe what happened.

DICK: Here, let me hang up that raincoat by the radiator. Tell us all about it.

LUCILLE: It was just unbelievable. There was a brawl right there in the lounge. Two fellows got into it at the bar...turned over tables, throwing glasses...they smashed the glass onto the jukebox.

DICK: Amazing! What started it?

LUCILLE: Oh, who knows? Probably fighting over some woman.

TOM: It figures.

DICK: I hope you weren't hurt.

LUCILLE: Not me. I stayed out of it. When two drunks get going at each other...I know enough to stay put...don't get involved. Brother, what a mess they made. We had to close early. It took until a half-hour ago just to sweep up the glass.

DICK: Tsk, tsk...terrible business.

LUCILLE: Whew, what a night! Any excitement around here this evening?

TOM: We were having an after-dinner drink with Mr McMurty before you arrived.

DICK: It was after your dinner, not mine.

TOM: He slept through dinner again...second time this week.

DICK: I can't help it. I get tired easily these days.

LUCILLE: Poor thing. *(She hands bucket of chicken to* DICK.*)* Have a piece of fried chicken.

DICK: Oh, no, I couldn't, Mrs. Sammons...it's your dinner.

LUCILLE: Call me Lucille. Go on, I've got plenty. Mac never eats more than a wing or two.

DICK: *(Taking a piece)* Thank you.

(LUCILLE *sits on one of the easy chairs, rises and extracts a golf ball from under the cushion.*)

LUCILLE: *(Holding the ball)* What in hell...

TOM: One of McMurty's toys...he's got them all over the hotel.

LUCILLE: *(Putting the ball in an ashtray)* Damn fool. Someone could hurt himself. How is Mac this evening, feeling well?

DICK: He looked O K to me.

LUCILLE: I worry about him. He drinks too much. Have two pieces, Dick. Go on. How about you, Tom? *(Offers the bucket)* Chicken?

TOM: No, thank you. I've already eaten.

(LUCILLE *takes a piece of chicken.*)

DICK: Umm. This is marvelous.

LUCILLE: It is quite good.

DICK: I was starved. I haven't been this hungry since we were in France.

LUCILLE: In France?

TOM: During the war.

LUCILLE: You were in France? "Oh, how lovely."

TOM: It wasn't so lovely then...there was a war going on.

LUCILLE: No, I guess it wouldn't be so much fun during a war. *(Sighs)* Paris in the spring. I've never been to Europe, but someday I'm going. Morty has been promising to take me to France for years...the bum, he never makes enough money...at least, that's what he says. "Next year we'll go," he says,

"Next year." When next year finally rolls around: one weekend fishing in the Ozarks.

TOM: Morty?

LUCILLE: My husband. *(Pause)* I should say my former husband...We separated...temporarily.

DICK: Oh, that's too bad.

TOM: Hmm, I thought you were a widow.

LUCILLE: No such luck. Never happen to this girl. If he ever did kick off... I'd end up with a pile of dough.... Then I could travel.... Ha! Fat chance. Instead I end up working six nights a week slopping tables in a crummy bar, dodging the gooses of dirty old men. No offense, boys!

DICK: We don't mind, do we, Tom?

TOM: No. *(Pause)* I don't pinch waitresses.

LUCILLE: *(To* TOM*)* Whatever gave you the idea that I was a widow? *(Laughs)* I better change my wardrobe. I didn't know that I looked like I was in mourning.

DICK: Earlier tonight he thought Mr McMurty had never been in love. Can you imagine that? *(To* TOM*)* But he set you straight didn't he? *(To* LUCILLE*)* Told us all about an old flame, a ballerina in Pittsburgh during the war...such a sad story... *(Realizes he has said the wrong thing.)* Ooops, I shouldn't have said that.

TOM: You always find a way to put your foot in your mouth, don't you?

DICK: Please don't tell him I said anything...

TOM: See the mess you've gotten yourself into this time. Big mouth?

LUCILLE: Don't worry. I don't care anything about other women Mac has known. Ancient history.

DICK: Are you sure?

LUCILLE: *(A lie)* Doesn't bother me a bit.

DICK: Whew, that's a relief. *(Trying to smooth things over)* Why don't you have a drink with us, Mrs Sammons.

LUCILLE: Why, thank you. You boys shouldn't be drinking in the lobby. You know what will happen if you get caught.

DICK: Giacconni's not here tonight.

TOM: Anyway, it's a special occasion.

LUCILLE: Really? What?

TOM: Don't you know what day this is?

LUCILLE: *(Thinks)* Uhh...November the 11th. *(Pause)* So? What's so special about today?

TOM: The Armistice!

LUCILLE: Huh?

DICK: World War I. It was over today. Forty-three years ago.

LUCILLE: Oh?...So, that's why you're wearing the costume!

TOM: COSTUME!

LUCILLE: I wondered...I thought it was a masonic lodge outfit or something.

DICK: *(Hurt)* This was my uniform. *(Pause. Sad)* We had a parade.

LUCILLE: *(She pats DICK's arm.)* I'm sorry, Dick. I didn't know. *(Pause)* Well, World War I was a bit before my time...but, just the same...let me propose a toast to two of the finest old gentlemen I have ever had the privilege of meeting.

DICK: That was very kind of you.

LUCILLE: To your health! *(She drinks and gags.)* God, what is that awful concoction?

DICK: Cooking sherry.

TOM: We did have some whiskey, but Mr McMurty took the bottle for your dinner party.

LUCILLE: Why, that conniving old bastard! Leaving you boys with cooking sherry to celebrate your holiday...Wait until I get hold of him...I'll give him...

TOM: It's all right, Mrs. Sammons. We'll manage.

LUCILLE: Will you stop being so formal, Tom? Call me Lucille. *(She begins to rummage in her purse.)* I just happen to have a little something with me. *(She pulls out a pint of vodka.)* One of the fringe benefits of working in a tavern.

DICK: Oh, you really shouldn't go to the trouble.

LUCILLE: *(Taking their glasses.)* Nonsense. If you're going to have a toast, it must be done properly. An important occasion like...Armistice Day certainly deserves a more civilized oil than this. *(She looks around for a place to dump the glasses of sherry.)* Now where can I dump this drink? *(She crosses to the potted plant.)* This will do. *(She pours the sherry into the plant.)*

TOM: Oh, no...not there, please!

LUCILLE: Don't fret, Tom...it will do that plant a world of good. *(She pours vodka into their glasses.)* Hope you don't mind vodka.

DICK: Vodka is fine.

LUCILLE: *(She hands them their drinks.)* Here you go... Now, let's try that again. To the Armistice!

TOM & DICK: To the Armistice!

(They clink their glasses together in a silent toast. TOM and DICK sip their drinks. LUCILLE leans against the fireplace mantel and drains her glass in one long swallow. She sets the glass down hard on the mantel.)

LUCILLE: Ahh, much better. *(Sighs)* Well, why don't you tell me all about the war.

DICK: Everything?

LUCILLE: Sure, why not? How many Germans did you kill? *(Pause)* It was the Germans we fought in that war?

TOM: Yes...and the Austrians.

LUCILLE: I remember..."Kick the Kaiser!" Right? Well, how many did you get?

DICK: I don't actually know. I never counted.

TOM: We were too far away to see what we were shooting.

DICK: The artillery...you know, big cannons.

TOM: *(He points to DICK's shoulder insignia.)* The 103rd Field Artillery, 26th Division. We fought on the Hindenburg Line.

DICK: Tom and I fired a howitzer. Couldn't see where the shells landed. When we went through a village and saw the rubble, only then did we know if we ever hit anything. *(Pause)* Of course, it could have been German shells. No way of telling. *(Pause)* The only Germans I saw were dead or prisoners.

LUCILLE: Sounds fascinating.

DICK: Actually it was pretty boring...loading a howitzer gets to be a routine job after awhile.

LUCILLE: I'll bet both of you were decorated as heroes.

TOM: I didn't get any medals.

DICK: Me either. *(Pauses)* Harry was the only one that got a medal.

TOM: *(To DICK, vindictive)* I warned you not to say...

DICK: I forgot.

LUCILLE: Who's Harry?

TOM: Harry Palmer. Our buddy during the war. He's coming here tonight for our reunion. Harry comes every Armistice Day...it's a tradition.

DICK: But he's late this year. Very late.

(TOM *gives him a look as if to suggest he be silent.*)

LUCILLE: How nice to have a good friend for such a long time. I hope he arrives in time for your party.

TOM: Harry missed the parade, but he'll be here before morning.

LUCILLE: So...Harry was a hero?

DICK: Yes, wounded many times...a real soldier.

LUCILLE: Were you wounded, Tom?

TOM: No. I made it through without a scratch.

DICK: I dropped a shell casing on my foot once. Almost got tetanus. (*Pause*) Tom had dysentery.

TOM: I did not.

DICK: Yes, you did. After you ate some French bread.

TOM: (*Correcting*) I was sick...but, I did not have dysentery.

DICK: He's being brave, but believe me, you never saw anyone so sick in your life.

LUCILLE: How awful! What happened?

TOM: Oh, those miserable Frenchmen. Some idea of a practical joke on the American liberators. It makes me furious to think about it. We entered this deserted town after a week of shelling.

DICK: Lamarche-en-Woerve.

TOM: Yes...Lamarche-en-Woerve. I'll never forget that rotten hole. We were looking for food, so we went into this deserted French bakery...I took a loaf of bread and some wine. There was no one around...so, we sat on a curb under a street lamp and began eating.

DICK: And then Tom turns to me after he finished half a loaf and says to me, "This bread tastes funny..."

TOM: I should have noticed it earlier...but, I was too hungry at the time.

DICK: So, Tom cracks open his loaf of bread, and sure enough, there was a core of horse shit right down the center of the loaf.

TOM: Those bastards baked it right into the bread.

DICK: He thinks they did it on purpose. I'm sure it was an accident. The bakery was next door to a stable.

TOM: Accidents like that don't happen. I know it.

(LUCILLE *starts giggling.*)

TOM: The Frogs were laying for us. *(Pause)* Don't tell me the dung just walked into that bakery and jumped into the oven. Someone put it there, dammit!

(DICK *and* LUCILLE *are laughing.*)

DICK: There wasn't any in my loaf.

TOM: Go on, laugh. It wasn't funny...not one bit. I nearly puked my guts out.

DICK: *(Laughing)* A pretty good way to catch a thief when the baker is away.

TOM: Very funny. If I ever catch the Frenchy that did that, I'll....

DICK: And ever since that night...Tom refuses to eat another piece of French bread.

(DICK *and* LUCILLE *howl.*)

TOM: Shut up, both of you! It wasn't funny.

(DICK *and* LUCILLE *try to stop laughing, but can't.* TOM *turns to* DICK.)

TOM: I'm going to punch you in the mouth if you don't stop laughing.

LUCILLE: I'm sorry, Tom. I just got tickled.

TOM: *(Snorts)* Hmpf.

LUCILLE: Don't sulk. We're laughing at the story, not you.

TOM: We'll see. *(To* DICK*)* Just you wait, big mouth!

DICK: You told the story!

TOM: Who brought it up?

(Silence. TOM *uses the inhaler.)*

DICK: You shouldn't do that.

TOM: *(Throwing the inhaler)* Why is everybody so damned concerned about my nose?

(Silence. TOM *sits sulking. All are quiet.* LUCILLE *dries away tears.* DICK *drinks quietly. Suddenly* LUCILLE *snickers and she and* DICK *break up again.)*

TOM: *(Furious)* All right, DAMMIT! ENOUGH!

(All sit quietly again. TOM *closes his eyes.* LUCILLE *tries desperately to subdue her chuckles. No sound.* DICK *and* LUCILLE *shake occasionally as they try to hold it in. A smile will break out from time to time.* TOM *is looking for revenge, finally he opens his watch and speaks.)*

TOM: I think you are going to be late for your dinner, Mrs Sammons. I'm sure Mr McMurty has heard you *cackling* down here and probably wonders what...

DICK: Tom! Don't be rude!

LUCILLE: That's all right, Dick. I can take a hint...The chicken is getting cold. *(Rises)* I'd better go.

DICK: Not until Tom apologizes. Well, Tom...

LUCILLE: Forget it. It's not important. Tom's right...I've overstayed my welcome.

DICK: Sometimes Tom can be so rude. He doesn't mean it.... He doesn't know what he's saying sometimes....

TOM: Oh, yes, I do.

LUCILLE: No explanations necessary. Well...see you later, gentlemen.

DICK: *(He hands the vodka bottle to her.)* Don't forget your bottle.

LUCILLE: You keep it. *(Pause)* It's a party!

(TOM *stares out the window.*)

DICK: Good night.

(LUCILLE *starts up the stairs.*)

DICK: I want to apologize for Tom since he won't do it himself.

LUCILLE: *(Without looking back.)* I've forgotten it.

(LUCILLE *is gone. Silence.* DICK *turns from the staircase and crosses down to* TOM.)

DICK: That was vicious and cruel!

TOM: She deserved it! *(Turns)* And you deserve a swift kick in the ass!

DICK: You have no concern for other people's feelings. You never think of anyone but yourself. You're a selfish bully! *(Pause)* Sometimes I wonder why I stay with you.

TOM: You are a simpering brat! No one else would put up with you. If you were half as concerned about Harry as you are about that whore's fried chicken...

DICK: Mrs Sammons is not a whore!

TOM: Oh! What do you think they do up there two nights a week?

DICK: They have dinner and talk...and she reads to him. I know, I've heard them.

TOM: Naive.

DICK: Well, so what if they do sleep together. Is it any of your business? They're in love.

TOM: *(Chokes)* Love! Is that what you call it? At McMurty's age, it's...disgusting!

DICK: Everything is disgusting to you. Who do you think you are? *(Pause)* Well...to me, you're disgusting.

(A scream is heard from upstairs.)

DICK: What was that?

TOM: *(Sarcastic)* Love.

DICK: Tom, if you don't apologize to Mrs Sammons, I'll... *(Bravely)* I'll move out of this hotel. Tonight! I swear it, I'll leave.

TOM: No, you won't. You've got no place to go.

DICK: I'm serious. *(Pause)* I'll move out tonight.

TOM: *(Laughs)* Ha, ha! Why don't you move in with Harry...that would be a good one.

(LUCILLE *appears on the landing of the stairs. She is shaking. Tears are on her cheeks. She moves slowly to the banister, staring vacantly.)*

TOM: Something wrong, Lucille?

LUCILLE: *(Hesitant)* Mr McMurty...is...dead!

DICK: Oh, my God! *(He slumps on the foot of the stairs.)*

TOM: *(Recites)*
In Flanders Fields the poppies blow.
Between the crosses, row on row.
That mark our place; and in the sky
The larks, still bravely singing, fly
Scarce heard amid the guns below.

(DICK *sits with his head in his hands, muttering to himself.* TOM *continues to recite* Flanders Field.)

TOM: We are the dead. Short days ago
We lived, felt dawn, now sunset glow,
Loved and were loved, and now we lie in
Flanders Fields.

LUCILLE: *(Hysterical)* There is a man dead upstairs and all you can do is recite poetry! WILL SOMEBODY PLEASE DO SOMETHING!

(No one moves. Pause)

TOM: What would you suggest, Lucille?

LUCILLE: Call an ambulance, dammit!

(Pause)

TOM: What for?

DICK: *(Mumbling to himself)* Oh, dear, oh, dear.

LUCILLE: *(To* TOM*)* What did you say?

TOM: *(Slow and deliberate)* I said...what for? He's dead isn't he? Why would he need an ambulance? A coroner would be more appropriate.

LUCILLE: You're an animal.

TOM: SLUT!

DICK: Tom...don't...

TOM: *(To* DICK*)* You stay out of this!

LUCILLE: If you're looking to tangle with me...

TOM: I wouldn't waste my time. *(He starts for the stairs.)* If you'll excuse me, now...I'm going to see if I can find my bottle of Scotch.

LUCILLE: *(Grabbing* TOM *by the arm.)* WHERE DO YOU THINK YOU'RE GOING?

TOM: Upstairs. *(Pause)* Take your hand off my arm, before I kick your teeth in.

LUCILLE: *(Releasing her grip)* You stay out of his room!

TOM: Believe me, I won't go near him. *(He goes upstairs.)*

DICK: I'm really sorry, Lucille. *(No response.)* I can't understand it. He seemed so healthy a few minutes ago...Must have been a heart attack... you never know.

(LUCILLE *lights a cigarette and stares out the window on the front door ignoring* DICK.*)*

DICK: What are you going to do now?

LUCILLE: I don't know...*(Long pause. She wipes away a tear)* Dammit!

DICK: Is there anything I can do?

LUCILLE: No...thanks. I'll be all right. *(Pause)* Damn him! I knew this would happen. That old bastard would never listen to me...I told him not to drink... but would he listen? Oh, no...even the doctors warned...but he never paid any attention. Mac never listened to anyone. He knew whiskey would kill him. How the hell can someone destroy themselves that way? It doesn't make any sense...Well, I hope he's happy...if he wanted to die that badly... I hope he's got what he wanted now! Jesus!

DICK: Lucille...before Tom comes back...I want to say one thing. Tom doesn't mean to say the things he does...I know, deep inside he cares a great deal about Mac....

LUCILLE: DAMMIT! Will you stop apologizing, Dick! Why do you have to be sorry for everything that happens?

DICK: But, you've got to understand about him...

LUCILLE: Oh, for Christ's sake! What is there to understand?

DICK: He doesn't mean everything he says.

LUCILLE: Oh, yes, he does! That son-of-a-bitch means every word that comes out of his mouth. Stop pretending that Tom is a nice guy, because he's not.

DICK: He's my friend.

LUCILLE: And you don't need to apologize for your friends. Tom is old enough to look out for himself.

DICK: Lucille...you don't understand...he needs me here...

LUCILLE: What for? His "yes" man?

DICK: No...

LUCILLE: What does he give you in return?

DICK: Companionship.

LUCILLE: That kind of companionship you don't need. What about your other friend?... What's his name?...Harry. Why don't you live with him? Certainly it would be better for you...

DICK: I can't...that's not possible.

LUCILLE: Why not?

(TOM *comes down the stairs with a bottle of whiskey.*)

DICK: *(He notices* TOM, *whereas* LUCILLE *does not.)* I...I can't tell you. I don't want to talk about it right now....

LUCILLE: *(She notices* TOM, *to* DICK.*)* Why don't you want to talk about it? What are you afraid of?

TOM: Leave him alone! He doesn't want to talk about Harry because I told him not to.... *(He crosses to table and pours a drink.)*

LUCILLE: Let Dick make his own decisions. Stop trying to run his life!

TOM: *(To* DICK*)* What did you tell her?

DICK: Nothing.

TOM: Your big mouth is going to get you into trouble.

(TOM *holds* DICK *by the sleeve.*)

DICK: *(Pulling away)* Stop threatening me! I didn't tell her anything...

LUCILLE: *(Noticing the bottle for the first time)* Where did you get that bottle?

TOM: On the nightstand in McMurty's room.

LUCILLE: I TOLD YOU NOT TO GO IN THERE!

TOM: Madame, I live in this hotel, not you. I'll go anywhere I damn well please.

LUCILLE: Don't you have any respect for anything?

DICK: Tom. This time you've gone too far.

TOM: *(To the room in general)* When I was in France during the war, and a solider died next to me in a trench...we didn't have time for burials and eulogies over the dead...just a quick prayer, then we took the dog tags, cigarettes, food, dry socks and anything else he wouldn't need...You'll do anything, and I mean anything to stay alive just one more day. *(He picks up MCMURTY's putter.)*

DICK: *(A devastating blow)* Even strip the clothing...

TOM: *(A warning to DICK)* War is war!

DICK: That's no excuse...There isn't any more war, TOM!

TOM: Yes, that's one of the problems in this country today...a good war, with trenches and gas would straighten out these jellybellies damn quick!

LUCILLE: *(Quietly, but with intense emotion.)* A man that I loved and respected is dead...and he is going to be given a decent burial. I will not allow his body to be picked over by vultures. *(To TOM)* Take your filthy hands off that putter.

TOM: *(Holding it away from her)* Mac promised this putter to me when he was gone...I'm claiming it now. *(To DICK)* You had better get your claim in now before she tries to pick the hotel clean...

DICK: *(Angry)* This is not time to argue about possessions. *(To LUCILLE)* We had better call someone....

(Pause)

TOM: *(Nonchalantly examining the putter)* I thought Mac looked very peaceful when I was up there...a little pale, but very peaceful. *(To LUCILLE)* Did you know that this putter was given to him by Bobby Jones? Did you know that?

DICK: Tom...How can you behave this way?

TOM: It's easy...Just watch me, and learn. You should know, BIG MOUTH. Just had to mention him, didn't you? Couldn't you have waited...oh, no...

(LUCILLE crosses to desk phone, lifts receiver and dials. TOM notices her suddenly.)

TOM: What do you think you're doing?

LUCILLE: Calling the police.

(TOM slams the head of the putter near the phone, narrowly missing LUCILLE's hand.)

TOM: No, you're not! Get away from that phone. *(He rips the cord out of the wall.)*

DICK: TOM*!*

LUCILLE: *(Frightened)* You could have killed me with that thing!

TOM: This is not a matter for the police.

(DICK *starts to protest, but is silenced by* TOM.)

TOM: You stay out of this!

LUCILLE: Put that club down, or so help me...

DICK: No. I will not stay out of this.

(TOM *raises the putter like a weapon.* DICK *and* LUCILLE *freeze.*)

TOM: SHUT UP! Both of you. *(Pause)* Now...very calmly...now, we are going to sit down quietly like civilized human beings and talk this out...SIT!

(They reluctantly sit.)

LUCILLE: You're insane!

TOM: QUIET! *(He relaxes somewhat.)* First, is the matter of claim on the deceased's possessions, notification of the next of kin and the proper authorities...Care for a drink? No? Well, when Harry gets here, he'll decide how to settle this affair. Harry is an expert in the matter of property settlements...He was once a lawyer before he retired...

LUCILLE: You're...a lunatic!

(DICK *rises.*)

TOM: I told you to sit down.

DICK: Put that golf club down, Tom.

LUCILLE: Be careful, Dick!

DICK: I'm not afraid of you. *(To* LUCILLE*)* He won't hurt you. *(He starts wearily for the stairs.)*

TOM: Dick, don't try to sneak off. *(Panic)* Where are you going?

DICK: I've had enough, Tom...I told you I was leaving...I'll pack a suitcase...and send for the rest of my things in the morning.

TOM: You are not going anywhere...Not until Harry arrives!

LUCILLE: *(To* DICK*)* Is there another phone around here?

TOM: *(Almost pleading.)* What is Harry going to think?

DICK: *(To* LUCILLE*)* There's a pay phone on the corner at the drugstore. I'll get my coat.

(LUCILLE *rises carefully, moves around* TOM *toward the door.*)

LUCILLE: I'm leaving, now, Tom. Understand? Don't you dare try to stop me... Are you coming with me, Dick?

DICK: Yes.

TOM: *(Blocking* DICK's *way)* No, he's not going anywhere.

DICK: Get out of my way, Tom.

TOM: You can't leave...You're not going with her.

DICK: Yes...yes, I am. You are not going to tell me what to do...or what to think, no more...It's over.

TOM: *(Defensively)* Harry will be furious if you're not here.

DICK: *(Crying)* Dammit, Tom, will you stop. There isn't going to be any Harry...

TOM: Harry will be here.

LUCILLE: I'm leaving. Dick, if you're going with me...

DICK: *(A realization that he must destroy* TOM *in order to save him.)* Lucille... stay for a few minutes...there's something I want you to hear.

TOM: *(Afraid of what is to follow)* NO!

DICK: Tom, it's over. Harry is not coming this year. Harry is not going to be here, like he wasn't here last year...or the year before...Harry is dead!

TOM: NO! HE'S ALIVE!

(Pause)

DICK: You took the gloves off his body at Coetquidan. You broke his frozen fingers to get get the gloves off his hands.... Remember?

TOM: No...it's not true. The face and chest were blown away...There were no dog tags...some unidentified doughboy...He escaped! Remember...I saw him in Paris riding in an automobile after the Armistice...and that time on the train outside London... It was Harry!

DICK: Someone who looked like Harry.

TOM: You can't say that.

DICK: *(Mainly to* LUCILLE*)* Harry died at Coetquidan in 1918 before the Armistice...

TOM: No, he did not.

DICK: And...we're responsible for the way he died.

TOM: This is not the truth!

DICK: Yes, it is! Shut up, Tom! I'm going to say it...the way it really happened....

(TOM *is crushed. Pause*)

DICK: It was a winter night, during heavy artillery barrage...Tom and I were pinned down in a trench...and near the barbed wire, about fifty feet away in another trench, was a wounded soldier...Harry! He was calling to us... he cried for help for almost an hour.

TOM: Pah! The oldest trick in the book. All the Germans used it...they all spoke English. They were trying to trick us...they call for help and when you stick your head out you get shot!

DICK: This was no German. It was Harry...I was going to crawl to him, but Tom wouldn't let me go. Tom said it was a German...and then... he threw a grenade into the other trench...and everything was silent. No more cries for help... It was Harry...calling to us...

TOM: We don't know that!

DICK: After the barrage...we crawled to the other trench and then we saw the uniform...it was one of our boys...The face was gone...we were freezing... we took the gloves and boots...so we could stay alive a bit longer... *(He sniffles.)* We never reported the killing...

TOM: It was an accident! Happens all the time in battle! It was someone else...Harry is alive! He will be here tonight! I'll show you...

LUCILLE: Oh, my God, I think I'm going to be sick...*(She goes out the front door.)* I've got to get some air...

TOM: *(Refusing to give in)* They never identified the body....

DICK: Dammit! Will you stop? *(He grabs the watch from* TOM's *vest.)* You took the watch off his body! This one!

TOM: Harry gave that watch to me!

DICK: No! I saw you take it....

TOM: That's a lie!

DICK: You didn't think I could see you take the watch...while I was removing his boots...Tom, you can't hide it from me...I knew it was Harry...and so did you! I know why you stole the watch...so I wouldn't know...I understand it was an accident, Tom...we don't need to pretend anymore.

TOM: I didn't steal it...Harry said...it was O K.

DICK: Admit it, please... Will you say...Harry is dead!

TOM: *(A last attempt)* But, there were no dog tags...

DICK: *(Quietly)* Tom. He's not coming. Let it go!

TOM: *(Breaking down.)* I am not responsible! ...Is it my fault some idiot doesn't know when to take cover...and gets himself wounded...? Huh? Serves him right, goddamit! Stupid idiot...I can't take the blame.

DICK: No one is blaming you...Let go, Tom.

TOM: I...I can't...

DICK: You have to... *(Pause)* Where was he last year?

TOM: I was not a coward! Never...you hear? I never got any medals... but I am no coward!

DICK: I know...I never said you were.

(Pause)

TOM: *(Vindictive)* And I thought you believed...all this time...and I thought you believed. Why? Why did you stay with me...deceiving me? If you never believed Harry was alive...then why did you stay with me after your wife died?

DICK: I don't know. *(Pause)* I was lonely...I thought you needed me.

TOM: Pah! I have never needed anyone. I managed without you during your marriages...I can get along without you now...Go, on...get out of here, you ungrateful...*(He breaks down crying.)*

DICK: And I needed you...*(Pause)* I wanted to believe...for you...I just couldn't...I'm sorry...I...*(He trails off.)*

(DICK *goes up the stairs. After a pause,* TOM *rises and crosses to get a drink and looks around the room. He notices the "Welcome Harry!" banner. He sets his drink on the register desk. He slowly takes down the banner and stuffs it into the fireplace.* DICK *comes down the stairs wearing an overcoat)*

DICK: I put a blanket over his face. The eyes were open.

TOM: *(Drying his eyes with handkerchief)* Where's your suitcase?

DICK: In my room. I'll pack it later. I don't know where to begin. What to take...I've collected so many things.

TOM: Where will you go?

DICK: I don't know. *(Pause)* We have to bury McMurty first. Lucille is going to need help...she...*(He trails off.)*

TOM: *(Handing the putter to* DICK*)* Give this to her...I never liked golf, anyway. *(Long pause. Then with great difficulty)* Will you stay...after tonight?

DICK: I don't know. *(Pause)* There would have to be a lot of changes.

TOM: I need someone to talk to...without McMurty around to argue with...well...

DICK: We'll see...I've got to help Lucille make a phone call first. We'll talk about it later. *(He goes out the front door.)*

TOM: I'll leave a light on for you. *(He stands in the middle of the room staring at the banner in the fireplace.)*

END OF PLAY

www.ingramcontent.com/pod-product-compliance
Lightning Source LLC
Chambersburg PA
CBHW061758110426
42742CB00012BB/1956